The Audio
Theater Guide

The Audio Theater Guide

Vocal Acting, Writing, Sound Effects and Directing for a Listening Audience

ROBERT L. MOTT

McFarland & Company, Inc., Publishers
Jefferson, North Carolina, and London

LIBRARY OF CONGRESS CATALOGUING-IN-PUBLICATION DATA

Mott, Robert L.
    The audio theater guide : vocal acting, writing, sound effects
and directing for a listening audience / Robert L. Mott.
        p.   cm.
    Includes bibliographical references and index.

    ISBN 978-0-7864-4483-0
    softcover : 50# alkaline paper ∞

    1. Voice culture.   2. Acting.   3. Theaters — Sound effects.
    4. Theater — Production and direction.   I. Title.
    PN2071.S65M68   2009
    792.02′4 — dc22   2009031699

British Library cataloguing data are available

On the cover: Keene Crocket creates sound effects during a live
broadcast of *Inner Sanctum*, 1944 (courtesy of Keene Crockett)

Manufactured in the United States of America

*McFarland & Company, Inc., Publishers
  Box 611, Jefferson, North Carolina 28640
  www.mcfarlandpub.com*

This book is a tribute to Norman Corwin,
who in addition to being a friend and inspiration
gave the radio theater's listening world
the words and sounds they could picture
in the privacy of their imagination.

Acknowledgments

To my wife Cinda, for all her encouraging and loving support. To Ruby and Patrick Raymond, for all their helpful assistance. And to you, the reader: I hope you enjoy reading what I've enjoyed doing for so many years. Then again, if I didn't really love it, would I still be doing it?

Contents

Preface

Voice-only acting? Is this really something new? Weren't the puppet voices of *Punch and Judy* entertaining King Arthur's Court long before Elmo's voice was heard on *Sesame Street*? And didn't Walt Disney's squeaky voice surprise early movie audiences that a household pest named Mickey could actually talk?

Later, but long before the creative voices of Tom Kenny (SpongeBob SquarePants) or Nancy Cartwright (Bart Simpson), there were a host of talented radio actors headed by the legendary Mel Blanc, who in addition to using his normal voice as an actor on numerous radio shows used his voice for such unusual vocal effects for everything from a polar bear to a clunky, old Maxwell car's motor. Then, when he wasn't using his versatile voice for radio, Blanc crossed over to movie cartoons and created vocal effects that included the exasperated quacking for Donald Duck. There was also the lovely June Foray, doing her versatile voice for the television cartoon *Rocky and His Friends* and Chuck McCann, doing the many voices on *Cool McCool*.

What did Mel Blanc, June Foray and Chuck McCann have in common? They all began their careers in live dramatic radio ... the birthplace of voice-only acting. It was there that they gained the experience needed for the demands of providing voices for cartoons, animations and anything else that required a versatile, talented and imaginative voice.

Mel, June and Chuck are only three out of scores of talented voices that pioneered the art of voice-only acting in the atmosphere that live radio generated during its golden years. Today those same opportunities now exist in your audio/radio theater. All that's needed is a normal voice, desire and the imaginative ability to pretend

The human voice is a magical instrument. Words on paper — cold words — have only as much color, as much power, as the reader gets out of them. But take these same words and have them performed into a microphone and they suddenly become pictures in the minds of the listeners.

The audio theater's microphone doesn't care a hoot what your gender is, what color your hair is, or whether you're skinny, fat, bald, or tall. Its only concern is the sound of your voice. Voices have the versatility to cry like a baby on one page, and on the next, sound like a creepy old witch whose screeches are so scary that the wicked witch of *The Wizard of Oz* would give her broomstick to have such a voice. Audio theater, however, isn't just a one-man or one-woman band. There are other cast members you'll be working closely with in front of live audiences.

Yes, *live* in front of audiences! It's like giving the audiences a backstage pass to see and hear the body and vocal motions the actors must go through to create a terrorizing scream, or what sound effects are selected to create a picture in the audience's imagination of a human body being turned inside out, or a head being chopped off!

This use of common household items being Foleyed (used to provide sound effects) is quite a departure from the way it's done in a modern recording studio with computers and time codes. One requires actors with years of voice-only experience, compared to the audio theater that provides this much-needed experience. Whether it's for a professional career, improving your ability to speak in front of an audience, trying your hand at writing a script, or using your imagination to create sounds, everything you need to know is included in this book. To get you started and show you some shortcuts, I've included some sketches and scenes that can be used for practicing or performing before your live audiences. Now all it takes is your imagination to create, and your determination not to be afraid to succeed.

1

Voice Acting

Have you ever given a thought to how important the sound of your voice is in regards to your appearance? If not, you should, because there are only four different ways we are evaluated and classified as to who we are.

1. How we look.
2. What we do.
3. What we say.
4. How we say it.

If you don't believe the power of your voice and speaking, consider former president Ronald Reagan who began his career as a radio sports broadcaster at WOC-AM in Davenport, Iowa, in 1932. Back then when an announcer was needed to broadcast the University of Iowa's homecoming game against Minnesota, Reagan was given five dollars and bus fare. Much, much later, after all his accomplishments as a movie star and his terms as governor of California and president of the United States, Reagan was asked the secret of his radio, television, film and political successes. He said, "I owe it all to my best friend, my voice."

Perhaps now you'll understand what makes audio theater so unique. Instead of spending years — yes, years — improving your voice, audio theater gives you the opportunity now. Whether your goal is a professional career, speaking in public, speech and debate classes, or simply having fun working with a group with similar interests, audio theater will give you the knowledge and experience needed to succeed.

Not only will you gain experience cooperating with others, you'll have the excitement and fun of performing on radio, television, in school auditoriums, dinner theaters ... wherever live audiences are looking forward to seeing entertainment that is new and exciting. Who else provides this training for inexperienced talent.... The Disney Studios? *The Simpsons*? Nickelodeon's

SpongeBob SquarePants? Sesame Street? I don't think so; and that in a nutshell is why I wrote this book ... to give you the much-needed experience ... *now*.

The Power of Our Voices

A voice is a powerful tool. It expresses your personality better than the clothes you wear, how your hair looks, or even if you're wearing a Rolex watch. And that's what audio theater is all about ... the sound of your voice. Not your age or appearance, just the sound of your voice.

EXAMPLE: SUPERMAN

The popularity of the *Superman* films of today began when radio listeners were amazed by what they could only see in their imagination way back in 1935!

ANNOUNCER: Faster than a speeding bullet!
SFX: GUNSHOT AND RICOCHET
ANNOUNCER: More powerful than a locomotive!
SFX: LOCOMOTIVE TRAIN EFFECT
ANNOUNCER: Able to leap tall buildings in a single bound!
SFX: FLYING EFFECT. STRONG WIND UP FULL AND UNDER.
ANNOUNCER: Look up in the sky! It's a bird!
ANNOUNCER: It's a plane!
ANNOUNCER: It's SUPERMAN!

Radio's opening for *Superman* is self-explanatory. Even if you had never heard of *Superman,* you would be tempted to listen just a little longer to find out what all the exciting sound effects and booming voice was all about. And once you did, Jackson Beck's voice captured another listener.

Beck's sonorous voice made him one of the most requested voice-only actors for anything that required a decisive and distinctive sound. How long was his career in radio, television, films, cartoons and animations? Long enough to have him doing Brawny Paper Towels commercials on television at the age of eighty-two! Why was a man of this age chosen? Because his voice was just as strong and no-nonsense as when he was doing Superman on radio. And since he wasn't seen on camera, appearance and age were not a consideration. It was the voice the Brawny Towel advertisers wanted.

Page 5 shows Jackson Beck with the author going over the sound effects needed for *The Cisco Kid,* a popular radio drama that Jackson Beck starred in on radio from October 2, 1942, until February 14, 1945. This particular reenactment was done at a convention given by the Friends of Old-Time

Jackson Beck, left, with the author, right, reenacting sound effects from *The Cisco Kid*, a popular radio drama that Beck starred in from October 2, 1942, until February 14, 1945.

Radio. (Conventions such as these are held throughout the country and attended by huge audiences. Check your computer to find out when one will be done near you, then find out how your audio theater can become involved.)

It may seem unusual that an actor so late in life is still doing commercials for today's television, but it isn't. It's just a new challenge for an actor's voice. Ernest Borgnine, who won an Oscar for his role in the film *Marty* and starred in the early television comedy *McHale's Navy,* is at the moment doing the voice for Mermaid Man on the popular television cartoon *SpongeBob SquarePants.* His age, a young 91! But just like Jackson Beck, voice-only actors, no matter what their ages are, still retain their trained voices that allow them to continue enhancing their acting careers, which often started during the golden age of dramatic radio!

Not being seen, but only heard, allowed Bud Collyer to be *Superman* on one show, while also being a television game show host, without even having to go into a phone booth to change his clothes! Because radio is a voice-only media, how did the radio listening audiences know that Clark Kent was changing from the *Daily Planet*'s mild-mannered reporter to the all-powerful Krypton Superman? Certainly not by seeing him change his clothes, but by hearing him changing his *voice*! All Bud Collyer had to do was say in his normal voice, "*This looks like a job...,*" and quickly change the next two words to the steely-edged sound of, "*...for Superman!*" Immediately the audiences knew the transformation of characters was completed!

Who, me? Act?

Yes, you. To begin with, "acting" isn't just a special talent or a profession, it's a way of life. There hasn't been a time from diapers to blue jeans when we haven't acted. We've "acted" sick to avoid going to school or to work and we've even "acted" hurt to get sympathy. Be honest — would you buy clothes from a salesperson who, instead of "acting" polite, growls truthfully, "Those jeans make your butt look like the back end of a school bus!"?

Now that you know that we're all actors at sometime or other, why not be a good actor? Your voice doesn't have to be so noticeable that you get compliments, or so compelling to be authoritative, or sweet-talking, or even sexy. All that's needed in audio theater is that your voice can do what it did as a child, be able to pretend.

Whether you've had acting experience in the theater, in front of a camera, or only in front of a mirror, acting in audio theater comes from your attitude as much as the sound of your voice. If you can visualize and feel, really feel, the part you're playing, your voice will reflect what you're feeling. Little wonder that audio theater audiences are surprised to hear the sound of a baby crying coming from a balding man, or the voice of a balding man coming from a teenage girl!

The best example I can give regarding the value of pretending involved Charlie Chaplin, who many regarded the consummate clown when he starred in silent films such as *The Little Tramp*.

One evening, Chaplin was entertaining some guests in his home and doing impressions of familiar figures. He concluded his performances by surprising his guests by singing a song in the same vocal manner as the world-renowned opera singer Enrico Caruso! One surprised opera lover couldn't help being overwhelmed by what she just heard and gushingly responded, "I didn't know anyone in this world could sing as beautifully as Enrico Caruso!" Chaplin just smiled and replied, "Actually, I can't sing at all, I was only pretending I was Enrico Caruso."

Voice Acting

Voice acting is somewhat misleading. Of course it starts with pretending you're something you aren't. But how do you do that with just your voice? You don't. As talented as your voice may be, it needs an awful lot of help from your posture, the shape of your mouth and your facial expressions. And nowhere else is this so apparent than in audio theater. Not only are the actors heard, but the audience can see it takes more than just a voice or making faces like a tiger. First you have to pretend you're a tiger and your voice and body will do the rest! None of this is ever seen done by voice-only actors in a remote commercial studio. And this is what makes audio theater so exciting. Audiences not only hear the sounds and voices, they're often amazed when they see how they've done and who is doing them!

What's Acting?

Acting is a double-edged sword. If an actor looks or sounds like an actor, the actor has failed. Yet if the actor just "acts" herself, she too has failed. Therefore, the consummate believable actor isn't in the business of acting at all; it's all about pretending with all your heart you're someone other than your true self. When this is done with honesty, you'll no longer worry how you'll deliver a line. It's only how the character you're playing would deliver the line, and that requires a versatile voice; not a special sounding voice, just a versatile voice that comes from being aware of some basic voice facts.

THREE HELPFUL SYSTEMS

There are three systems that make up the sound of our voices: breathing, resonating and articulating. These three systems can be broken down further:

- How your outgoing breath carries and supports your voice.
- How your voice box turns these outward breaths into sound.
- How the sound is amplified in your chest, throat and nasal passages.
- How your mouth, tongue, lips, teeth, palate and cheeks shape the sound into words.

Now it becomes more catchy. As you breathe in and out, air goes between two membranes called vocal cords. These vocal chords remain as loose as unstretched elastic bands during your normal breathing and require a strong current of air coming up from your diaphragm. To locate this important muscle, sit in a chair with your lower back against the chair. Now place the palm of your hand three inches above your navel and at the bottom of your rib cage. Go through the motions of standing and sitting, and notice how the muscles under your hand tighten. In addition to the work done by the surrounding chest and upper abdominal muscles, is the vital and dynamic breath support center. It's this vital air exhalation support system that gives us the ability to speak intelligibly. It's a fact that intelligible words can only be spoken when you exhale and not when you inhale. Don't believe me? Try saying the following words while taking an incoming breath of air: *"Is what I'm saying just a bunch of hot air or not?"*

More Than Just Hot Air

Before you can talk, or make the vocal sound of a dog barking, the force of the air from your breath support center vibrates your vocal cords and gives it pitch. Once the air has been given pitch and this tone is resonated, it's time for the lips, tongue, teeth, cheeks, palate and uvula (small fleshy-looking tongue at the upper entrance of your throat) to form words from this pure current of air. Now you know why your voice is so much a part of you and is so distinctive.

Moving Your Mouth

Learning how to move your mouth and all it's moving parts is especially important to the vocal actor. Getting your mouth open to an actor is as important as "moving your feet" is to a tennis player. Neither can afford to be lazy with their movements if they want to be successful.

To get your mouth moving, try relaxing your jaw and moving it up and down as if it were being pulled by strings like a marionette. Now try saying "blue" without emphasizing the "oo" sound. Repeat 20 times.

Once you get your mouth open and moving, you have to wake up your tongue. Try saying "licorice" ... slowly at first, and then as rapidly as possible, 20 times. Next say "lee" as rapidly as possible. You can even try singing a song using only the word "lee." Now try humming a note with your lips barely touching one another. If you're doing it correctly your lips will vibrate and tingle. Say "p" and your lips make a popping sound. Say "mmm" and your lips close. Say "f" and your upper teeth touch your lower lip. To prove how important it is not to have a lazy mouth, try saying: *"How much wood can a woodchuck chuck, if a woodchuck could chuck wood?"*

Not too difficult, was it? Now try saying a slightly different version. *"How much wood can a woodchuck chuck from Woodside, Wisconsin, if chucking wood paid a workable minimum wage?"*

Quite a difference. By breaking up the rhythm so you can't slide over the words, demands that your mouth not be lazy and needs to move even more.

Are You a Whiner?

Not only do you have to move your tongue, teeth and lips, your nose has something to say as well. It may sound nasal because you either have a cold or you're talking through your nasal passages. Not that this is all bad. If you want to sound "whiney," talking through your nose and stretching the sound of your words will do it.

EXAMPLE

Supposing you're asked to play the part of a "whining teenager."

TEENAGER: Go to the mall? We go there all the time and never meet anyone except those that are just like us.

If you read those lines slowly and through your nose you might get the job. But is there another trick you could use? When we say words we dislike, don't we often give them a more emotional reading? It's almost like you're leaving out, "Yuuuk!"

Try reading those sentences again, replacing the words "mall" and "us" with "yuuuuuk."

TEENAGER: "Go to the yuuuuuk? We go there all the time and never meet anyone except those that are just like yuuuuuk."

By dragging out the word, *yuk* in a nasal voice as if you're in pain, you've enhanced your chances of getting the acting assignment immeasurably.

Perhaps you already have a nasal voice and are not aware of it. Say the letters "m," "n," and "ng." These are the only three nasal sounds that you can expect to hear when you sound these letters. Try it by pinching your nostrils shut and saying: "Moon over Miami in the morning." With your fingers still pinching your nostrils closed, say: "Happy birthday to you." Notice the difference?

Remember, if you don't open your mouth when you speak, the words will come out through your nose. Good to know if you are playing a character that is dull, lifeless and whiney ... bad to know if that's your normal voice.

Back to Childhood

Remember how many times you got yelled at for sucking your thumb? Not anymore, at least not if you want your mouth to move correctly. I once worked with a brilliant actress named Nancy McLoughlin, who surprised me when I found her sitting alone and seemingly sucking her thumb just before going on the air. At first I thought she might be sulking because of something the director said that hurt her feelings. But that didn't make sense as she was the star of the show!

I finally got the answer from an actor friend who knew Nancy. Prior to going on the air, she would put her thumb in her mouth and *gently* bite down on it to make certain her mouth, lips and tongue were moving properly. If she felt her teeth were interfering, she knew she wasn't moving her mouth enough for getting the words out clearly.

If you find thumb sucking inappropriate for your age, try it with a pencil, or anything that will alert you to the fact that your teeth are too close together.

Proper Breathing

Although audio theater frees you from memorizing your lines, it requires that you read them from the all-important script. And as you will see, knowing how to breathe properly is extremely important, especially when you have long speeches.

EXAMPLE: BLONDIE

BLONDIE: (blurting it out) "If you think you are going to get away with anything as two-timing and double-dealing as dumping me for this other broad, you ain't seen the other side of me that will go to the district attorney and open my mouth wide open about just how upstanding and honorable the stupid public was to vote you in to judge their crimes after the money you took to free the biggest crook in the country! (louder) And don't tell me to keep my voice down, 'cause what I'm saying now is going to be heard tonight on the Six O'clock News!"

Did you gulp down gobs of air before reading Blondie's tirade? If so, you're not only wasting your breath, gulping air will make you tense. To give you an example of how little air you actually need, a single exhalation can carry you through eight or more lines on a single sip of air.

> Sing a song of sixpence
> a pocketful of rye,
> Four and twenty blackbirds,
> Baked in a pie.
> When the pie was open,
> The birds began to sing;
> Was not that a dainty dish,
> To put before the king?

In giving your words more intensity without straining your voice, read the nursery rhyme again. Only this time put your hand back to those three inches above your navel to your diaphragm. Not only will it assist your energy to speak, it is the secret of projecting your words without shouting and harming your voice. But first, a few simple abdominal exercises.

Speaking More Effectively

All words start with an exhalation of our breath. However, if you only say words with your mouth, you've bypassed a series of amplifiers — the throat, the nose and the sinus cavities. Together they raise the level of your voice as much as twenty times.

Although nothing in your mouth is wasted in the formation of words, the busiest by far are the lips and tongue. Say "ah" and your tongue just kind of lays there. Say the "a" as in bat, and it bends over forward. Say "oh" and the tip of the tongue points downward. Say "oo" and it digs further down. Say "t" and your tongue pushes against the top row of teeth. Say "r" and the tongue flattens out and it gives your voice an almost growling or trilling sound. Say "s" and your tongue pushes up to your front teeth and makes a sibilant (hissing) sound.

Your lips are equally busy. Say "p" and your lips make a plosive (popping) sound. Say "mmm" and your lips close. Say "f" and your upper teeth touch your lower lip. First there is the breath, then the sound, then the resonance and, finally, the articulation. But always keep in mind the importance of an erect posture so your diaphragm will be in the best position to provide the exhalation your voice needs to do its work.

DIAPHRAGM EXERCISES

In order for this all-important diaphragm muscle to function properly, it needs to be exercised. Anything that will tighten your abdomen will work, including blowing up a balloon. Only, instead of gulping air and blowing with just the air from your mouth, put your hand on your diaphragm and feel your stomach tighten as you inflate the balloon with one steady breath. If you don't have a balloon handy, blow in your clenched fist.

Another excellent breathing exercise requires nothing more than your imagination. Pretend your index finger is a lighted candle and is ten inches in front of you. Now make a "W" shape with your lips, and while holding one hand under your rib cage, take a sip of air and exhale a thin stream of air towards the "candle" without blowing out the flame.

In doing this, you should feel the tightness of your stomach muscles supporting your thin stream of air the further you move your finger away. You might want to wet your finger to make it more sensitized to your air stream. Now see how long you can maintain a steady flow of air against your finger while extending the distance from your face. You will soon notice that as the distance increases, so does the support from your body, and at arm's length even your hips and buttocks will become involved.

Are you surprised that this support system is also needed even when you speak on the cell phone, or into a microphone?

Speech Problems

The trouble with many speech problems is that most of us don't have any idea we have them. I always thought I had a great speaking voice until I auditioned for a radio announcer's job. It was then I was told I gave certain words a "glottal" pronunciation. Racing to a dictionary I found glottal comes from "not moving my tongue." Try it. Put your tongue in back of your bottom teeth and say "cattle." Did it come out sounding "catuhl"? Now move your tongue. You have just cured yourself of "glottalitis."

One of the advantages of knowing about speech impediments is learning how they can be put to use. If, for instance, you want your voice to sound lazy, you simply don't move your tongue — "Hey, you gottuh problem with dat?"

Become a Good Watcher and Listener

The first requirement of being a good vocal actor is that you must first and foremost be a good listener and observer. By picturing and concentrating on the sound your voice needs to create, don't forget how important the rest of your body is. For instance, you are in your teens and are asked to be the voice of an old man, or old woman, or even a cartoon character. By twisting your face in various positions so that your lips are wrapped tightly over your teeth, and you're stooped over, begin talking and picturing how old you are when you say the following sentence: "Peter Pan produced a prized pretty purple pear."

It doesn't matter how fast or slow you say the sentence, by not moving your lower lip you've aged in facial appearance and vocal sounds. Whenever you come across someone with an interesting dialect, notice how they fix their mouth and even their face and body movements when they talk. Make it a habit of becoming a good listener and observer of your friends, co-workers, people in the supermarket; wherever there are people. You'll soon be acquiring character information an actor must have when the demand is needed.

Does that strike you as strange? It shouldn't. How we stand, the shape and position of our faces, all affect the way we feel and the sound of our voice. Why do you suppose that entertainers who mimic famous people's voices also mimic their facial and body characteristics?

"Having a good ear" is nothing more than listening carefully and it should be practiced in your daily life wherever you find people talking. If you listen carefully, you're bound to hear someone with a special, interesting, or strange sounding voice. And when you do, you have the potential to imitate it or take the various parts from it and adjust as required to fit your acting needs. Because that's what you do, listen and create with your voice. The more voices or sounds you can call upon, the more it speaks to your vocal acting capabilities and the value you bring to the audio theater and perhaps to your professional career.

IT'S ALL ABOUT TEAMWORK

Although writers are always looking for a new way to present their characters, they often depend a great deal on what the vocal actors will come up with regarding how the character sounds. Many of the characters in today's cartoons aren't drawn to be realistic, therefore the vocal actor must be equally outrageous as to what these characters sound like.

Coming up with a voice for a lobster might not be the easiest task. But you must look for whatever clues that will help. The fact that the lobster wears a top hat might indicate that the lobster is vain. A second clue might be that lobsters come primarily from Maine and Massachusetts and speak a "*Bah*-ston" (Boston) accent.

Now that you know what it takes to have a compelling voice, let's find out what's holding you back from using it.

Stage Fright

If our nervous system had the ability to discriminate between which fear signals were real and which were imagined, it would most likely ignore something as trivial as sweaty hands, a dry mouth and wobbly knees. But since it seemingly can't, when it receives the same fright signals from your nervous system as you prepare to go on stage as when you're in serious danger, you're leaving yourself open to stage fright.

Our nervous systems appear to be like a computer. Unless you punch in the correct information, it doesn't have the ability to properly respond. Therefore, if you give your nervous system the same signals going on stage as being chased by a Tyrannosaurus Rex dinosaur, be prepared to have an awful lot of nervous energy in the form of "stage fright."

But what is this thing called "stage fright"? In the theater it certainly isn't a fear that the stage is going to open up and swallow you. But what about audio theater? Are the actors afraid of dropping their script, losing their place in the script, knocking over the microphone, or the fear of looking foolish? *Bingo*!

Foolishness comes in two parts. Fear of being thought a fool (losing your reputation, and actually *being* a fool (a shot in the heart to your ego).

Although stage fright is triggered mentally, it also causes a tightening of muscles. It's as if we are trying to make ourselves as small a target to danger as possible. Our shoulders hunch up to our ears and our neck suddenly becomes rigid. These symptoms are common not only to actors, but to NFL football players as well. In fact, they're common to anyone who is putting their self-image on the line.

Keep in mind, our feelings don't have a mind of their own. They respond in direct relationship to what they perceive as danger. Therefore, if you feel that facing an audience is going to be a dangerous, "killing" experience, your nervous system will send a flood of adrenaline to help you defend yourself. Therefore, doesn't it stand for reason we can control that energy in our nervous system by not allowing our expectations to govern our thoughts?

What are expectations? Aren't they perceived thoughts about what *might* or *could* happen? Therefore, instead of trying to get prepared for the worst, why not fool your jittery nervous system by sending it relaxing messages. You can do this by following some of these brief exercises:

- Breathing in rhythm ... slowly and deeply.
- Opening your mouths and yawning.
- Rolling your head clockwise and counter clockwise slowly around your shoulders.
- Relaxing your shoulders and stop wearing them for earrings.
- Shaking your arms vigorously.

These exercises are excellent for getting rid of the jitters. The rest is being properly prepared. I once asked a doctor friend of mine how doctors keep from getting nervous before a serious operation. He smiled and answered, "If we weren't properly prepared and didn't know what we were doing, we wouldn't be operating in the first place."

Knowing what you're doing and being properly prepared. Not bad things to remember before you go on stage, or even if you're just doing something easy, like a heart transplant.

Summary

1. The voice is perhaps the most ignored quality of beauty.

2. The ability to make sounds occurs when air is forced from our lungs causing our vocal cords to vibrate.

3. The ability to say words requires the combined efforts of the tongue, teeth, lips, cheeks, palate and uvula.

4. In speaking, sips of air are more effective than deep breaths of air.

5. The diaphragm is a muscle located in your chest.

6. Because of the location of the diaphragm, a good speaking voice needs the body to be erect.

7. When using your diaphragm to speak, your voice will have the energy to be heard at great distances without shouting.

8. Not moving your tongue gives your words a glottal sound.

9. Speaking through your nasal passages gives your voice a "whiney" sound.

10. The main cause of "stage fright" is fear of looking foolish.

11. Stage fright is both mental and physical. The best way to fight it is to lower your expectations of what you don't have control over, and shake the jitters out of your muscles.

12. A lazy mouth is the cause of most speech impediments and dialects. Proper breath ... the way you exhale ... is the foundation of a good voice.

13. People who have dialects are often unaware that they have them; and those that do are reluctant to lose them because it identifies who they are.

14. People often look the way their voice sounds.

15. If you ever hear an interesting voice, listen carefully. You never know when you might need to imitate it.

16. In reading a script, don't let your eyes get ahead of what you're saying. Remember, we read faster than we talk.

17. Stage fright, like any seemingly debilitating emotion, is only evidence that we are human and alive and perhaps didn't prepare properly.

18. Read aloud with your hand on your chest as a test for resonance.

19. To find the "girdle" of your breath support, place the palm of your hand four inches above your navel. In a sitting position, with your navel against the back of the chair, stand and sit and feel the tightening of your girdle of breath support.

20. Mispronouncing words is due to a lack of the accepted or popular pronunciation of a particular word. Dialect is different. It's more of a way of pronouncing words that is influenced by historical, social, or geographical implications.

21. Put a finger to your larynx and say "zzzzz." Zs must be vocalized. Now say "ssssss." Notice your larynx doesn't vibrate because the letter "s" doesn't need to be voiced. It may be whispered. Now try and whisper "Zebra." You'll find it ends up "See-bra."

22. To strengthen your voice, take a sip of air and try making a "hisssss-ing" sound for as long as you can.

23. There are two kinds of actors; those that get paid to act, and the rest of us.

24. The most difficult part of being an actor is not acting, but simply being.

25. Having trouble focusing? Try picturing the Statue of Liberty and a watermelon at the same moment. If you can't do that, stop thinking of mak-ing a fool of yourself and focus on something positive, like breathing from your diaphragm.

26. Becoming the part you're playing takes the guesswork out of how to act.

27. It isn't the fear of failing that's so terrible. At least that teaches us our mistakes. The one to watch out for is not trying. That teaches us noth-ing but wonder.

28. When you really know the character you're playing, acting suddenly becomes being.

2

Microphone Acting Techniques

Acting for Your Microphone

There are a tremendous number of advantages acting solely with the audio theater's microphone. You don't have to worry about bumping into furniture, or remembering your lines. You don't even have to worry about hitting your stage marks, or being in place for the cameras. And what about getting fitted for costumes, or getting your face made up? Nope, not in the audio theater; it's all done with the microphone and the audience's imagination. And not just "talking" into a microphone, but acting and creating sound effects. Before all that can happen however, there are a few things you should know that will help the microphone operate at its optimum efficiency.

DOS AND DON'TS WITH MIKES

At times the microphone seems frightening, while at other times, it's the actor's best friend. To allow a microphone to help your voice perform to the best of its ability, here are some things you should avoid doing with a microphone.

1. Never blow directly into a microphone.
2. Never tap a microphone.
3. Never drop a microphone.
4. Never cough, or sneeze into, or near a mike. Turn your head and fold your arm and cough or sneeze inside the crook of your arm.

Today's mikes are very sensitive and expensive. Therefore, whether you're doing a show for the audio theater, in a recording studio for commercials, or in any media that requires microphones, always have the people with technical knowledge handle your mike.

17

THE MIKE'S SIMILARITIES

One thing all microphones have in common is their capability for converting acoustical energy (air vibrations) into electrical energy. Here the similarity ends. Each type of microphone (and there are many) is designed to perform a particular function.

One mike might attenuate the highs in a singing voice, while another will boost the lows. Another will emphasize the bass quality when the voice is placed close to the mike (proximity effect), or add more presence (your personality) to the voice when it's moved farther away.

Our Hearing Versus the Mike's

The microphone has often been compared with our own auditory system. Although this might seem logical, it isn't quite true. Our hearing is very selective and the elements of a microphone are not. Humans can hear a number of noises at the same time and focus only on one, whereas the microphone will record any and all sounds made within hearing distance.

It isn't that humans don't hear all the sounds that microphones do, it's just that our brains are more selective as to what they allow are ears to focus on. This ability to focus on certain sounds, to the exclusion of others, is what makes living or working in a noisy environment bearable. Therefore, to get the best results from a mike, select the one that best serves your needs.

RF BODY MIKES

RF (Radio Frequency) mikes, or "body" mikes, have a miniature radio transmitter in the form of a body pack that is attached to the actor's body. This is used to take the signal (voice) from the mike concealed near the actor's mouth and transmit it to the receiver that is plugged into a separate sound system. RF mikes serve a much-needed purpose for stage actors by making certain that everything they say, or sing, reaches the proverbial "last row of seats in the balcony."

Unlike the stage actor's need to move freely and still be heard, the mike in the audio theater stays stationary to allow the actors' voices the illusion of movement. This is possible because all microphones have distinctive sound patterns that either accept or reject sounds.

The Microphone's Three Patterns

There are three basic polar patterns for microphones: unidirectional; omni-directional; and bi-directional. The patterns indicate the microphone's area of sensitivity. The most sensitive area is referred to as "on axis" or the "live" side of the mike. The area that is least sensitive is said to be "off axis" or the "dead" side of the mike. Each microphone is most effective when used for the particular purpose it was designed for.

In order for actors, or sound effects people, to get the proper sound from their microphone, they should carefully study the diagram below.

Unidirectional

The diagram below shows the sensitivity pattern of a hypercardioid, or unidirectional, microphone. You can see why it is called "hypercardioid" because of the mike's heart-shaped lined pattern. It also indicates that the mike is most sensitive at 0 degrees, or at letter A, and least sensitive to the sides B, C and D. Because of this one-sided sensitive area, it is called a unidirectional mike. This is the mike most often used by a narrator, or the sound effects people who don't want noises from the audience leaking (being heard) into their microphones.

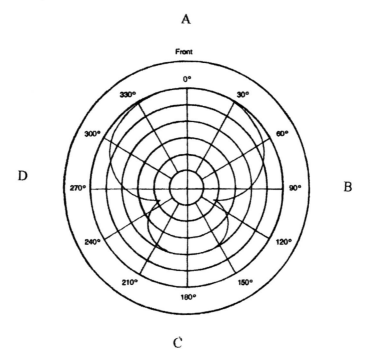

The sensitivity pattern of a hypercardioid, or unidirectional, microphone. The name comes from the heart shape of the pattern, which depicts the sensitivity of the microphone. It is the most sensitive at 0 degrees (A) and less sensitive at B, C and D.

Omni-Directional

An omni-directional microphone picks up sound in a circular fashion that is sensitive to sound not only from the front part of the mike, but from the back and sides as well. Because of this circular sensitivity to sounds this is a good mike to use if you want to record the applause and laughter that the actors are receiving.

Bi-Directional

The advantage of this mike over the omni-directional mike is that two people can face each other and speak without having noise from the mike's sides leaking into the microphone.

Now that you know the more technical microphone terminologies, rarely does a director ask you to "get more on axis, or off axis," they will simply say to move more on (closer) or off (farther away) from the mike.

Microphone Arrangements

The manner in which microphones are arranged in the audio theater will basically be done for the cast's needs. Once the actors, music and sound effects have given the engineer their normal sound levels they will use on the air, they should not change them once the show begins.

It makes no difference whether your voice acting is done in a studio or in front of an audience; if your voice needs a microphone, the only person who truly knows what your voice sounds like is either the audio engineer or your director. It's for that reason it's important that when you're asked to give a voice level, you give the normal level you'll be using on the air, either live or recorded. If you're told your voice is too loud, the engineer will either adjust his pot (potentiometer) to your voice level or simply ask you to back away from the mike until your voice level is acceptable. Once the show is in progress in front of an audience, or being recorded in a studio, an engineer doesn't have time to keep adjusting the sound levels coming from the various microphones.

Microphone Holders

The audio theater isn't a theater where the actors are all the same height standing in a row reading words into a microphone. If it were, there would only be a need for one type of mike and one type of holder for all mikes. This isn't the case. Actors come in all sizes and scripts require special needs. One script may require a dozen actors in a scene; another may require only two actors seated at a table. Then, there are sound effects. They may need four mikes at different heights to cover all the manual effects that are required for the show. Fortunately, there are microphone holders that can accommodate all these various needs the audio theater might have.

Banquet Stands

As the name implies, it's a very short stand used on podiums for speakers at a banquet. It's also used by actors who need to be seated at a table, or the sound effects person who needs this type of mike stand for footsteps or other Foley effects.

Boom

A boom is a metal rod attached to a stand. It can be heightened, lowered, or extended for whatever audio needs are required by a microphone.

Floor Stands

This popular mike holder allows the mike to be raised and lowered simply by regulating the tension that holds the mike's inner rod in a fixed position. This is the mike stand most used in the audio theater because it allows the actors and sound effects people a fixed position for the microphone while allowing the actors and sound effects people the needed movement for their voices and sounds.

Getting Help from the Mike

Now that you know how important your voice is, it's time to know the different ways a microphone can be of help. To begin with, think of the microphone as someone's ear. When you want to speak low, or whisper, you get closer to the mike. When you have to shout, you lean back. Now the question is, how many mikes does it take for two actors to do this? The answer is, it's all according to where the audio theater is being done. If it's being done for radio with no audience, one mike. This way the actors can "play" (act) off one another's facial reactions and not worry about ignoring the live audience in the theater.

If the audio theater is being done in front of an audience, there should be enough mikes so the audience can see the actors' facial expressions. The same is true in a professional studio. The number of mikes are dependent on how many actors have to keep their eyes on a monitor while they are lip syncing (matching mouth movements with words) to a commercial or cartoon.

Microphones for Different Cast Members

The audio theater often does scripts written by one of the cast, or recreated from a script done during radio's golden age. Very often these scripts require cast members of different heights and voice levels. If there are children in the cast, you can have them stand on apple boxes (boxes used to give actors height), or short two-step ladders. Because young actors require so much help having their voices heard, their voices are normally done by actors playing the parts of children.

Adult actors playing the parts of children started back in the days of live radio. In addition to the microphone problems, directors had to abide by the many laws protecting children from the abuses that occurred during the overworked days of vaudeville. Underage children were only allowed to work a number of prescribed hours, and have a tutor for their school lessons. Plus they had to have the child's mother there to take care of the child's other needs and behavior.

Because this was in the days of live radio, directors had enough on their hands getting a show on the air with adult actors, therefore, the less people the director had to deal with, the better. As a result, many of the adult actors could, and would, double as children. In addition to the reduced worry and stress the director had, audiences in the studio were always surprised and enjoyed seeing the role of five-year-old junior played by a graying fifty-year-old actor.

Normally a play requires more than just two actors. Very often there are three or four actors, or even a crowd scene, where all the actors have to be heard in the same scene. Do you have to put out more mikes to accommodate everyone? It's all according to how big the various major parts are, or how many speeches the cast members have. In all cases, keep the number of mikes to a minimum and the movement from the cast at a maximum.

Keep in mind, although you're accustomed to seeing rock bands, where even the drummer may have a number of mikes for his bass, snare, tom-toms and cymbals, each mike must be plugged into a very expensive and complicated audio mixing console and operated by the audio mixer. Although these audio consoles are similar to the ones used by the networks during the live days of radio, even then, the audio mixers kept the number of mikes they used to a minimum. In fact, the NBC Symphonic Orchestra, conducted by Arturo Toscanini, often conducted a live radio broadcast by not having any instruments singled out for microphones but having only one microphone for the entire orchestra!

Perhaps the audio theater could use only one microphone if it was a singing group, where all the singers stayed in one place, but it isn't. The scripts performed in the audio theater require mikes that can accommodate a great deal of movement done by actors of different heights and voice levels. But even then, if there is a crowd scene where many of the actors have only one line, there must be a great deal of cooperation from the actors saying their lines into the one mike designated for this crowd scene. They must jump in, say their line, jump back, and make room for the next actor as quickly as possible. One thing they can't do is remain at the mike when they're finished!

MIKE HOGS

Hogging a mike is lingering at the microphone and making it impossible for the next actors to get a clear opening at the mike so their voices can be heard properly. I once did a soap at CBS that had an actress in the cast who was a notorious mike hog. On this one show, everything was going smoothly until the mike hog said her line and didn't back off quick enough for the next actor. The actor, rather than not having his line heard, took matters into his own hands and goosed her.

Problems Our Microphone Hears

We all have them. They're just not as noticeable until the microphone gets a hold of them. Whether we leave phone messages on someone's cell phone or an answering machine, in the audio theater or a high definition recording studio's microphone, if there is any blemish to your voice, the mike will find it.

This is especially true of the old bugaboo of popping the Ps in prices, peaches and parsnips. This bad habit is right up there with blowing into a microphone to see if it's hot (open); it's called "P popping"! This "plosive problem" is caused by getting too close to the microphone and expanding too much air in pronouncing words like "pigs, pineapples and pelicans."

Many recording studios put a screen either over, or a short distance from, the mike to correct this popping-problem; the best way is opening your mouth. If you think you do have this problem, put your open hand in front of your mouth and say "punctuate." If you feel a puff of air against your hand, try opening your mouth more and using a less forceful amount of air to pronounce, perplexing, problems ... particularly the "P" words.

THE ART OF NOT SPEAKING CORRECTLY

The United States is a very large country made up of different states, many of which have their own unique way of pronouncing certain words. As a result, these words identify people with a dialect or regional accent that identifies where they originated from, whether it's from the United States or from somewhere outside of the United States.

People from Boston often give a hard sound to any words that end in "*ar*," such as "bar" and "far." While people to the north of us in Canada pronounce "out" as "*oot*," or "*aboot*" instead of "about." While people from India speak slower: "Ah denk you weddy much." And why do people from Germany always begin a word that begins with a "W" as if it's the letter "V?" Vhy do they alvays do that?"

Being able to do dialects is an art in itself and should be practiced whenever possible. You can never tell when you'll be asked to give a cartoon's lobster a Bostonian way of speaking. Therefore, when you hear someone with an interesting accent of any sort, notice how they fix their mouth and even their face and body movements when they talk. Another good way of attaining a particular dialect is to rent a film you have seen that has a dialect you're interested in doing. Notice how the characters move, and start recording your voice until you too can imitate the sound.

Both of these suggestions are good, but the best way is to make it a habit of listening and observing your family, friends, co-workers, people in the supermarket. You'll soon be acquiring character information an actor must have when the demand is needed.

Acting with Your Scripts

Although acting with a script has many advantages over memorizing your words, a script must be handled carefully for the best results. Remember, your audience is dependent upon hearing your voice clearly and distinctly, whatever character you may be playing. In addition to keeping the pages away from your face, hold your script up to eye level so that your face is always pointed directly at the mike. When you have to turn the pages of your script, be careful to do it quietly.

Although I have seen actors drop their script pages to the floor when they're finished reading them, I don't recommend it. Trying to find an unread page that accidentally got dropped into the pile on the floor is more than just a trifle stressful.

MAKING NOTES

Because audio theater has less rehearsal time than any other media, a script is often used for more than just saying the written lines. Therefore, you should make notations on your script in any way you choose to remind you of the words that need to be emphasized, given the correct pronunciation, or simply cut. When this happens, always use a pencil, never a pen! The changes or cuts you were just given might be changed once again minutes before your scheduled performance!

Unlike deleting words or sentences on your computer, you can't push the "delete" button. The cuts must be made by simply drawing a line through the word or sentence to be cut. Never scribble a word or mark out part of a sentence so it can't be read; it may be reinstated. If a whole paragraph is to be cut, you start with the first word to be cut and draw a line down to the last word of the cut. Now if the director changes her mind, the "cuts" can still be read easily.

Giving Voices Movement

Normally, the proper distance for speaking into a mike is six to eight inches, or the width of your hand. This distance is considered to give your voice an "on" mike sound and gives the audience a point of view that enables them to picture where they would be standing if they were in the same room.

The same is true with sound effects. If a door is opened or closed, or footsteps are heard, they are always in reference to that person speaking closest to the mike. On television, or in the movies, it would be the person the camera is focused on. In audio theater, because of the perceptiveness the listening audience has to the loudness of what they hear, it also gives them a picture of where the actors are located.

To avoid audio theater from falling into the trap of being "talking heads," their voices have to have movement. This can be done in a number of ways, both with head and body movements or the audio mixer fading your microphone down to the proper sound level. However, this can only be done if all the other microphones are closed. Therefore, given a choice, I would suggest the actor do his own scream.

- Falling from a great height can be accomplished by starting the scream on mike and slowly turning away from the mike and letting your voice fade out.
- If the height is a great distance, one actor starts the scream and in the middle, and at the same volume level, a second actor continues the scream. This is best done by a director cueing the actors when to start their screams.
- Walking away from the microphone shows the audience in the theater you are both physically and vocally fading out from the scene.

- Remaining in place at the mike, but only turning your head, gives the vocal illusion of fading off.
- Leaning your head back slowly is another way of having your voice sound as if you're fading off.
- Turning your back to the microphone, and slowly turning to face the microphone, gives the illusion of fading on mike from a greater distance. If two actors did nothing more exciting than standing opposite one another reading words from a script, the golden age of radio never would have lasted, or been so popular.

EXAMPLE

These next two short scenes will demonstrate the importance of voices being "on" and "off" mike to the audience's perception of movement. It's the difference between just *hearing* the words and *picturing* the words. In films, what the camera sees is referred to as the audience's POV (point of view); in the audio theater, it's what the microphone hears that becomes what the audience imagines.

SUSAN: What do you feel like doing?
GAIL: I don't know.
SUSAN: Wanna go to the mall?
GAIL: I guess so. I got a pair of shoes I can take back. They're right here in my bedroom closet ... if I can find them.
SUSAN: How about digging out what I loaned you last month?
GAIL: That old sweater?
SUSAN: No, my new surfboard.

This scene could be funny, but the way it is now, it's a good example of "talking heads." In order to give the audience a sense of movement, and their imagination an idea of the size of the bedroom, all that is required is how the microphone perceives the voices.

I use the words on microphone only as an example. Normally scripts simply indicate "on" and "off" and the writer assumes that the actor is familiar with the terms. Speaking "on" microphone is the movie equivalent of the camera term POV. It refers to the actor in the scene that the camera is focusing on.

The same is true in audio theater except it's from the listener's POV. Only instead of calling it the listener's POV, the audio theater's term is perspective. Perspective always refers to what is important to the scene. It indicates the place where the audience is listening from, just as POV is what the audience is hearing and seeing through the eye of the camera.

EXAMPLE

SUSAN: What do you feel like doing?
GAIL: (On mike) I don't know.
SUSAN: (On mike) Wanna go to the mall?
  (*By the characters both speaking on mike we know they are together and the scene could be taking place anywhere.*)
GAIL: I guess so. I got a pair of shoes I can take back. (fading off) They're right here in my bedroom closet ... if (slight irritation) I can find them in this junk closet.
  SFX: Movement of clothes, etc.
SUSAN: (On mike) How about digging out what I loaned you last summer?
GAIL: (Off mike) You mean this old sweater?
SUSAN: (On mike) No, that new surfboard.

Having Gail's voice fading slightly indicates she is "walking" to the closet. We know this because Susan has remained "on mike" when they were both talking at the beginning of the scene.

This is important in audio theater. You must establish where the microphone, or home base, is at all times. Voices that move farther away, or closer, indicate not only movement, but give additional information to the audience as to the size and type of the room ... also referred to as the acoustic, or proximity, effect. In the previous scene, the size and sound of the room was given to the audience by the amount of time and the fading of Gail's voice from home base, or from Susan's POV.

A word of caution; always be aware of where your head is when speaking on mike. You just saw how the slightest movement of your head indicates you are either leaving or entering a room. Therefore move your body as much as you like, but be extremely careful that you don't confuse a listening audience as to where your character is by being careless with head movements while talking into the microphone.

Acting with Actions

Audio theater isn't simply a combination of distinctive words spoken from the actors. It also requires a great deal of emotional acting that are outcries from your whole body. The best way to have a poor show in audio theater is to ignore these unspoken body expressions that mean so much to the audience's imagination.

If a script is written that involves a great deal of sound effect patterns (related extended sounds), and the actors only read their lines and sound effects only does their sounds, you're missing what makes audio theater so unique.

EXAMPLE

1 SOUND: TWO FAST GUNSHOTS FOLLOWED BY GUN CLICKS.
2 GOOD GUY: Those were your last two shots. You're finished, Slade!
3 BAD GUY: Maybe that gun is, but this knife ain't!
4 SOUND: STRUGGLE.
5 GOOD GUY: Drop it! Drop it!
6 BAD GUY: You're breaking my arm!
7 GOOD GUY: I said drop it!!
8 SOUND: KNIFE HITTING FLOOR.
9 BAD GUY: There ... I dropped it! Now I'm gonna drop you!
10 SOUND: PUNCH AND STRUGGLE.
11 GOOD GUY: You had your turn ... now it's mine!!
12 SOUND: PUNCH AND BODY FALL.

Although there is plenty of action in this scene, what's lacking is emotion. It must be shown the two men are fighting with their fists, knife and for their lives, not having a social debate. And the best way to show emotions is not to talk about it, but go deeper, where a grunt and groan is worth a thousand words.

EXAMPLE

1 SOUND EFFECTS: TWO GUNSHOTS FOLLOWED BY CLICKS.
2 GOOD GUY: Those were your last two shots. You're finished, Slade!
3 BAD GUY: (Breathing heavy) Maybe that gun is, but this knife *ain't!*
4 SOUND EFFECTS: STRUGGLE.
5 GOOD GUY: (Straining with effort.) Drop it! (Effort) ... Drop it!
6 BAD GUY: (Painfully) You're breaking my arm....
7 GOOD GUY:(Effort) I said drop it!!
8 SOUND EFFECTS: KNIFE HITTING FLOOR.
9 BAD GUY: There ... I dropped it ... (Effort) ... Now I'm gonna drop you!
10 SOUND EFFECTS: PUNCH AND STRUGGLE. *(Grunts)*
11 GOOD GUY: You had your turn, now it's *mine!*
12 SOUND EFFECTS: PUNCH AND BODY FALL. *(Reactions)*

In doing a fight scene, grunts, effort and reactions come with the fight. But what about reacting to a physical effort in a more serene scene?

EXAMPLE

1 SOUND EFFECTS: CAR DOOR SLAM
2 CATHEE: How far are we going?
3 PETE: We just got out of the car.
4 CATHEE: But where are we going?
5 PETE: I told you we were going to take a little walk.
6 CATHEE: Walk? That's a mountain! They'll never find us!
7 PETE: Will you come on. The view from up there is worth it ... c'mon.

8 CATHEE: These bushes have thorns and the dirt is getting in my sandals.
9 PETE: We've only got a little ways to go and then we'll be able to see forever.
10 CATHEE: Forever? What if there's an avalanche?
11 PETE: Only loud noises cause avalanches and we'll have one if you don't
   stop (louder) *complaining*! (quickly and softer) complaining. Hey, where
   are you going?
12 CATHEE: Back to where a hot tub's bubbles don't cause (softly) avalanches
   (beat) make that ... (shouts) *avalanches*!

SUGGESTION

Simply reading that scene should take 45 seconds, but is that "acting"
the scene? Going up a mountain is not like a walk in the park, and this couple don't appear to be seasoned hikers. It's indicated in the lines that are written, but the audience needs even more information for their imagination,
from both sound effects and the actors' reactions to the sounds.

In this next version, I've italicized the changes that would be done to
the actors' reactions to sound effects, and sound effects' reactions to the actors'
words. Because of these changes, a few words have been added by the actors
because now they are hearing the sound effects accenting their spoken words.

EXAMPLE

1 SOUND EFFECTS: CAR DOOR SLAM.
2 CATHEE: How far are we going?
3 PETE: We just got out of the car.
4 SOUND EFFECTS: FOOTSTEPS ON GRAVEL.
5 CATHEE: But where are we going?
6 PETE: A little walk up there.
7 CATHEE: Up there! (steps stop) That's not "up there," that's a mountain!
   They'll never find us!
8 PETE: Will you come on ... (Breathing). The view from up there is worth
   it. C'mon.
9 SOUND EFFECTS: BUSHES FOLLOW ACTION.
10 CATHEE: These bushes have thorns ... (ow) ... and the dirt is getting in
   my ... sandals. (Breathing)
11 PETE: We've only a little ways to go and then we'll be able to see forever!
12 CATHEE: Forever? What if there's an avalanche?
13 PETE: Only really loud noises cause avalanches and we might just have
   one if you don't stop (louder) complaining (quickly and softer) so loudly.
14 SOUND EFFECTS: WALKING STOPS.... CATHEE STEPS GOING OFF
15 PETE: Hey! Where're you going?
16 SOUND EFFECTS: STEPS STOP
17 CATHEE: Back down the mountain and into my hot tub ... where the
   bubbles won't cause an (yells) Avalanche!

In reading the revised script, notice how both of the actors' words being Foleyed by sound effects (sound synchronized with the actors' words) has helped what the writer had written. This is the advantage of having the actors and sound effects interacting and not having the sound effects done later in post production, as with most voice-over, audio-only media.

If the script requires the actors and sound effects to interact their lines and sounds, it helps both the actors' voices and the sound effects if they both watch each other so that the words and movements coincide. Unlike the movies, where the sound effects are Foleyed to the actor's movements on a screen in post production, in audio theater the Foleying is done live by sound effects matching not the actors' movements, but the actors' words. This is made even more effective if the actors watch the person Foleying some footsteps and they silently move their feet as if they are making the sounds.

Just because the actors in audio theater act with the sounds of their voices, doesn't mean they have to stand at the mike like their feet are nailed to the floor. Even the actors in movies don't normally run around when they're saying their lines, but they aren't emotionally frozen either. Therefore, remember that whatever you do with your body affects the sound of your voice.

Auditioning

Auditioning for parts in audio theater is excellent experience, especially if you intend to make acting your career, or even for just facing new audiences for any speaking occasion. And the best way to reduce the stress is by being properly prepared. Daws Butler, a brilliant voice-over actor, summed up being prepared by observing the 5 Ps — "Proper Preparation Prevents Poor Performance." I strongly recommend you take this talented actor's advice.

The stress actors go through when auditioning goes by an assortment of names. To play on your school's football, baseball, basketball or cheerleading team, you must try out — stressful. To get into college, you must have the proper scholastic requirements — stressful. To receive the job you want, you must be interviewed, or take a written or physical test — stressful. Are you still concerned about auditioning being stressful? Then, when you do all this and you're still feeling stress, remember no one wins them all, not even the legendary Orson Welles.

REPLACE ORSON WELLES?

The Shadow, like *Superman,* and so many of the early radio shows, first became popular in magazines. In *The Shadow*'s case it was, *Street and Smith's*

Detective Story magazine. Frank Readick was the first actor to play the role of the Shadow and created *The Shadow*'s signature laugh. Later, when Orson Welles, who at the time was a radio actor, took over the role, the creator of the series, Walter B. Gibson, loved Welles' voice, but hated the way he did the Shadow's all-knowing laugh! Therefore, throughout the time Welles was on the show, the signature opening Shadow's laugh wasn't done by Welles, but instead a recording of Frank Readick's more acceptable evil laugh.

This is a valuable lesson for those who are thinking of making a career out of voice acting. Whether you are doing an audition or acting in a popular cartoon, you must be ready to hear criticism. That doesn't mean you have to accept it. When Welles was criticized about not being able to get the proper sound for the Shadow's laugh, Orson Welles was tactful enough to accept the criticism of his laugh with a smile. Then, a short time later, he went on to become legendary in both radio and Hollywood as an actor and director.

As you can see, uncertainty about whether you're going to be successful with all your efforts is something you have no control over. Therefore, auditioning often creates stress and jitters. But if that's the problem, isn't the answer not to go after anything you want real badly? I don't think so. Do you?

Summary

1. Think of the microphone as someone's ear.

2. When only two actors are at the mike and one has finished her part, it is polite to remain at the mike for the other actor to get reactions from you.

3. Keep the script to one side of the mike instead of in front of your face for a better voice quality.

4. If you must cough or clear your throat on air, press your forearm back to your upper arm tightly and cough while pressing your face against the V in your arm.

5. Never just read or say your lines ... act them.

6. Avoid being a "P" popper by not using your cheeks on such words as: "puffing" and "Proper Preparation Prevents Poor Performing."

7. To widen your ability to do dialects, cultivate the habit of listening to the voices when you are watching cartoons or animated films.

8. Because the sound of an actor's voice often influences what the animated characters *look* like in a film, instead of singing in the shower, practice doing dialects.

9. Can you imitate a cat, dog, pig or baby crying? Listen, listen, listen

... and then practice, practice, practice and you'll be amazed what your voice can accomplish.

10. The three general pickup patterns for microphone are: omni-directional, bi-directional, and uni-directional.

11. The microphone pattern most used for actors is the bi-directional.

12. Sound effects normally uses the cardioid, or heart-shaped, pattern.

13. Recording your voice with a hand-held recorder as you read material from this book or newspaper will help you analyze the sound of your voice.

14. If someone is hogging a mike when your cue comes, it is polite to push them aside.

15. Never scratch over a line that has been cut so you can't read it ... at the last moment, they may want it read.

16. With a large cast it's not a good idea to drop your script pages after you've read them. They can not only cause paper noises, but how would you find it if you've mistakenly dropped a page you haven't read into this mess?

17. Speaking rates vary between 120 and 160 words a minute. Slowing the word rate down, or speeding it up, is a useful device in indicating the type of character you're portraying.

18. Our voices, or "voiceprints," are so unique they may soon outdate fingerprints. But it's still up to us to make them interesting.

19. Recording your voice as you read paragraphs from a book or newspaper will help you analyze the sound of your voice. Is it a type of voice you would enjoy listening to on the radio or television?

3

Barkers, Burpers, and Screamers

Can You Digitalize Imagination?

Today, many of the more adventurous and creative sounds you hear in films, or television, are done with digital sampling (sounds recorded for computer-readable numbers). Although digital sampling is very effective for the big screen and television, it has no place in the intimacy of the audio theater.

Audio theater is a theater where the emphasis is on imagination, where audiences have the option of closing their eyes and picturing what they are hearing, or keeping them open and seeing the creativeness it takes to be so imaginative. Neither of which would be entertaining if the sound of a dog barking was done with a CD, and not a teenage girl with a megaphone.

Vocal Effects for Cartoons

Cartoons today are more popular than ever. Although some amazing innovations have been done with the characters' surrealistic appearances, they still need voices, or sounds, that give the characters a recognizable personality. Because unless they do, the cartoon characters are just a bunch of drawings.

Stephen Banks, writer for the Nickelodeon Network, explained: "Once the written script and the storyboard (still drawings) for the cartoon have been drawn (but not filmed) it goes to the actors before it goes to animation. The reason being that, in recording the actors' voices first, the animators are often inspired as to how the characters should look simply by the sound of the actors' voices."

Perhaps now you can appreciate all the vocal ad-libbing you will be required to do for scripts in your audio theater. It makes no difference where the acting is done; it's the experience you acquire doing the acting itself. Your voices are the same, the microphones are the same, all that is lacking is the opportunity to acquire vocal training and experience working with other cast members. All of which is offered in the audio theater performing before the all-important live audiences.

The old humdrum whining of, "How do you get experience if no one will use you unless you have experience?" doesn't apply here. Your audio theater will get you in front of an audience, both where you live and often nationally, whenever you feel you're ready. There are even audio theater organizations around the country that hold conventions, festivals, and even award money for the best script submitted during their many script contests! (Search National Audio Theater on the Internet for more detailed information.)

KNOWING WHEN YOU'RE READY

How do you know when you're "ready"? When your audio theater group is working as a team and you can show audiences how creative and imaginative a theater experience can be that doesn't need settings, costumes, or makeup. Just imagination!

Still not certain your group is ready? How about when your audio group actors have stopped concentrating on perfecting just their one voice, and begin welcoming the numerous vocal challenges that make audio theater unique from visual media.

THE NEED FOR VERSATILITY

Daws Butler, an extremely talented vocal effects artist, did hundreds of different voices over his lifetime of voice-only acting. One of which was the voice of the Kellogg's® Corn Flakes® tiger roaring "They're Grrrrrrrrreat!!!" Not only did that distinctive roar sell a lot of Corn Flakes, it made Daws an awful lot of money. Not that he didn't earn it.

When Daws was handed the script by the agency representative the conversation probably went something like this: "Daws, we want the sound of a tiger roaring that will sell a lot of Corn Flakes."

A commercial audition is often as brief and quick as that. You'll get a few minutes to study the script and perhaps a picture of the tiger. But don't count on it. However, if your vocal tiger roar is so unusual and exciting, the advertising agency might just change the tiger's cartoon image to fit the sound of your voice.

Whether or not this was the case with Daws' interpretation of what the Kellogg's cartoon tiger should sound like is very possible. Because when Daws interpreted these words that were written on the script, *"They're great!,"* into

... *They're GRRREAT!*," it became one of the most recognizable commercials in breakfast food history!

Were animal sounds the only type of vocal sounds Daws Butler did? How about those classic Hanna-Barbera characters: Yogi Bear, Huckleberry Hound, Quick Draw McGraw, Elroy Jetson and hundreds of other voices? Wow, was that man's voice talented! The secret of Daws Butler's success? No one could ever say, "Give me an actor who sounds like Daws Butler." Why? Because no one ever knew what Daws Butler's, Mel Blanc's, Chuck McCann's, Nancy Cartwright's (voice of Bart Simpson), or June Foray's normal voices really did sound like! And when I asked June Foray how she could have done hundreds of normal-sounding voices one minute and then do Rocky the Flying Squirrel on *The Bullwinkle Show*, and hundreds of other voices and sounds for Disney, Hanna-Barbera and countless films and commercials, she just looked at me and said, "That's what I get paid to do, hide my real voice so no one gets tired of hearing it."

If you're thinking, "Oh sure, I could do that if I had June Foray's or Daws Butler's voice!" well, you can't. You have something better: your own voice. This comes from what Daws Butler had to say: "Regardless of the type of voice-only acting that you do, what is really needed is a versatile voice; and the only way to get that is by watching, listening, imagining, and practice."

PRACTICE, PRACTICE AND MORE PRACTICE

"Plenty of practice!" And that's exactly what you'll get in your vocal theater. Your vocal theater isn't just a "voice-only" theater of *reading* scripts, it's *interpreting* with words, or vocal sounds, what the words are intended to mean. In the Kellogg's commercial, the written words "*They're great!*" could be read in a dozen different ways, but would they match the message and reach the vast cereal-buying audience? This is extremely important. Make certain, if your vocal effects are for commercials, to make your vocal words or sounds satisfy what the written words are trying to say in a manner that will most impress the interests of your audience.

GETTING MORE AUTHORITY IN YOUR VOICE

One of the ways of making your voice more versatile is by giving your voice more tonal qualities. Even before the air leaves your windpipe, it has begun to resonate, using your chest as a sounding board. Resonance is basically the vibrations that follow the principal tone in a series of almost instant echoes.

After the vibrations of your voice box determine the pitch, resonance determines the *quality* of the tone. If your primary resonance is in your nose, you will have a nasal tone. To avoid this, practice having your vocal tones come from your chest.

EXAMPLE

Sit in a chair with your feet about 12 inches apart. Next, place a script between your heels and bend over in your chair with your head dangling and your arms hanging in a relaxed manner loosely by your side. Now begin reading from your script using just a single breath. It isn't necessary to read the script to make sense, it's the sound of your voice you're after. Then as you straighten up, your speech should resonate in your chest and your pitch should be lower.

To find out how much lower your voice can be, place your open hand on your chest beneath your collar bone and groan as you say "aaaaah" as if you were in a doctor's office. Now as you leave the doctor's office you have to walk down a flight of stairs. Continue groaning until you reach the bottom step. Be aware of your chest's vibrations as you descend the steps. With your hand still on your chest, say, "I don't believe it is going to snow." Continue making sure you keep lowering your voice, step by step, until you reach the lowest pitch you can maintain naturally. You are now ready for a cereal company to pay you big bucks just for using your deep, growling voice to roar ... "They're Greaaaaaaaaaat!"

Looking Like You Sound

"Voices" aren't singular movements with just your mouth when creating vocal effects, your face has something to say as well. As you might imagine, your face often has to look weird in order to get just the appropriate vocal sound. This goes for the rest of your body as well. After all, if you're asked to crow like a rooster don't you have to put your script on the table, fold your arms for wings, and flap them proudly as you cock-a-doodle-do? What about the sound of a gorilla? Throw out your chest and pound it with both fists. The more you can make yourself look like a gorilla, the more you'll fool your brain into thinking you *are* a gorilla! And isn't that worth making a monkey out of yourself?

CAN YOU ROAR LIKE A TIGER, HOWL LIKE A WOLF?

The first requirement needed in becoming a successful vocal effects artist is a desire to do more with your voice than just talk. If that's the case, you have a good start in becoming a successful vocal effects actor.

When we think of the "sound" of an actor's voice, do we ever imagine sounds such as a mosquito buzzing, lions roaring, dogs barking, an old automobile chugging, baby cries and blood-chilling screams? If you don't, you're neglecting a very special group of talented actors. These are the actors who in addition to using their normal voices for saying words, or speaking lines, have the ability to make all sorts of interesting, unusual and sometimes weird-sounding vocal effects.

The one huge advantage about doing vocal effects for animals is that you don't have to worry about doing different dialects. No matter where the animals come from, a puppy from Germany will whimper the same as one from Hackensack, New Jersey.

This doesn't mean there is only one kind of whimper, anymore than a dog barks the same way when it's glad to see you, or when it wants to eat, or hears a strange noise at night. This is where vocal acting comes in.

The second requirement is that your desire and love to roar and howl like animals, hiss like snakes and buzz like bees is stronger than your fear of looking foolish.

Afraid of Looking Foolish?

The one bugaboo about doing vocal effects in front of an audience is being afraid of looking foolish. If you are, you just aren't putting your heart and soul into it. Because, if you're sincere in what you're asked to do, whether it's a "sinister-snake-with-a-sibilant-speech- and sinus-problem who simply loves succotash," or a "kitten lapping up a dish of cream," you can't be focused on what you're doing and feeling silly both at the same time.

I once worked with a sound effects artist who had an amazing ability to mimic effects with his voice. He credited it with growing up on a farm and enjoyed imitating all the animal sounds. He'd coo like the pigeons, cackle like the hens, crow like the roosters, whinny like the horses, grunt like the pigs, but never in front of an audience where he could have been paid for his talents. I often asked him why he didn't become a vocal effects actor with his tremendous ability and he'd just shrug and reply, "I'm okay doing them when it isn't important, but I couldn't do them in front of an audience; I'd feel like a nut!" And yet all he had to do was stop thinking of what he *looked* like, and concentrate on what he *sounded* like, the proper choice all successful vocal effects actors have to make.

But isn't that what vocal effects or acting is about? If you're sincere about what you're asked to do, you can't be focused on the effect you're doing and what the audience is thinking of you at the same time. It doesn't matter how much makeup or costumes you wear, you can't hide your feelings from an audience. If you feel like an idiot, you'll look like an idiot.

Therefore, if your mind has such a strong control over your feelings, isn't it better to have it focus on what you're doing? And when it does, the audience will respect and appreciate your ability and talents to be so imaginative and entertaining that you can imitate a rattlesnake sniffing around some sizzling bacon!

Hissing Snakes and Sizzling Bacon?

In addition to doing roaring tigers for commercials, vocal effects actors are also often called upon to snore, hiccup, scream, whimper, whistle, or laugh hysterically. What about roaring like a bear, lion, hisssssssing like a snake, or sizzling bacon? Absolutely. After giving it some thought, what sound is similar to that of sizzling bacon? Is it air hissing out of a car's tire? No, that hissing is too high in sound and too steady and forceful. But what about the sound of an angry hissing snake? Don't they both have the same sibilant sound as that of sizzling bacon? They would be if those vocal effects had been done by Brad Barker.

Brad Barker was working on a live radio show as a straight actor and found out it would take too long for the person doing sound effects to get what was needed for the added sound of bacon frying (a hot plate and wet rag). Barker, because of his acting popularity, had a conflict (another acting assignment) and, not wanting to be late for his next show, quickly volunteered to do the sizzling bacon sounds vocally. Without batting an eye, he slightly gargled air through his clenched teeth and saved the day both for that show and got himself to his next live show on time.

As distinctive and talented as Barker's and our voices are in doing certain vocal effects, we can always use a little help. Therefore, when you use your nose as a resonator, it will give your voice a nasal sound. Whereas, if your chest is the resonator, your voice will have an authoritative quality to roar like a tiger. But that's only a part of the ultimate sounds that your voice will be required to do, so in addition to the help the microphone will give, what about an empty milk carton?

Milk carton? Sure, or a conical shaped plastic orange juice container, or the empty cardboard tube from paper towels or toilet tissue; anything that gives your voice the much-needed help for a difficult vocal effect. Didn't Marlon Brando put apple halves in his cheeks to effect his speech for his role in *The Godfather*? And if Brando can use apple halves, can't you use a conical-shaped, plastic orange juice container for the roar of a bear?

THE BEAR AT 30,000 FEET

Not just a bear you see in a zoo, what about an angry, grizzly bear breaking out of a cage in an airplane at 30,000 feet? It was the first time I had ever worked with Brad and was often told what a genius he was as a vocal effects artist. I would soon learn the truth.

In rehearsal I did the sound of the plane flying in stormy weather and shook the jail gate I was using to simulate the grizzly bear's cage. The bear wasn't happy about the cage or flying at 30,000 feet and showed it by angrily shaking the iron-barred cage and roaring his grizzly bear hatred of the confinement!

During the rehearsals I didn't think too much of my job of rattling a heavy jail gate to simulate the sound of the bear cage. In fact there wasn't even a reason, not if Brad Barker's angry grizzly bear wasn't going to get any more ferocious sounding than whimpering. I was even surprised that the director wasn't being critical of either me or Brad when we took the break after dress rehearsal and got ready for the air show. Then, thirty seconds before air time, Brad came walking over holding an empty conical orange juice container and smiling. "You rattle and I'll roar and we'll scare the hell out of the audience!"

At first I thought he was going to use the orange juice container to hold water in case his voice got dry. Did I get a surprise? The first thing I learned was that Brad had been saving his voice during all the rehearsals. The director knew this and assumed I had enough experience to realize this too. Then, as the clock ticked away the final few seconds, suddenly the whole atmosphere in the studio changed! As I revved up the small plane and took off, Brad put the orange juice container to his mouth and his voice no longer came from an actor in a grey suit thinking about how much money he was going to make! Because, out of this polite actor's mouth, came the sound of a frightened and enraged, shaggy-haired, seven-foot-tall, growling, grunting, grizzly bear!

Watching Brad use the container to help with the various growls and roars was like a musician playing a strange-looking instrument capable of scaring your pants off! Suddenly I grabbed the jail gate bars and for the rest of the show both Brad and I had become not actors or sound effects men, but a seven-foot, frenzied, grizzly bear! How hard and long I shook the bars depended on the intensity of Brad's roars that continued throughout the entire show!

When it was finally over, Brad's roars and my desperate efforts to break out of the iron-barred cage, was the first time I ever had the emotional experience of knowing how a terrified, caged, grizzly bear must feel, frantically wanting his freedom at 30,000 feet! All because of Brad's voice and an empty orange juice container that *demanded* I feel that way.

I soon learned that other vocal effects actors had their own methods of giving their voices a helping hand. Some used pillows for baby cries, others did the crying into the creases of their folded arms. But what will it take for you to do the barking sounds for a dog? Not just any dog, but a big, big, big dog?

GIVING ANIMALS A PERSONALITY

Doing vocal effects for animals in the audio theater is not like simply doing voices for animals drawn in cartoons. It's *being* that animal you're portraying. First of all, you don't say words. You bark, growl and pant. Half the time with your tongue in your mouth, and the rest with it just hanging out. And don't mistake these facial expressions as "mugging" for laughs, it's what you have to do to become that animal you're portraying.

And it's also what makes vocal effects artists so valuable. Yes I've used records and tapes for animal sounds, but never to give them a personality. As excellent as many of these animal effects are on CDs, they are only effective for background sounds, or sounds that don't require interactive responses.

The following sketch is an excellent opportunity to improve your ability to do animal sounds. In doing it, if you feel foolish, you're going to have a hard job convincing an audience you're a dog, let alone a great big, big, unusual dog; so, forget you're an actor barking like a dog and bark because that's what dogs do ... especially big, big, big dogs!

SFX OR FOLEYING?

At one time the term "Foleying" referred to the manual sound effects provided for the movies. Prior to that these types of manual effects were called "sync effects," meaning they were done in synchronization with the movements in the film. Although these Foley effects of the big dog's paws aren't indicated in the script, they should accompany any movements the dog makes ... or we imagine the dog makes. The person doing the Foley paw effects needs to work very closely with all action that requires movement from the big dog; what name or color you choose for the big dog is up to you.

This sketch is to be played for laughs. Therefore the pace and timing between George's lines, Lassee's barks and paw sounds and the normal SFX must be done without any thought that what they are doing is funny. That's up to the audience to decide. Above all, the vocal artist doing the barks and growls must not feel uncomfortable, or appear foolish. Instead, he or she must act, look and sound, like a big dog protecting the house against George, a seeming intruder. While George, fearing for his very life, tries everything possible including acting he isn't one bit afraid of this big, big, dog.

THE BIG, BIG, BIG
DOG SKETCH

ANNOUNCER: Tonight's scene opens with George arriving home a day early from a weeklong business trip. What George doesn't know is, while he was away his wife offered to pet sit for a neighbor's dog, let's make that a very, very, large neighbor's dog. His wife has just left to get more, much more, pet food as George opens the front door.

SOUND EFFECTS: DOOR CLOSES

GEORGE: (Calling) Hi honey, ... I'm home! (pause) Honey? (thinking) I'll bet she's downstairs in the playroom watching television. Won't she be surprised to see me. I'll just sneak this playroom door open ... close my eyes and give her a great big kiss.

SFX: DOOR OPENING ... KISSING SOUND

GEORGE: (Opens eyes and trying to be brave) You're not honey, are you? No sirreee! You're bigger than a linebacker for the Dallas Cowboys!!! (forced laugh dries up) But you don't have to be afraid of me boy, no sirrreee. If there's one thing I love is small dogs, big dogs ... hot dogs...

BIG DOG: (Growl)

GEORGE: Sorry! Could you step back a hair big fella? One of your dog tags is still caught around my throat! (cautious) Just a teeny bit more...

SFX: DOOR SLAM AND BOLTS

GEORGE: Whooeee is he big! But this solid oak door will hold him!

SFX: MUFFLED POUNDING SLIGHTLY OFF

But just to make sure! (SOUNDS FOLLOWS ACTION) I'll put a chair, a table, and the television in front of the solid oak door...

SFX: DOOR POUNDING SLIGHTLY LOUDER

GEORGE: They sure don't make these solid oak doors like they used to! Or the chairs ... (EFFORT) or the mahogany dining room table ... or the television ... or the solid brass parrot cage!

POLLY: (PARROT SCREECHES)

GEORGE: Better you than me, Polly!

SFX: SUDDEN BIG CRASH

GEORGE: (trying not to be afraid) Hi big fella ... here I put all this stuff against the door and you came through the wall! (GRASPING AT STRAWS) But you don't have to be afraid of me big guy! No sirreee. What's your name fella? Spot? Bowser? Teeth?

BIG DOG: (SNARLS)

GEORGE: Whoops! There I go again! Wanna play, big fella? You do? Okay, gimme your paw ... gimme your paw ... gimme your paw!!!

SFX: LOUD SLAP

GEORGE: That's not what I had in mind, big guy ... but you did it very well ... yes you did! (idea) How about playing a game of "go fetch?" First, let me get this log from the fireplace. (effort)

GEORGE: There. Now I'll open up this door and throw it out as far as I can!

SFX: LOG BUMP

GEORGE: Right on my foot! (hopping on one leg) No, big fella this isn't a game! Fetch the log, not my leg, big guy ... the log! Let go, let go, let go!

SFX: CLOTH RIP

GEORGE: Okay! You can have my pants, just give me back my underwear!! That's a good boy! Now I'll open the door. DOOR OPENS (effort) Lift the log and here we go boy ... go get it!!

SFX: DOOR SLAMS AND RAPID LOCK SOUNDS

GEORGE: And just to be sure!

SFX: NAILING DOOR SHUT IS INTERRUPTED BY DOORBELL

GEORGE: (Finally curious) Who is it?

SFX: DOOR SMASHING

GEORGE: Hi boy ... I was just going to open the door ... come in, come in ... and look what you've gone and done! I threw out a log and you brought back a *Volkswagen!*

GEORGE: (Hardly able to get the words out) Wanna play again, fella?

BIG DOG: (happy barks)

GEORGE: Now what can I throw? How about the spare tire you're chewing on? Now I'm going to take this tire and I'm going to roll it down that big, big hill that doesn't end until the next town. Won't that be fun?

BIG DOG: (happy barks)

GEORGE: Okay ... one for the money, two for the show, and away it goes!!

SFX: SLAMS DOOR. PHONE RINGS AND OFF CRADLE

GEORGE: Hello? (relieved) Thank goodness it's you.... Of course I knew it was your voice, who else would be calling me??? (desperate) Honey, I know what you have to say is important but not like I've got to.... What? You're pet sitting for a dog in the basement because you know I'm frightened of big dogs. He's what? First in his class and is worth 15,000 dollars?!! Wrong? What makes you think that something's wrong? Here boy, here boy ... (imitates the big dog) woof, woof, woof ... does that sound like he's unhappy ... he's calling me now.... I gotta go, honey!!

SOUND: PHONE HANG UP AND DOOR OPEN

GEORGE: (calling and fading off into music) Here boy ... here boy ... (hiding his terror) you don't have to be afraid of me boy, no sirree ... cause I love all kinds of dogs ... little dogs ... big dogs ... even big, big big, big dogs!

MUSIC: HOW MUCH IS THAT DOGGIE IN THE WINDOW?

APPLAUSE

Some Tips

Although this sketch has a small cast, it's an excellent example of the versatility of audio theater. Where else could a sketch of this nature be done that requires the audience to imagine a dog of this size ... or any dog?

Even when dramatic radio was live back in it's golden age, not all actors were capable of doing a dog barking, or any animal effects. That is why those few actors who specialized in doing animal or unusual vocal effects had very, very, very successful careers ... just as they do today.

But even these vocal effects actors don't rely entirely on their naked voices. They use pillows for baby cries, empty paper towel holders for big growls, empty toilet paper tubes for smaller growls, or simply pull both facial cheeks apart with their hands for monster roars. All of this to be done emotionally so that audiences can literally see what your sound looks like! Now do you wonder why these vocal effects actors have such successful careers? With these talented actors, "being happy as a clam" is more than just a saying ... it's a vocal effect challenge!

A Few of the Unsung Heroes of Howling and Barking

The following actors have been heard by millions of people over the years but their names have rarely or ever been publicized:

Brad Barker (MGM lion), David James (Cheetah in Tarzan films), Earl Keen (Lassie), Madeleine Pierce (baby cries), Mel Blanc (Bugs Bunny), Ray Erlenborn (animal sounds in Doctor Dolittle), James MacDonald (Mickey Mouse), Nancy Kelly (screamer), Daws Butler (Yogi Bear), Donald Bain (mosquitoes to chirping birds), Nancy Cartwright (Bart Simpson), Chuck McCann (Cool McCool), June Foray (Rocky the Flying Squirrel) and Alan Reed (Fred Flintstone) are just a few of the talented voice-effects actors who have entertained us for so many years.

Many I knew by working with them, others I knew by reputation. Finding and getting the names of the hundreds of others would be difficult enough, listing all the vocal effects they did would be impossible. If I left you out, I apologize.

Summary

1. Animal imitators and vocal effects artists are all vocal actors who have the ability to either talk about a tiger, or be the tiger.

2. To become a voice-only actor requires listening and imitating, not any special kind of voice.

3. Vocal actors require as much movement with their faces and bodies as they do their voices.

4. Many vocal actors play the part of an old man and a young puppy in the same show. This imaginative casting is what sets audio theater apart from visual media.

5. Creating sounds vocally can be helped by milk cartons, megaphones, or whatever prop is needed to get the job done.

6. Although we normally exhale while we're speaking, inhaling makes a very effective sound of a dog barking.

7. One vocal effects actor was so serious about his ability to create sounds, he wouldn't think of buzzing like a mosquito unless he knew whether it was a male or female.

8. If you don't feel like singing in the shower, why not practice sounding like a wounded dinosaur.

9. Walt Disney was one of the first cartoon vocal-only actors when he created the sounds for Mickey Mouse in 1928.

10. Making the vocal sounds of a grunting pig will only make you look foolish if you think of anything other than being a grunting pig.

11. A famous stage actor once told me, nothing succeeds like practice ... not even practice ... you must both practice your art form and have the desire.

4

Writing Tips for the Audio Theater

Before people wrote a sentence, or spoke a word, they did a lot of thinking and imagining. And isn't that what writing is all about, expressing your thoughts in such a way as to ensure there is some record of what those thoughts are, or were? Whether those thoughts were once scratched on a cave wall, written on paper with a quill, or keyed into a word processor, the craft of creative writing hasn't changed. It's the same for you as it was for Shakespeare and Mark Twain. I can't think of a quicker or more challenging way of having your thoughts heard than in your audio theater in front of a live audience!

Now the question is, how do you know that you even have the talent to be a writer? Is being a successful writer something you have to be born with, or can it be taught and learned? The answer is, how badly do you want to have your thoughts expressed? If you just "like" to write, it isn't enough. You can like a Pepsi, or like to talk on your cell phone, or like to watch sports, but you can't just "like" your dream. Therefore, instead of worrying if you have to be born with the talent to be a writer, actor, or doctor, ask yourself whether you have the burning desire to do whatever it takes to become a writer. If you honestly believe you have, the worst thing you could ever possibly write will be better than not having written at all.

Style

Style is what your imagination brings to your heart. Only you have lived your life, and only you can put it into words with your true emotions. Putting words together for the audio theater, or for cartoons, monologues, pantomimes, television, magazines, or books, is only a visible outlet for your

45

thoughts. Expressing those words is your style. Just as your style is unique, there are different requirements in order for what you wrote to be accepted.

FORMATTING YOUR SCRIPT

The audio theater script is probably the easiest script to format. No need for camera angles, just a few suggestions to the actors and sound effects. But in order for a voice-only script to be accepted, either in the audio theater or in other media, it must follow a few rules.

An acceptable script for audio theater (or most other media) must be written on pages no larger or smaller than letter-size paper (8½ × 11 inches) and should have ample margins on both sides of the paper for the following information:

1. Page numbers are in the upper right corner.
2. Actors' names are to the far left of the page.
3. Sound effects and music cues instructions should be in capital letters and underlined.

SUBMITTING A STORY

Submitting a story to be done in your audio theater couldn't be easier. There are little restrictions as to what you write, as long as it appeals to your audience's imagination. Other markets are not quite so lenient. Their requirements focus rigidly on a particular format. This is as true with a surrealistic cartoon such as *SpongeBob SquarePants* as it was during the golden age of dramatic radio with shows such as *Suspense*.

If you had an idea for a story and wanted it heard on *Suspense,* you would first have to write to the show and find out if they accepted scripts from freelance writers (writers not under contract to the show). Once that was done, they would read your script and send you a format sheet of what was demanded of your script.

Ross Murray, a writer of a number of scripts for *Suspense,* was kind enough to allow me to show you what a format sheet looks like; included are two opening pages to one of his broadcasted scripts.

The Theory of "Suspense"—What Is Desired and What Is Not Desired in Scripts Submitted

Suspense attempts to keep its own heft and dimension among programs devoted to the general subject of crime and punishment.

1. It is not a detective show. This does not mean that a detective cannot figure importantly in the plot. It does mean that we do not go in for a

crime committed, followed by a tracking down of a criminal by means of a detective's analysis. Suspense is thus not a "Whodunit?".

2. Suspense is not a Horror Show. There can, of course, be an element of horror in a Suspense drama, but it must have believability; it must be conceived with taste and class.

3. Suspense is not a ghost story show. We feel that our most powerful examples have been those in which the listener could easily identify himself with the central character being enacted. "Sorry, Wrong Number," is simply the horrible predicament of a woman desperately trying to get someone to believe her over the telephone.... Other of our broadcasts have observed similar urgency and simplicity.

4. Suspense requires that a criminal meet with retribution. However, no poor guy or gal should come to a bad end through no fault of his or her own simply by dint of circumstances.

5. Suspense uses stars. In this connection, a starring role is not created simply by the number of words per page uttered by a character. The character must have a definite profile. If he is a killer, or heavy, he pursues his machinations too far and is hoisted by his own petard. If he is a hero, fighting against insuperable odds, he is ingenious enough to extricate himself from this difficulty.

Suspense scripts should be twenty-four playing minutes in length of the drama proper — including music cues. Orchestra is available for any musical effects desired.

William Spier
Producer, Director-Editor

That was a *Suspense* format sheet that writers had to follow to have their script aired on one of the most popular shows during radio's golden age. In return, if your script was accepted, it could be done by some of Hollywood's biggest radio and film stars and heard by an audience of millions of listeners. Jimmy Stewart, for instance, was cast as a paralyzed war veteran driven to murder by the sight of a man who resembled one of his former Japanese torturers! How is that for keeping an audience surprised and in suspense? But isn't that what screen stars are doing today in cartoons and animations? Eddie Murphy playing the part of a donkey?

First Things First

As important as having your script idea done in your audio theater, the manner in which it is written is equally important. Each media has its own writing requirements whether it be for the screen, television, cartoons, animations, stage, or the audio theater. And because the audio theater's words and movements depend upon what they sound like to a microphone, the script must be written in the most practical and accommodating form.

Now that you know the type of story *Suspense* would accept, the following two pages are included to show how your story would need to appear on paper for the director, actors, music and sound effects. If it didn't, your chances of having your script even being read beyond the first page would be very small.

EXAMPLE: WINNER LOSE ALL

SUSPENSE
(pg 1)

1   <u>MUSIC:THEME AND UNDER</u>
2   BOB: Las Vegas ... Sucker City ... land of the money cow. And in my pocket
3   I had a permit to milk it ... a system to beat the wheel. But first I had to
4   convince one of the farmers tending the cow that I wasn't going to take too
5   much ... and that wasn't going to be easy. (<u>MUSIC OUT</u>) (BEAT) After
6   about a week of nosing around I decided on the place I was going to hustle.
7   (SOUND: GAMBLING B.G.) The owner was a guy named Carlin, Walter Carlin,
8   and he wasn't doing as well as he wanted ... but then, who does?
9   <u>SOUND: STEPS TO DOOR ... KNOCK</u>
10   CARLIN: (FROM INSIDE) Come in!
11   <u>SOUND: DOOR OPENS ... STEPS IN ... DOOR CLOSES</u>
12   BOB: Mr. Carlin?
13   CARLIN: (SLIGHTLY OFF) Yes, who are you?
14   <u>SOUND: FEW STEPS IN</u>
15   BOB: My name is Bob Richards and I've got a proposition for you.
16   CARLIN: Goodbye, Mr. Richards.
17   BOB: Listen to me for one minute.
18   CARLIN: (A LITTLE EDGE) I said goodbye, Mr. Richards.
19   BOB: But I want to give you something for nothing.
20   CARLIN: Nobody in this world ever gave anybody something for nothing.
21   BOB: I will ... guaranteed.
22   CARLIN: All right ... you've got one minute ... make your pitch.
23   BOB: When was the last time you had a spread in the *New York Times*?

(pg 2)

1   CARLIN: Come on son, quit playing. This is a small place compared to
2   the palaces on the Strip.
3   BOB: And you're not only small, but your business is bad.... Isn't
4   that right, Mr. Carlin?
5   CARLIN: I said I'd give you a minute to make a pitch ... not to discuss my
6   business affairs.

7   BOB: That's part of my pitch. I can get nationwide publicity at a small
8   fraction of the cost.
9   CARLIN: Keep talking ... you have thirty seconds.
10 BOB: Okay, but don't interrupt me no matter how crazy it may sound at
11 the beginning.
12 CARLIN: I won't.
13 BOB: I have a system for roulette. Oh, I know everybody has some kind of
14 system, but I've got one that will win. The only trouble is when the
15 house finds somebody's got a winning system the table is closed for a
16 while ... or the betting is limited. Now here's my pitch. You let me win
17 two hundred thousand dollars.
18 CARLIN: (BEGINS TO TALK)
19 BOB: Let me finish. It'll take about a month to forty days. During that
     time
20 every paper in the country will have a spread on the guy that's going to
21 win almost a quarter of a million! Then when I bet 200,000 at the end
22 of my tour of duty, all I want is fifty thousand grand in cash for my
23 share. But you've got coast-to-coast publicity and I've got fifty grand
24 clear! We got a deal?

EXAMPLE

In reading those two pages you can see how the writer's ideas are expressed, not only for the listening audience to hear, but for the director and cast members to best understand how the words are to be performed most effectively.

1. *Music cues are capitalized and underlined.*
   1. MUSIC: THEME AND UNDER

2. *Actors' names are at the far left of the script.*
   2 BOB:

3. *Sound effects are also capitalized and underlined.*
   3 SOUND: STEPS TO DOOR ... KNOCK

4. *Technical information is put in parentheses.*
   4 CARLIN: (FROM INSIDE)

5. *How the writer suggests a line is to be read is called a "reading" and put in parenthesis. Any other information the writer wants to give the actor is also put in parentheses.*
   5 CARLIN: (A LITTLE EDGE)

6. *The advantage of numbering your lines becomes obvious when you're editing.*
   6 DIRECTOR: On page 1, line 26 of Carlin's line, cut: "you've got one minute." Then on page 2, line 17, cut: "Now here's my pitch." On page 3, line 14, cut: "huh."

EXAMPLE

Comparing this next example that doesn't have numbered lines shows how difficult it is to communicate information regarding cuts, notes and suggestions from the director, especially when time is a factor.

> DIRECTOR: On page one at the bottom of the page after Bob's line, "I will guarantee," cut Carlin's "you've got one minute" in the middle of his speech. Then on page 2 in the middle of the page after Carlin's line, "I won't," go down five lines of Bob's speech and cut "Now here's my pitch." Then on page 3, Bob says, "huh" in the middle of the page, cut it.

Although numbering the lines are a matter of choice, one formatting rule that never should be broken is double-spacing your sentences to make room for the inevitable cuts, changes, or notes that need to be included.

Another rule is never use a pen ... always a pencil with a good eraser when making cuts. To prove how important these tools are in making last-second changes, I've included a page from *You Can't Take It with You*, starring Walter Brennan.

Please note that despite attempting to include the original script pages from the various shows done in radio's golden era, the condition of many of their script pages made it impossible. Therefore, although I've included a few of these to give you the feel of what it was like doing live dramatic radio, I did the next best thing ... copy everything, exactly as was on these hurried edited pages with their cuts and time changes.

You will see in reading the next page why it was so important to have double spaces between the lines for deletions and changes in the dialogue.

Breaking All Rules

If records are made to be broken, I suppose rules are as well. See if you can find some of the format errors for a script that was supposed to be written for radio.

SCHEDULED FLIGHT

SOUND: AIRLINER REVVING UP AND TAKING OFF WITH NARRATION

NARRATOR: (simply) On the runway of a commercial airport, a modern airliner is poised like a giant dragonfly. Along her silver body is painted, "Citadel Airlines."

SOUND: SPURT

NARRATOR: With a sudden, thunderous surge of power, she sweeps forward on her way into the vastness of blue sky and white clouds.

SOUND: UP AND AWAY.

NARRATOR: Now, our main title and production credits will appear. Then we fade into our opening live-action sequence.

YOU CAN'T TAKE IT WITH YOU
August 12, 1951

SPOT THREE

ANNCR: "Every week, NBC and its affiliated stations bring you a
          world of entertainment. But there is more to network
          radio than that. Radio is a more efficient and less
          expensive way to advertise. The increased sales resulting
          from the advertising mean more production of goods and low
          prices for you. In addition, the keen competition inherent
          in advertising shows up every day in new products, in
          better products -- for your use. Every program broadcast
          by NBC and its affiliated stations, whether it contains
          an advertising message or not, is paid for by the revenues
          gained from advertisors. So--when shopping, remember
          the brand names you've heard on NBC. These manufacturers
          believe in their products enough to urge the greatest
          possible number of people to test them in their homes.
          Only quality products can survive this test. Only quality
          products can continue to advertise."

Radio script page from *You Can't Take It with You*, starring Walter Brennan (August
12, 1951).

MUSIC: BUILDS AND OUT
SOUND: FADE IN MOTOR SOUNDS AS HEARD INSIDE AIRLINER
       LOUNGE
NARRATOR: We are now in the main passenger cabin of the airliner in flight.
    A stewardess, trim pretty and efficient, is coming down the aisle, checking
    the names on her passenger list. Sitting alone, is Mary Ann Hughes, a pub-
    lic school teacher, very attractive and dressed in good taste. She is writing a
    letter and her face looks troubled. The Stewardess moves up to Mary Ann.
    She senses the schoolteacher's abstractions.
STEWARDESS: I beg your pardon — Miss Hughes?
MARY ANN: Oh, yes, Stewardess. (in recognition) Well, hello, there! Remem-
    ber me?
STEWARDESS: Of course, Mary Ann Hughes! Last summer on our Chicago
    flight.

MARY ANN: That's right. On last year's vacation.

STEWARDESS: Still teaching school at Heightstown?

MARY ANN: Yes, and I'm on my vacation again, thank goodness.

STEWARDESS: We all need them, don't we — — when we have a job to do.

MARY ANN: (Hesitatingly) Well, the way things are with me, I may not even go back.

SOUND: BUZZER OFF

STEWARDESS: (fading off) Pardon me, Miss Hughes, I'm wanted.

MARY ANN: (close on mike) I may not go back. (more emphatically) *May* not? (with decision) I *won't* go back, ever! I just can't take it! (normally) Am I running away? I hope not. I hope I'm running toward a solution — that will make me feel of use to something, or someone. Anyway, I'm not going back there — — not after what happened that last day of school — —(whispering) not after that!

SOUND: FADE OUT PLANE SOUND

NARRATOR: (intimate) As Mary Ann speaks, our camera moves in, closer and closer, until her face fills the screen, whereupon our picture dissolves to another scene — a schoolroom — and we witness the event which Mary is recalling.

SOUND: FADE IN, SCHOOLYARD OF CHILDREN'S VOICES OFF MIKE.

MARY ANN: Joey, I just don't understand! You have been one of my best pupils and I thought you liked me. I thought you'd be *glad* that I was moving a grade ahead and that I'd be your teacher again next term.

Simple Carelessness

How did you do? Did you find those mistakes that had no business in a radio script? Here are a few I found on the first two pages!

1. Breaks the double-spacing rule between sentences.
2. There is no indication when the music starts, only when it, *Builds and Fades.*
3. How do you make the sound of a *spurt?*
4. NARRATOR: *Now our main title and credit will* appear...?
5. NARRATOR: As Mary Ann speaks, our camera moves in closer and closer, until her face fills the screen, whereupon our picture dissolves to another scene.

Perhaps the writer had written some films or a play and thought radio didn't have a special format. If that was so, it was simple carelessness on his part. All of the different media have their own special formats that best suit their needs. And it's up to the writers to find out what they are if they want their scripts done ... or even read.

The same is true for audio theater. Basically audio theater is one that stimulates the audience's imagination ... not simply by what the audience hears, but what they see as well. And in order to do this, there are a number of ways of making an audio script different from the other mediums simply by following some creative and imaginative tips. But first, you must see that your story gets on paper properly.

Some Audio Theater Shortcuts

After your script has been written in the proper format, there are a number of shortcuts available with information that will help the actors and directors.

ELLIPSIS

A series of dots ... used to indicate slight pauses that writers use when they want to show how an actor's character feels without putting emotions into words ... or simply searching for words ... correct words ... for something emotionally difficult for them to say ... or how they're feeling at the moment to register in the listener's mind.

By using the ellipsis method for emphasis, you make the line strong without the emotional excitement that the exclamation mark implies.

Example
A different use for the ellipsis is shown with this sound effect cue.

Sound Effects: Door Opens ... Steps in ... Door Closes
In this case the dots are used for slight pauses to indicate timing. You can see how simpler and more effective they are than if the writer had to indicate the word "pause" to indicate the time between the actors reading their lines and sound effects producing their effects.

Sound Effects: Door Opens (Pause) Steps in (Pause) Door Closes
The use of ellipses in the sound effects cue indicates more than just pauses, it indicates the person entering a strange office is not intimidated. He doesn't stop after opening the door and ask to enter the office ... nor does he leave the door open. As you can see, the use of the ellipsis does an awful lot of work for just being three little dots.

BEATS

"Beats" are very similar to ellipses but more of a hiccup rather than a pause. This difference in length is just long enough to think to yourself the word "BEAT." The problem with indicating this written word (BEAT), even though it's in parentheses, is if it is written in the middle of an actor's speech, it could throw the actor's timing off, or even worse, she could read it as if it was part of her speech.

Example

> NANCY: (Painful) Cathee (BEAT) this isn't going to be easy (BEAT) but (BEAT) well (BEAT) if I don't say it (BEAT) well (BEAT) here's the truth.

As you can see from Nancy's speech this could easily happen and is why actors dislike having a script with (BEATS) written in them. The other is they clutter up a script and are often penciled over. By using the simpler ellipsis method, those sentences would look like this:

> NANCY: (Painful) Cathee ... this isn't going to be easy ... but ... well ... if I don't say it ... well ... here's the truth.

Notice that by the writer using dots between words they serve another purpose by indicating what sort of emotional readings the writer suggests.

READINGS

"Readings" are often written by writers to indicate to the actor how a word or sentence should be said. After spending so many hours over a sentence, or even every word, writers often are afraid the actors won't give their precious words just the precise emotional meanings. As a result they parenthesize these reading suggestions to the actors and directors and sometimes go a little overboard with their parental concerns.

EXAMPLE

> 1   MARY: (not certain this is wise) Do you really think we should go, Bob? I don't have a thing to wear ... (groping for excuses) ... and my hair is a mess...
> 2   BOB: (Firm) We're going if you have to wear a wig!

Readings are fine ... but only if they are really needed and deserved. Oftentimes writers use them to make certain the actor will give a worried reading for words that are in opposition to how the actress feels her character would react. Perhaps rather than being (not certain this is wise) she feels more comfortable reading the lines the way it's most realistic to her character ... which is simply in a nervous tone of voice. The same is true of Mary's other readings: (groping for excuses).

Not only is the number of readings in that short scene unnecessary, the amount of words the writer uses to get his suggestion across is often unnecessary. Long, drawn out readings can become a problem for the actors. Normally not only will the actors cross them out and give their script a messy look, they often make the embarrassing mistake of reading them as if they were part of their normal lines. Actors work as hard at making their characters believable as the writer does in creating the characters. Therefore actors often interpret reading suggestions from the writer as a criticism of their abilities as actors. Therefore use readings only when absolutely necessary, but not as an excuse for writing characters that are so vague that they need them.

Normally at the first dry rehearsal (rehearsing without technical facilities) the director will give the actors her feelings about how certain lines should be read if she feels the actor is losing the character's proper attitude. Therefore, the writer should be very careful and use their readings wisely unless they want to step on two sensitive toes ... the actor's and the director's.

Readings present yet another problem. They're often put in by the writer who can't quite find the proper word to indicate how one of his lines should be read. Then, instead of searching a thesaurus for the proper words, they stick in the first word or words that come to their head.

Example

> JOEY: At first it was cool. All the kids liked you! But lately it's just like we were a nuisance, and...
> JANE: (imperatively) *Joey!*

Why "*imperatively*"? Why not imperious or peremptory if the writer wants to confuse and send the actors searching for a studio dictionary. Why not simply write:

> JANE: (angry) *Joey!*

"Angry" might not be as impressive as "imperatively" but isn't the writer after a certain emotion, not a vocabulary quiz? Then again, perhaps the writer wanted a more subtle anger and hopes by indicating "imperatively" that the actor and director will come up with just the proper and subtle emotion that he can't find the proper word for?

This is a big and lazy mistake on any writer's part. Many actors and many directors take whatever the writers put in their scripts is to be done exactly as the writer indicates. After all, didn't the writer sweat over each and every word, comma and period? Therefore if the writer puts a request for a certain emotion that only the word "imperatively" will give him, who should know better than the writer? Exactly ... "who *should* know better?" ... most often the director and actors. If the writer has done his work, the character he wrote will have a mind of its own, and now it will be up to the actor to see the audience hears it ... imperatively or not imperatively.

The only thing worse than writing readings that are vague is writing words that are too precise. Sometimes a writer's love for their characters makes them go just a little over the edge with their worries and fears by being over-protective, over how one of their precious words should be read.

Example

   1   MARY: (Torn between her gut emotion and what's expected of her to say and how to say it ... she simply murmurs an uncertain) Hello.
   2   HARRY: (Uncertain how to react to Mary's reply, responds in guarded tones) Hello.

As you can see, a writer can be carried away giving the actors and directors too much help that isn't needed. Therefore, if you find yourself writing a script and giving the actors too much advice as to how your words are to be read, perhaps what needs to be done is to improve the way lines are written.

Keep Your Script Moving

An example of keeping your script moving is to be aware you don't have the luxury of time to develop your characters to the point where the audience feels sorry for the bad guy because he came from a dysfunctional family. Even the names of your characters should be an indication as to who they are. You wouldn't expect a character named "Spike" to be a rocket scientist, or a girl named "Trixie" to be a brain surgeon.

Writing for a wimpy character takes more than just a "wimpy" name and voice, it needs help from the written words. Words that help make the actor's voice *sound* wimpy should always be more relied on than just their name.

Example

MATT: Let's check out what's happening at the beach club, Bull.
BULL: Really, Matt? Why now? You know there's never anything going on when we go there and ... well, why not hang out here?

In identifying the characters that were saying these words, wouldn't you say the names given to the characters were mixed up? In the writer's mind "Bull" might be the one who is overbearing and aggressive but it never gets down on paper. Simply by picking out a name like "Bull" won't convince any audience as to the nature of your characters unless they hear it in their spoken words.

Estab-BG-and Out

"*ESTAB-BG-AND OUT*" simply means: "Establish the sound effects, Background the sound effects, and take them Out." Dramatic license is asking an audience to suspend their judgmental demands of realism for the sake of art. How much dramatic license an audience allows sound effects is often an indication of how much they are enjoying themselves. If a story requires a church bell to toll the midnight hour, the first several rings should be in the clear, and the rest faded down under dialogue. This may not be the way it happens in real life, but it's far better than having the bells tolling to twelve so loudly that it makes the actors have to shout to be heard.

Films give something for audiences to see, the audio theater gives audiences something to imagine. And you'd be surprised how quick your audience comprehends a sound and wants to know what's next. This is particularly true of background sounds.

If a film takes place in the woods and there are crickets chirping, the audience has the woods for distraction. This isn't the case in the audio theater. Here the crickets are used to indicate the woods with no other distraction than the actors' dialogue. And once audience's imagination has heard the crickets and formed a picture in their minds, the crickets can be faded under the dialogue and the audience will never wonder or worry about what happened to those woodsy, chirping denizens.

TIMING WHAT YOU WRITE

Whoever came up with the axiom "time is money" must have been a director in broadcasting. Where time isn't measured in hours, or minutes, but seconds. Where ten-second commercials at the Super Bowl may run in the hundreds of thousands of dollars, having the ten-second commercial run only nine seconds cheats the sponsor out of an awful lot of money.

Knowing the value of time is important, whether it be for the Super Bowl, or doing a radio commercial on your local station, or getting started in your audio theater. And the best way to get along with the confines of time is to be aware of what can happen if you don't.

A rule of thumb in timing a script, whether it be for the theater, film, television, cartoons, or radio, is to allow one minute per page. Whether this is fair or not, it's reality. If a producer, editor or director picks up a script for a one-hour show and it has ninety pages, chances are it will never get read. The same is true in our audio theater. If you write a five-minute show, don't stretch it out to ten pages. To avoid overwriting, read the lines to yourself and time them. If there are a great deal of sound effects, they must be imagined. Together, the sound effects and dialogue may take only three pages on paper, but will time out to five minutes when being acted. Better you do the editing than leaving it for the director during the stress of rehearsal.

SEGUES/CROSS FADES

The term "segue" is normally used in a musical sense as "segueing from one song to another without interruption." It's understandable that the terms segue and cross-fading can be confusing, but they are often used interchangeably. What cross-fades are to sound media, the term "dissolve" is for films.

Dissolve is used to fade the camera's picture out from one scene to another; whereas in the audio theater, cross-fading is the term used to fade out one scene to either another scene or a different time period. The term "segue" is more direct in changing the scenes. In films it's "cut to the chase," in the audio theater it's changing a scene at the same sound level without utilizing fades. Both offer a sense of movement.

Example: Cross-Fading

GRANDSON: What was the war like, Grandpa?
GRANDFATHER: It's been so long ago, son, (thinking) but one thing comes to mind I'll never forget. I was about your age (start fading) and I went to the recruiting office to ... (fading up)
RECRUITER: How old are you, son?
YOUNG BOY: (Brightly) I'm older than I look, and I'm as big, or bigger, than any of these others, sir!

As you can see cross-fading not only gets you to another scene, but another time period very smoothly. However, if you want your script to go from one scene to another quickly without a fading interruption, select two sound effects that are somewhat similar in sounds for the transition.

Example: SFX: Wind and Footsteps in the Snow

JOHN: Will that wind ever stop blowing?
BUD: It's better than the heat and mosquitoes of the Amazon River.
JOHN: I guess you're right.
SFX: SEGUE FOOTSTEPS IN SNOW TO PADDLING WATER
PHIL: As bad as this river's mosquitoes are, at least we're not freezing our butts off in this boat.

The more unusual the sound effects are, the more interesting the script becomes. Just make sure that the two sounds are identified in the dialogue.

SFX: CLAP OF THUNDER
MOTHER: (worried) Listen to that awful thunder! And all Mary's wearing is her skimpy cheerleader's outfit! She must be having an awful time!

SFX: CLAP OF THUNDER SEGUES TO BOOM OF BASS DRUM FOL-
LOWED BY CYMBAL CRASH AND CROWD CHEERS
MARY: Another touchdown! What a night! What a night ... what a beautiful
 night! (megaphone) Let's hear it for the Giants!

Notice that the Mother refers to Mary but in the segue the audience can
only hear a feminine voice. Is this Mary's? In order to make certain the audience is aware that the voice is Mary's, the writer included the information
that Mary was wearing a "cheerleader's outfit." Then in the following scene,
Mary supports this cheerleader reference by using a megaphone and leading
a cheer.

Cross-fades and segues are just two tools you can use along with sound
effects to make your scripts more visual and exciting. Another is hearing what
a character's mind is only thinking.

STREAM OF CONSCIOUSNESS

The technique of listening to what a character is thinking is referred to
as a stream of consciousness and can be used effectively with cross-fading.

Example

SOUND: CHILDREN'S VOICES AND STREET NOISES OFF
JIM: Listen to those kids waiting for the school bus ... (remembering) and that
 smelly, noisy (start fading children's voices) old school bus that I used to (fade
 in bus sounds) have to take and that jerk that thought he was so tough...
BULLY: All right, stupid, you know better than to sit in my seat!
JIM: (young and protesting) It isn't your seat and I was here first...
BULLY: You want another bloody nose, you little jerk?

In writing any forms of fades from one scene to another, be sure you get the
important information heard before you start the cross-fading. This will ensure
that the audiences will have some knowledge that will make sense as to why
the two scenes are connected.

A Writer's Fear

Writing for audio theater will start you on the road to overcoming a
writer's biggest fear: running out of ideas. The fear that if you put too much
originality in one script, will you have another idea for another script due
next week? And if not the next week, how about the next day?

To prove how productive the writers for radio's *Lone Ranger* had to be,
I've included only a partial listing of *The Lone Ranger* programs, heard for 30
minutes, three times weekly!

A-2773 **THE LONE RANGER**
"Toughest Kid in Town" by Dan Beattie 10-11-1948
A-2776 **THE LONE RANGER**
"The Black Gang" by Dan Beattie 10-25-48
A-2779 **THE LONE RANGER**
"Tenderfoot Sheriff" by Dan Beattie 11-8-1948
A-2780 **THE LONE RANGER**
"The Red Mask Outlaw" by Dan Beattie 11-12-1948
THE LONE RANGER
"Trail for the Iron Horse" by Dan Beattie 11-15-1948
A-2782 **THE LONE RANGER**
"Tennessee Moody" by Dan Beattie 11-22-1948
A-2783 **THE LONE RANGER**
"The Hidden Herd" by Dan Beattie 11-29-1948
A-2784 **THE LONE RANGER**
"Double Trouble" by Dan Beattie 12-3-1948
A-2785 **THE LONE RANGER**
"The Second Frame-Up" by Dan Beattie 12-8-48
A-2788 **THE LONE RANGER**
"The Lone Bandit" by Dan Beattie 12-20-1948

Had enough? Fran Striker, was even more prolific writing as many as 156 *Lone Ranger* Scripts, 104 *Green Hornet* episodes, 59 *Sergeant Preston of the Yukon,* 12 *Lone Ranger* novels and a number of movie scripts!

Partial listing of *Lone Ranger* programs.

The listing above was given to me by one of the many old-time radio organizations throughout the world, SPERDVAC (The Society to Preserve and Encourage Radio Drama, Variety and Comedy).

Don't be fooled by SPERDVAC's funny name, they're located in Los Angeles, and have an informative monthly newsletter and a yearly convention where radio scripts are performed over a three-day weekend period. There's even a story competition open to anyone who wants their script done in front of a live audience. If your script is accepted, you will receive prize money and the satisfaction of seeing your story done at the convention, often by professional actors, seen by a huge, live audience, along with a CD copy of your hard work!

The amount of *Lone Ranger* scripts those few writers turned out each week proves nothing has changed today. In order to be a successful writer in any media—films, television, cartoons, animations, books—you can't sit around waiting for an idea to fall in your lap, it must become a way of life. Writing requires activity; the more active your mind is in your everyday life, the more successful your writing will be.

Set a time period every day when you sit down for at least one hour and write. Write about anything, even the weather, just put your mind in the habit for that one hour, or five pages, you are going to write! What better reason to write than your audio theater? By getting in that habit, you have the advantage of having your hard work heard and seen by live audiences. Won't that look good on your resume, and an advantage few other writers trying to get their scripts read would love to have.

GETTING IDEAS

Now that you've gotten into the habit of writing and you're writing a great story, give it all you've got and don't hold back. Don't hold any ideas for a rainy day! Don't confuse ideas with money in the bank. The more withdrawals you make with ideas, the richer your writing becomes. That's as true in your audio theater as it is for a movie, television series, cartoon, animation, or a pantomime. And there is no better place to have your ideas listened to or seen than in the audio theater. It gives you experience in getting the most out of your idea in the least amount of time. It also gives you an opportunity to have your ideas performed in a specific, demanding media; your audio theater. You'll soon find out that writing for audio theater is more than just ideas; it gets you thinking and imagining ... and isn't that what writing is all about?

To prove this, I've included just one page from the amount of *Lone Ranger* shows that can be rented from SPERDVAC. Notice (and this is just one page) the amount of scripts that were written by Dan Beattie.

Just reading the amount of scripts that were written by these two writers should give you the confidence to know "running out of ideas" isn't a problem you may have thought it was. Now that you know it isn't, don't fall into the trap of using it as an excuse for putting off the discipline a writer must have to be successful. I can't think of a career that is more personal than putting your thoughts down for everyone to read, watch, or hear. I also can't think of a career more personally gratifying.

Summary

1. By overwriting instructions to sound effects and the actors you only clutter the script with unnecessary words.

2. Giving the actors too many "readings" is often upsetting to the actors and time consuming for the director to cut, or change.

3. As you write beware of the time. If you're overwriting, start cutting. It may even make a better and tighter script.

4. Use words in an audio theater script that are descriptive, not deceptive.

5. Do not prolong the action with a lot of exposition.

6. If you ever get stuck for something to write about ... take any subject and ask yourself two simple words of curiosity ... "What if?"

7. Identify the sound effects as soon as possible.

8. In choosing between words and action, always choose action.

9. Keep sound effects cues brief and to the point.

10. When writing your script keep an eye on the clock.

11. Don't write long and complicated sound effects patterns that require five people to do them successfully.

12. Be aware of the equipment available to the people doing sound effects.

13. In writing sound effects cues, the amount of people you need to do sound effects isn't the number of cues you write, it's how far apart they are in the script.

14. To avoid confusing an audience, keep your sentences brief, meaningful and the words chosen for their ability to be seen by an unseeing audience.

15. Writing scripts for audio theater is an excellent way of preparing you for whatever your writing interests might be.

5

Picturing What You Write

Putting Voices into Words

Writing for audio theater is different from writing for television, cartoons, animations, films, or any other visual media. It's writing so that what the audience hears is pictured in their minds' imagination. Once you have mastered this technique, the freedom that audio theater offers is unequaled in any other media.

As important as what audiences can comprehend in a visual media, that's the work the imagination must do in the audio theater. But how can audio theater compete with the movie's special effects department that can create multi-million-dollar explosions by pressing a button on their computers? Very simply, by not pressing buttons. By not pressing buttons and appealing to something more powerful ... the audience's imagination.

DO YOU LOOK BEFORE YOU WRITE?

If rock drummers only needed the sounds of their drums, they wouldn't need the number of drums, or the manner in which they played their drums. Drummers have become the centerpiece of a rock concert not only for the beat they provide, but for their movements with their sticks and cymbals. The same is true of the people doing sound effects in the audio theater. If the sounds required were just for a listening audience on radio, it would be done in an entirely different manner than before a live audience. The writer should always keep this in mind. In order for a script to be entertaining to a live audience, writers must keep the action moving in what they write, what the actors say, and how imaginative the sound effects are to the audience.

Pages 64 and 65 show two sound artists doing the same effect of horses' hooves. See if you can pick out which one is doing the effects for a home-only audience, and which for a comedy show with a theater audience.

Ray Erlenborn created sound effects for CBS comedy shows such as *Blondie* (1944–1948), which often had live audiences. Here he creates the sound of hoofbeats.

The photos above and on page 65 show the manner in which horses hooves were done by two excellent sound effects artists. The question is, which artist was doing his hoofbeats for a comedy show? If you selected Ray Erlenborn, you were right. Ray did many of the comedy shows, such as *Blondie* on radio, and *The Red Skelton Show* on television at CBS in Hollywood, that

George O'Donnell, sound effects artist at CBS who worked on *Let's Pretend* (1934–1954), a children's show, creates the sound of hoofbeats for a show without a live audience.

had audiences. George was also an excellent animal-effects artist who was too shy to do his creative imitations in front of a live audience ... don't let it happen to you!

The director of *Let's Pretend* was Nila Mack, who believed that most all the parts were played by children. Not just their own age either; a 12-year-old girl might be called upon to play an 80-year-old witch!

Does that come as a surprise? It shouldn't. Don't let the name "audio" theater fool you into forgetting the "theater" part as well. Simply because the audio theater doesn't need costumes, settings, or cameras, the entertainment it brings to its audiences is unique, because it plays on the imagination of the audience.

Keep Thinking

Once you get your ideas, you can start thinking about everything directly or remotely connected with them and start jotting them down. It may call for research, or just laying on a couch and letting your mind take you where it wants to go. If it does, let it! Now that you have some tips for putting your ideas down on paper, keep in mind there are always two sides to every story ... just don't try to straddle them. Writing isn't a debate. Take a topic for the audio theater and give it all you've got.

Some Words for the Wise

Too many writers believe it's their business to write an interesting story and their work is done. Not so, if they are wise. This was particularly important to know during the years of live radio, and it's just as important now in the live audio theater.

Writers, in addition to writing a saleable script, must take the time to investigate whether or not their script is practical. Writing a great story that requires twenty actors, ten microphones and four sound effects people is a script that rarely if ever gets done.

If the twenty actors could be reduced to ten actors and they doubled their parts, this would leave at least five microphones for the actors, not counting those needed by sound effects. Even if the stage or studio was large enough, and you had the budget for all the technical equipment needed, your story would soon lose the audience's interest in a maze of technical equipment.

Today's audiences probably know more about technical equipment they need for their computers, cell phones, iPods and what-not-pods. What they don't know is all the non-technical things that can create the sound of a face being slapped with just two pieces of wood. It's the curiosity of what the audience sees and what an audience hears that makes the audio theater so interesting and amazing. It's also historical, listening to a modern story being accented with sound effect props used when the story was written as far back as Shakespeare.

Therefore, when you write a story requiring sound effects, you should have some idea how they will look as well as sound. Would you write a sketch that requires your sound effects to be done electronically by a Synclavier perfected in 1975? Or would you rather have them done manually like Keene Crockett, firing off a gun with one hand, then breaking down a door with his foot, while still able to look at his script for his next cues. All done during a 1944 live broadcast of *Inner Sanctum*.

Think of the people that do sound effects as popular as the drummers in a rock group. Although you didn't pay the big bucks just to watch the drummers, it's difficult not watching them. The same is true with the people doing sound effects in the audio theater. Creating sounds with manual effects requires movement and movement draws attention. And if this movement is creating hiking in snow by squeezing a bag of corn starch ... it's not only creating a sound that is vital to the script, it's also entertaining as to how the sound is created.

Writing scripts that call for sound effects requires some serious thought. Perhaps your audio theater is just starting, or you don't have storage space for a large amount of manual sound effects. Writing a script that calls for a "bulldozer uprooting a giant oak" could cause a problem if attempted to be done with manual sound effects.

Manual sounds have their limitations when it comes to the sounds of jet planes, firework celebrations, racing cars competing ... and, of course, a "bulldozer uprooting a giant oak." The rule of thumb is, don't try to create any sound effect if it doesn't sound realistic to your story. By that I mean, if a sound requires authenticity and it can't be done realistically with manual effects, don't sacrifice the believability of your script with a poor manual imitation simply because it looks creative to the audience. What's most important is the authenticity of the sound to your story. The only exception to this is when you've written a comedy. Then if you want your Fibber McGee closet crash to end with ducks quacking vocally, by all means do it, but only if it gets those all-important laughs.

Listed are a number of suggestions that a writer might use when it comes to writing sound effects cues that offer information, interest, and often amusement for the audio theater's audiences.

RULE 1: SFX SHOULD BE CONCISE

All sound effects cues are written in capital letters and underlined. The next step is to keep them simple. Numerous sound effects that don't have the support of narration, or dialogue, are called *sound patterns*. A sound pattern is a series of uninterrupted sound effects. As a result, they should be brief and easily understood. Although writers like to offer them as a teaser at the beginning of a show to attract an audience, they can often become confusing enough to irritate an audience.

> SOUND EFFECTS: CITY TRAFFIC. CAR TO STOP. DOORS OPEN/CLOSE. STEPS ON SIDEWALK UP CEMENT STOOP. PICKING THE LOCK. DOOR OPENS AND CLOSES. TRAFFIC OUT. STEPS UPSTAIRS SLOWLY. DOOR KNOB BEING TURNED. DOOR OPENS. THREE FAST GUN-SHOTS. STEPS RUNNING DOWNSTAIRS. DOOR OPENS. TRAFFIC IN. CAR DOOR OPENS AND CLOSES AND CAR SQUEALS OFF.

As a teaser, the above sound pattern has too many sound effects that require identification to be effective. How does the audience know it's the sound of a "lock being picked?" Even an audience watching the sound effects person doing these effects would be confused enough, to a listening-only audience this would just be a bunch of confusing noise. A teaser without words demands that every sound must be immediately identified with excitement.

> SOUND EFFECTS: KNOCK, DOOR UNLOCKS, OPENS, GUNSHOTS, BODY FALL.

RULE 2: ESTABLISH THE LOCALE AS SOON AS POSSIBLE

Once your teaser has captured your audience, you have to keep the momentum going or you'll be surprised at how quickly you can lose them. If the title of your story is "Murder on the Amazon River," you certainly don't want the characters sitting around having coffee and talking about the remoteness of the jungle. And if the action does start in the jungle and the characters are in a boat, the audience must know this by what they hear. That doesn't mean you have to reveal the color of the boat, or the manufacturer's name, but the audience must know that a boat exists and that it's in the jungle on the Amazon River.

RULE 3: HAVE YOUR SFX INFORM

Any sounds at the beginning of a scene should establish where the story is taking place. It isn't enough to write elaborate sound effects cues so the actor can read them on his script and understand what the jungle is like ... audiences must hear what the jungle is like. Therefore the writers must ask for sound effects that offer the listener the information that is useful to their imagination. Therefore keep your SFX cues short and concise, and not like this following short story about the Amazon River.

> SOUND EFFECTS:THE PIERCING SOUNDS OF JUNGLE BIRDS ECHO DOWN THE AMAZON AS THE THREE EXHAUSTED EXPLORERS STRUGGLE WITH THEIR PADDLES AGAINST THE STRONG CURRENT AND THE SWARMS OF MOSQUITOES THAT ATTACK EVERY INCH OF THEIR BARE SKIN. BUT DESPITE THEIR BONE-TIREDNESS THEY ARE GRIMLY REMINDED OF WHAT HAPPENED TO THE PROFFESSOR'S BOAT WHEN HE BECAME TIRED AND THE STRONG CURRENT SWEPT HIS BOAT AGAINST THE ROCKS AND TOSSED HIM INTO THE PIRANHA-INFESTED WATERS.

This might make an excellent beginning for a book, but it certainly isn't a cue for sound effects. All those wordy instructions the person doing sound effects has to read can be boiled down to one sentence.

> SFX: ESTAB&BG, JUNGLE BIRDS AND PADDLING.

Which means: "Sound Effects: Estab *(Establish)* & BG *(background)* the sounds of jungle birds and paddling."

RULE 4: MAKE EVERY SFX MEAN SOMETHING

In real life we're subjected to all types of sounds. We might be attending a funeral in the cemetery, while nearby a crowd is cheering and a school band is playing high energy music for a football game. This type of behavior certainly isn't respectful to the family mourning the loss of a loved one ... it's simply the way things are at a football game that just happens to be within hearing distance. It's the way real life often happens to be, unexplainable.

Listening to this same scene in the audio theater, would an audience be that tolerant? I don't think so. More likely their first reaction would be, "What in the world is that I'm hearing?! A brass band at a funeral?!! Is this a joke or what?!" Realism simply for the sake of "realism" is not excuse enough to be in a script unless it is directly related to the story.

A movie or television camera might even show the football game in progress next to the cemetery for the contrast in emotions, with cheerleaders screaming and tearful mourners. But how would the audio theater justify these reactions? Although the audio theater depends a great deal on the dialogue between actors to give audiences information, it would just take too much valuable time and talking explaining why a music band is being heard at a funeral.

One of the mourners might say, "Some people are heartless." But where does that go? Another mourner might have to say, "Isn't that the truth. Just the other day...." Whoa! We're at a funeral, not killing time waiting for a bus. Of course that's a nice touch of "realism," but who cares? We started out paying our last respects to a friend, and now we're talking about everything but our last respects to a friend!! The lines may be realistic, but who in the audience cares? What do they have to do with moving the story? Never sacrifice your writing with anything that is not related or doesn't move your story. No matter how brilliant or realistic your words and sound effects are, being *real* is never a substitute for being *interesting*.

RULE 5: WRITE EASILY IDENTIFIED SOUNDS

The quickest way to set a scene in your audio theater is with some readily identified sounds. Read that sentence again and this time emphasize *readily identified* sounds. Nothing is more annoying to an audience than to hear sounds they can't identify. Some sounds, as we already discussed, such as a clap of thunder, need little identification as long as there is a reason for it to occur. But the sound of rain alone needs all the help it can get, including a clap of thunder. Most sounds do, therefore make certain you accompany your sound effects with words, no matter what the sounds are.

RULE 6: TIMING YOUR SFX

In timing your SFX, saying the words "breaking down a door" takes far less time than the actual sound effects. This normally requires a pounding on the door first, and then comes the crushing sound done with a series of thin, wooden, berry baskets. Therefore, instead of just "saying the words" keep an eye on the people doing sound effects and see how the various sounds are created. Then the next time, when you need a more accurate SFX timing, you won't have to just say the words, you can picture them.

RULE 7: INTERACTING WITH SFX

In writing words that suggest sound effects, actors should feel comfortable Foleying with the effects. If the sound requires walking through the woods, it both helps your voice and sound effects to move your feet and allow sound effects to Foley (synchronize the manual walking sounds) with your movements. The same is true with the actor watching sound effects so they can give their words an appropriate reading.

RULE 8: KNOW THE LIMITS OF YOUR SOUNDS

Writing for the audio theater is not like writing for a movie that has seven-figure budgets. The best way to do that is to be knowledgeable and practical with what sound effects your script requires.

The audio theater is not in competition with movies or television, but offers an exciting audio alternative. Therefore in writing scripts the emphasis should be on what movies and television don't do and appeal to an audience's imagination.

Whenever possible write sound effects that can be Foleyed rather than done by pushing buttons on tape recorders and CD players. Some of the larger sounds must be done by electronic means, but they should be kept at a minimum. After all, it's one thing to hear an ocean wave, but it's another to hear it and see it being done with a drum head and BBs. If you are not familiar with the advantages of using manual effects, a list of them and how to create them are explained in the final chapter. By studying the many ways of creating sounds, they could even give you many interesting story ideas.

RULE 9: SFX FOR LAUGHS

Writing sound effects for a comedy show just about violates everything you have just read. In addition to sound effects being used for atmosphere, or to indicate information and movement, sounds such as a door slam are often used as an audio exclamation mark.

> FRED: Before you go, what happened to you and your wife, Tom?
> TOM: We got in an argument and she said, (mimicking) "I don't have to stand here to be insulted...."
> FRED: So what did you do?
> TOM: What could I do? I got her a chair!
> SFX: FOOSTEPS AND DOOR OPEN AND CLOSING.

Question

What unforgivable mistakes has the above sketch made with regard to the sound effects cue?

Answer

The closing sound effects cue takes too long. The "Tom" character has just got a big laugh from a joke and is exiting. See if you find which is the right sound from these three sound effects options.

1. SFX: STEPS TO DOOR OPEN AND SLAM SHUT.
2. SFX: DOOR OPENS AND SLAMS SHUT.
3. SFX: DOOR SLAMS SHUT.

The answer is #3. On a comedy show, despite how the cue is written, competent sound effects artists would never interrupt the pace of the show by taking the time to realistically open the door! As far as the audience is concerned, the character walked through the door! But who cares, as long as it gets laughs!

Summary

1. For everyone to best understand the problems the other skills face, it's a good idea to have the actors, directors, sound effects and music people switch skills once in a while ... if not on the air, in rehearsals. You never can tell when one of the cast members may get stuck in traffic.

2. In writing the sound effects cues, the writer is forced to write the most descriptive words in the smallest spaces, which in turn improves their awareness of self-editing what they write.

3. Don't clutter your pages with long, descriptive sound effects cues ... be concise.

4. Don't leave it up to the person doing sound effects to make your decisions, say what you want and make it short.

5. Sound effects in the audio theater are more than just phone rings and footsteps, think of situations that require your sounds to be creative and informative.

6. It is more entertaining watching and listening to an effect being created than just hearing it from an electronic box.

7. Creating sounds from manual effects is an excellent opportunity for the actors to do some Foleying with the sounds.

8. In selecting the sounds for your script make them readily identifiable.

9. Sounds that need help being identified, such as rain, should be referred to as quickly as possible.

10. Sound effects provide the audio theater's movement and action.

11. If brevity is the soul of comedy, sound effects are its exclamation marks.

12. Sound effects ease the pain of physical humor.

13. All sounds may be grouped into one of two categories: natural, or characteristic. A natural sound is that of an actual source. A characteristic sound is what a sound should be according to someone's perception of the sound.

14. Inasmuch as we all perceive sounds in a personal manner, there are no standards regarding how a sound effect "should" sound. If it doesn't stick out like a sore thumb ... it's most likely the "right" sound.

15. Never be carried away with the creativity of manual effects if they aren't doing their job. It's entertaining for an audience to see a balloon being popped for the sound of a gunshot. But would you still do the gunshot that way if it was for the sound of Abraham Lincoln being assassinated? I don't think so.

16. I strongly recommend the writer gets their script to the director as soon as possible so the director can, in turn, get the script to sound effects and music. These are the three people who need the most time to cast the actors and acquire the proper sounds and music.

17. Every year the National Audio Theater Festival holds a juried script contest for cash prizes. Check the NATF out on the internet.

6

Can Sounds Create Emotions?

Before studying the importance of movement that sound effects gives to the audio theater, you should be aware of the emotional influence certain sound effects have. This is especially true if you've always associated sound effects with car crashes, explosions and gunshots. Because, as you're about to see, there's a much more subtle, even psychological, side to the sounds we hear.

To begin with, in order to find out what's going on in a patient's mind, doctors often have them interpret a series of ink blots known as the *Rorschach* test. Although there isn't just one correct answer, it's simply what they mean to the person taking the test.

The same is true with sounds. Sounds are to our hearing what ink blots are to our eyes. Both stimulate an emotional reaction. The difference being, unless a sound is accompanied by another source of information, the brain is often unsure of what emotion is appropriate. Or as Walt Disney once said: "Sound effects are an 'earical' illlusion."

Imagine you are hearing the sound of a "crackling" fire. What emotion does that create? Not sure? How about if the sound is combined with the following conversation?

> MICHAEL: Listen to that fire, Susan ... you'd never know it's freezing out. What a great idea it was to build this fireplace last summer.

Is that better? I think it's reasonable to assume the "crackling fire" sounds create a feeling of security, and sleepy, cozy contentment. Now let's take that same winter's night and change things around. Instead of that crackling fire being in your fireplace, it's outside your bedroom door. You can't see what's causing the crackling sounds, you can only hear them. Would you still have the same cozy feelings you had when you actually saw the fire burning safely in the fireplace? Probably not. Although both sounds were exactly the same, one provided comfort, while the other created anxiety. One sound was seen, while the other imagined.

Sounds Are a Learned Experience

It may come as a surprise but our brains weren't born with the ability to identify a "crackling fire" sound anymore than they can a "mooing" sound. What they are capable of doing is the ability to learn and remember. When the brain receives a "mooing" sound from its hearing nerve center and nothing from the optic nerve as to what is visually creating that sound, it's immediately curious as to what the sound is, what's causing it, and whether it's friendly, or dangerous.

The brain, like our computer, immediately goes into its gray-celled data base and reports, *"I'm getting that mooing sound again. The last time it came from a gentle, four-legged, large, black and white animal we labeled a "cow" ... please confirm!"*

The brain will then go through a catalogue of sounds that it has on its hard drive that might possibly come close to identifying what this "mooing" creature is. But just suppose it wasn't a cow that made this sound and it was done by a vocal-effects actor? Would the brain still be fooled if it couldn't make a visual observation?

And that's where the audio theater has the visual media beat by a country mile! Not only does the audio theater create sounds, it doesn't need a cow to show the audiences how the cow sound was made! And as one young boy once said when television first came out, "I liked the pictures I saw on radio better."

SFX That Affect Our Feelings

Sounds that are familiar offer security. Sounds that aren't, or come as a surprise, or are too loud, don't. If a young girl is lost at night and approaches an old house to ask for directions, the soft, chirping sounds of crickets would be peaceful and reassuring. How do we know this nighttime sound is peaceful and reassuring? Because it's a sound we're familiar with. In addition, if there was danger, or even the threat of danger, the crickets wouldn't want to disclose their presence to predators and would be silent.

Therefore, as the girl approaches the house we are tricked into a sense of security by a sound normally associated with a friendly nighttime sound. Then, just as we relax and assume the old house isn't really sinister, as we first suspected, our security is snatched away. Not by the frightening noise of a witch's scream, or a clap of thunder, or by any noises, but by the silence. With the silence comes your imagination suddenly switching from peaceful thoughts to fearful apprehensions.

Manipulating Sounds

Silence is just one way sounds can be manipulated to affect our feelings. The following list offers a number of others that are less obvious, but just as effective.

- *Sustained Sounds:* Sounds that are steady and continuing give us a sense of stability. A volcano merely rumbling at a low level over a long period of time becomes familiar and non-threatening. As the rumbling suddenly stops, there is concern as to why it suddenly stopped. It never did before ... why now?
- *Intermittent Sounds:* Sounds that stop and start without a sense of rhythm, or reason, are a danger signal that something is wrong.
- *Increases in Volume:* A gradual increase in loudness indicates impending danger.
- *Sudden Fades in Loudness:* Indicates an abrupt change in intentions, as if the danger is having second thoughts.
- *Gradual Fades in Volume:* Sounds that fade slowly are an indication they are reluctant to leave and can still cause trouble. Much like a wild wolf that slinks away after losing a fight, but is still looking over his shoulder for another, and better, opportunity.
- *Wavering Sounds:* A steady wavering sound is one of alarm and meant to attract attention.
- *The Element of Boo!:* Having someone say "BOO" when they're facing you is more idiotic than startling. Having someone say "BOO" in back of you on a dark night is more than just startling, it's frightening. And the closer the person stands where they can't be seen, adds immeasurably to your fright. As you can see, the sudden attack of a sound adds to the sound's perceived loudness and loudness creates tension.

Although loud claps of thunder and flashes of lightning are used both for mood and add tension to a mystery story, they're also used as audible punctuation marks.

Example: Clap of Thunder

WOMAN: (terrified) The door's locked from the outside. I'm trapped!

Notice how the sudden clap of loud thunder punctuates the woman's line ... "I'm trapped!" This is especially effective at the end of a scene ... just as an exclamation point is used to stress something important at the end of a sentence.

Catching an Audience's Curiosity

Camping out in an unfamiliar forest can also be stressful. You've just snuggled down for a long and peaceful winter's nap, when suddenly you hear a scratching sound outside on your tent. Would you be startled, frightened, or simply curious?

Let me ask you another question. If you were doing the sound effect of the scratching sound in your audio theater, what sort of scratching noise would you make for this short scene?

EXAMPLE

JANE: Why couldn't we have stayed at the lodge in a comfortable bed, instead of out in these creepy woods in sleeping bags?

BILL: Because our sleeping bags aren't in a "creepy woods" but in a big protective tent.

JANE: But will it protect us from those big, black bears the park ranger said are all over the park?

BILL: The bears in the park are just as afraid of us as we are of them. Now will you turn off the lamp and go to sleep.

Sound: Sneak in Crickets

JANE: (frightened) What is that?!

BILL: Crickets ... harmless crickets that prove there are no mean bears around.

Sound: After Several Beats, Crickets Suddenly Stop

JANE: What was that!?

BILL: What was what?

JANE: Those crickets ... they stopped!

BILL: Even crickets go to sleep. Now will you stop worrying!

Sound: After Several Beats Scratching on Tent

EXAMPLE

Which of these tent scratching sounds would be most appropriate?

A. Soft scratching sounds?
B. A slight single scratch?
C. Loud persistent scratching?

If you made up your mind as to what sound you would select, you'd be getting ahead of yourself. There can't be a correct choice until you learn what the writer wants the scratching sounds to represent. If the writer wants to build suspense with the scratching sounds, which of the above sounds would you now have selected, A, B, or C?

My choice would be (B). A slight single scratch indicates curiosity. While (A) indicates further investigation, and (C) is more than just curiosity or investigation, the loud persistent scratching sound indicates whatever is making the sound wants to know what's inside this strange material. Perhaps something good to eat?

What sound would you use for this next example?

EXAMPLE

JANE: What was that!?
BILL: (getting bored) What was what?
JANE: That scratching sound against the tent!
BILL: Probably a branch from a bush. Now will you...

Sound: One Longer Scratching Sound

JANE: (interrupting) There! Does that sound like a bush?!

This is the beauty of the audio theater, the interactions between the writer, the actor and sound effects. All must work together to see that what is asked for by the writer is created by sound effects, and reacted to by the actor. If sound effects make the scratching sound too loud, it indicates anger and action. If the scene is long, the scratching sounds would have lost the tension and suspense the writer was trying to create. What about the actors? Does that affect how their lines are to be read? If, however, the scratching sound is barely heard, as the writer indicates, sound effects must create that particular sound to arouse the audience's uncertainty as to whether the campers are in danger or not.

Sounds That Provide Information

Most singular sounds provide information. A door knock tells us someone wants us to open the door. But, should we? Supposing the knocking sound is from your outside front door? It can be any one of the following type of informational sounds: timid, bold, angry, urgent, firm, rapid, or a dozen other different types of door knocks. All of these knocking sounds provide information about someone who wants the door opened, and more importantly, should we open it?

ATMOSPHERE AND INFORMATION

Atmosphere and information are inseparable. Rarely do we ever hear any sound that doesn't create an emotion. And the better the reason for a sound in the writing, the more effective the sound will be.

Example: Downpour of Rain

The sound of a downpour of rain drumming against a roof can provide a number of different responses. Will it provide the needed water to break a drought? Will it provide a comfortable, even romantic, sound to lovers snuggled up in front of a fireplace, or will it cause panic for fear of a possible mud slide? Sound effects, like music, enhance a story and provide the sounds that best fit a scene's emotional atmosphere.

Knowing When to Leave

As effective as sounds are in setting the atmosphere and information for a scene, one pitfall to be avoided with sounds such as crickets, rain, and the hum of an automobile running, is that once they have been established, their reason for being is finished. They should either be faded to a very low level or taken out completely under the dialogue.

There are, however, exceptions. If there are holes (long pauses) in the dialogue, the volume levels of the background sounds become more music than sound effects. This does not mean noticeably see-sawing the sound levels up and down but instead tastefully and gradually fading the levels in and out under the actors' dialogue in keeping with the scene's mood.

These are just a few of the ways sounds effects have the ability to alter our reaction to them. In addition, to the steadiness, or rhythm of a sound, simply by making a sound louder (impending harm) or softer (soothing and safe) influences our feelings.

SCARY AND UNCERTAIN SOUNDS

We discussed how frightening it can be not to be able to identify a crackling sound outside of your bedroom, as opposed to hearing the same sound and seeing it cheering up a room in the fireplace. This same confusion with a sound's identity was used as a frightening psychological tactic on the U.S. Marines on many of the Pacific islands during World War II.

Before a mortar shell explodes, it makes a "whooshing" sound as it travels through the air, causing the Marines to run for cover. The problem was, not all the mortar shells exploded, but they still made the same warning "whooshing" sound.

Perhaps the enemy was running short of mortar shells, and someone found that by putting an empty bean can on a springy sapling tree they could catapult the empty bean can through the night air and it would make the same "whooshing" sound as a mortar shell. If so, the plan worked. Now the Marines had to make the determination of whether the familiar "whooshing" sound could blow them up, or simply come clinking harmlessly against their tents.

It was this psychological use of sounds, and the pulling back and forth of the Marines' nerves, that caused the Marines so many stressful and sleepless nights.

FEELINGS

It's one thing to be fearful of a terrifying sound that's life threatening, but in what category would you put a small drop of water? Supposing I said there was more than one drop of water and they came from a faucet that suddenly decided to become leaky and dripped ... dripped ... dripped ... dripped in the middle of the night?

Did this sound concern itself that you had an important school test in first period, or you had a job interview the first thing in the morning? Now how would you feel about these little drops of precious, life-sustaining water? Of course it doesn't have to be water dripping. It could be any sound, loud or soft, if you felt these sounds' only reason for being was directed at your discomfort. Now how annoying would this make their sounds?

Are there such things as friendly noises? What's the difference between the piercing sounds of ambulance sirens in a large city when we're trying to sleep, or listening to the sound if you are having a medical emergency? A sound's appropriateness is far more important than its loudness. It's how we perceive a sound that is more important than the sound itself. In order to make the sound of a dripping faucet, a buzzing mosquito, or the popping of bubble gum annoying, you have to get it into someone's mind that a sound is done, whether it is or not, for the express purpose of aggravating, angering and antagonizing the listener. Therefore, the appropriate level of a sound is not its loudness, but how it affects the listener, or the atmosphere of the scene.

THIS IS PARADISE?

Television and films often depict paradise as an island with gentle waves and tropical birds, but in reality, can too much of a good thing be that good for us? Supposing you were out in the middle of the ocean alone fishing and your large powerboat sprung a leak and sunk. You, being the good sailor you are, were prepared for that emergency and hop in your dinghy and start paddling for a small island in the distance.

As you paddle, you see the fins of sharks circling your small boat. Thank goodness you didn't have to swim to the island and had the safety of your small boat! And even from your distance in the ocean, the lush, tropical island looked like paradise!

Upon reaching the safety of the sparkling sandy beach, you look up at the coconuts in the tree above you and again think how lucky you are! A beautiful island and plenty of food! You might not be rescued for months, but who cares, this is paradise!

Then, as you lay in the comfort of the warm sand, staring up at the blue sky you spot an orange, black-and-yellow-beaked bird the size of a seagull perched in a nearby palm. At first it just stares down at you and then it begins making a friendly whistling sound. Wow! Not only do you have food, but you have company as well!

As you continue gazing up at the sky, you notice what looks like a dark rain cloud. Excellent; now you'll even have fresh rainwater to drink! But as you continue looking at the cloud there is something wrong. The dark cloud is moving too fast, much too fast! Suddenly, what you thought was a storm cloud is suddenly making noises! Not thunder like an oncoming storm, but whistling like the friendly bird in the tree. But now there are hundreds of birds, thousands of birds! Tens of thousands of wildly, whistling, screeching, screaming, squawking, black-and-yellow-beaked birds!

As they circle the island and begin landing and making nests, the noise from their whistling, scream-like cries becomes ear-shattering. To escape the maddening sound, you race to the beach for your small boat! But it's nowhere to be seen! It's gone! The waves and current have taken it far out to sea! You're marooned on an island with the relentless, raucous cries of thousands upon thousands of squealing, squawking, screeching, screaming birds that make this small island their home night and day, day and night, night and day! All because one beautiful, pleasant-sounding bird just had too many noisy friends.

When Little Means a Lot

You just saw how something as familiar as too many songbirds threatened a man's sanity. How do you take something as familiar as a cell phone and make it into an instrument of terror? Simple; you take the normal small inconveniences you encounter with your cell phone and turn it into a life or death situation. Lucille Fletcher did it when wired phones were still popular and titled it "Sorry, Wrong Number."

Interestingly enough, this terror-filled radio drama was a so-so mystery novel about an invalid woman who is accidentally plugged in to a private telephone line and hears two men plotting to kill an invalid woman! Desperately trying to avoid this planned murder, she is confronted with an uncaring phone operator and police who don't believe her story. Too late, she realizes the invalid that is to be killed in a matter of hours is her.

The timing had to be exact between Ms. Moorehead's words and the sound effects. Berne Surrey (the sound effects artist) followed her every move, including Foleying the sounds of her imaginary phone dialing and the phone being slammed down on the receiver. At the dramatic and thrilling ending, Ms. Moorehead even pitched the sound of her scream to match the sound of Surrey's train whistle, making her scream more frightening.

The Power of Sounds Over Sights

Today, television and films show many gruesome sights far worse than what was heard during radio's golden years. Yet one sound effect was banned from radio during that time because so many listeners called the network and complained how horrible the sound was they just heard on their favorite program. What was this horrible sound? An old, soft and squishy pumpkin left over from Halloween that pretended to be a body falling from a tall building and hitting the sidewalk. The sound was made by dropping the pumpkin from a ten-foot ladder and hitting a slab of marble.

The writer originally wrote the scene as a woman screaming and, as she fell from the top of the building, her scream could be heard fading to silence. This would have been fine if the director didn't insist on reversing the perspective by having the mike at street level and wanting the scream to fade on until the body hit the pavement with the gushy sound of a Halloween pumpkin.

It's most unlikely that anyone listening had ever witnessed something as tragic as this, let alone heard what sound a body actually makes when hitting a sidewalk from those tremendous heights. But seemingly thousands of listeners had and complained so vociferously that poor Mister Halloween Pumpkin was never heard from again over the imaginative airwaves of radio.

What happened to that innocent pumpkin sound? It was snatched up by the Hollywood Foley artists and was heard in a movie where the bad guy accidentally backs into the whirling blades of a helicopter and his head was decapitated in front of a blasé audience accustomed to gory sights; proving the sight, coupled with the sound, didn't receive the emotional response that the radio listeners perceived with their imagination the night a pumpkin fell from the height of a ten-foot ladder. This is the power of audio theater and the ability to reach an audience's imagination, with or without a squishy, old, Halloween pumpkin.

Summary

1. The psychology of sound is how we perceive sounds and how they affect us emotionally.

2. Sounds are a learned intelligence.

3. Any sounds that can't be recognized are capable of causing stress.

4. Unusually loud sounds are not only harmful to our hearing, they cause irritation and stress.

5. A sound that has a sudden attack and quick decay commands our attention.

6. Add the combination of loudness and surprise and the sound becomes frightening.

7. Because we are so accustomed to everything coming to an end, a repetitive sound that goes on and on and on, regardless of its loudness, causes stress wondering when it will stop.

8. One of the most stressful and frightening of all sound is ... silence.

9. Any sounds that can't be recognized are capable of causing stress.

10. Think of sound effects as a placebo. If you do your sounds realistically enough, you'll be surprised what you can fool your brain into believing.

7

The ABCs of Directing

Directing the Audio Theater

Audio theater is a group effort where everyone has an opportunity to act, write a script, do the sound effects, select the music and especially to direct. Although your preference may be only one of the skills offered, this is an opportunity to have even a brief experience doing, or at least observing, all the various skills that make audio theater unique.

Is audio theater radio, or theater? The answer is ... yes. And to make certain these two imaginative art forms come together as just one is the job of the audio theater's director. They're responsible for cueing the actors, sound effects, and music, making script cuts, adding or deleting words, keeping an eye on the clock for time purposes, and making certain that all the voices, sounds and music are in the proper perspective (special relationship) to the microphone at all times! Who is this talented person we call a "director"? And what must you know if you decide you want to direct a script in your audio theater?

A director may be many things; a writer, actor, musician, or a sound effects specialist. He, or she, may be someone with none of those backgrounds and yet have the ability and talent for organization in seeing that all the various skills work together as a team. This is done in three ways, with all the sounds from the voices of the actors, the sound effects, music and how creatively they are all mixed into a microphone. First a director must have an understanding of just what a microphone can and cannot do in providing all this important information for the audience's imagination.

The All-Important Mike

Earlier we learned some of the important characteristics of the microphone. This is important for all the audio theater's skills, and most important to the director. If, for instance, you were doing a show at a new location and the house sound mixer asked you what your microphone needs were, you must know more about a microphone than just the basics.

The sound mixer would have to know more about how they're being used. Are the two actors standing, or sitting? Are they facing each other, or the audience? If they are facing each other, they only need one bi-directional mike. If they are facing the audience they'll need two bi-directional mikes. And if the two are sitting, the one microphone will be between them on a very short stand called a "banquet stand."

Then when the actors are reading their scripts, the director must see that the actors keep their scripts off to one side so the pages don't block their voices from the mike. Looking pretty at the mike is not as important as being properly heard. Remember, your listening audience is dependent upon hearing your actors' voices clearly and distinctly.

This is especially true for some of the most ardent fans of audio theater, the visually impaired. Therefore, in addition to keeping the pages away from the actors' faces, have the actors keep their script at eye level so that their faces are always pointed directly at the mike.

THE MANY USES OF A MIKE

The microphone, in addition to being the ears of the listener, is where all the action takes place. In stage theater it would be the spotlight; in films and television it would be the camera; but in the audio theater it's the all-hearing, all-seeing microphone. All-seeing microphone? Of course, in the audio theater it's what the audiences hears that influences what the audience's imagination sees.

Selecting a Script

In selecting a script for the audio theater, it should have appeal for both the listening and watching enjoyment of the audience. This is what they come to hear and see. Many are fans of old-time radio and have only heard all the exciting radio shows done during radio's golden age. Now, thanks to audio theater, they are given an opportunity to both listen and see how those shows are done. The same is true with the larger audience that has never had the chance of either seeing or imagining their entertainment. This is the job of the director, to select scripts that not only challenge the audience's imagination, but also surprises and perhaps even educates them on how versatile our voices are.

The Next Step Up

After selecting a script, the director's job in the audio theater begins. And first on the list, before even the actors are chosen, the script is now ready for the people who are doing the sound effects and music. Directors should be aware that the audio theater doesn't have the extensive music library or sound effects department that the radio networks once had. Therefore, the sooner the scripts are given to personell handling sound effects and music, the better chance music and sound effects will have of getting exactly what is needed.

If this surprises you, it shouldn't. Although the actors should have their scripts in advance, they can read them in a subway, on a sandy beach, or in bed. There is no further preparation other than their characters' voices. Whereas in the glory days of radio drama, the networks had several rooms filled with every imaginable manual sound effect for the sound people to choose from.

The same is true today in the Foley recording studios. There's even one room the size of a basketball court just for doing every imaginable-sounding footstep. Need the sound of dirt for a mountain climber scaling Mount Everest? No problem. A huge mound of rock and earth can be found over by a tree log that's used for chopping down a tree!

Although you might wish to have all these Foley advantages for your audio theater, dragging a tree trunk or dumping a truckload of dirt on the stage wherever your audio theater is appearing is obviously not possible. What is possible is for the director to determine what is needed sound effects-wise, and how many people they will need to do the effects.

Example

> SOUND EFFECT: <u>POUNDING ON DOOR. AFTER BEAT DOOR BEING SMASHED OPEN. GUNSHOTS. BODY FALL. PHONE RINGS AND OFF CRADLE</u>
> DETECTIVE: (on phone) No, this isn't Franco, or will it ever be Franco again.... He's dead.

Quite a busy scene. But how many sound effects are needed? The door knocking sound will be done with the audio theater's small portable door. Breaking down the door is created by crushing a berry basket, followed by the gunshots and body fall. Then after a beat, the phone rings and is taken off the cradle. As busy as this scene sounds, it could all be done by one sound effects person. That's because each sound follows one another and the sounds don't overlap and conflict with each other. Compare this scene with the next one and try and see why this second scene needs two sound people.

Example

SFX: <u>PHONE RINGS PHONE OFF HOOK</u>
GAIL: (whispering) Oh, hi, Marge. You'll be coming?... Great, but not a word
   to your husband.... This is a surprise for John.
SFX: <u>DOORBELL OFF</u>
GAIL: (hurried) I have to hang up, Marge, before John sees what I got him for
   his birthday!
SFX: <u>DOORBELL OFF AND PHONE ON CRADLE</u>
JOHN: (calling off) I'll get it.
SFX: <u>DOORBELL AND FOOTSTEPS</u>
GAIL: You stay upstairs, I'll get the door.

Although the sound effects in this scene are not as exciting as the previous scene, because of the different perspectives of the sounds, the scene
should have two sound people to ring the phone and doorbell. Could it be
done by only one? Of course, but instead of creating the proper distance perspective between Gail and John, it would sound to the audience like they were
right next to one another. Therefore it isn't the amount of sound effects that
are so troublesome to a scene, but it's how and why they are needed that is
so important.

Are all these technical things such as "perspectives" the job for the director? Yes, but only if they have help from the writer. Did the writer picture
the scene in their imagination? If they can visualize what they write, and are
aware of the market they are writing for, it saves the director a great deal of
time and trouble.

VOICE MOVEMENTS

One important responsibility the director has is to make certain the
script they select has a feeling of movement. Where stage actors have the ability to walk up an actual flight of stairs, vocal actors in the audio theater must
make their voices and sound effects do the climbing. This is done by changing the perspective (spatial relationship) of the actors' voices through the use
of the microphone.

The microphone, in addition to being the ears of the listener, is where
all the action takes place. In the theater it is the spotlight and in films and
television it will be the cameras, and in the audio theater it's the microphones.
Having to make decisions as to how close an actor or a sound effect should
be to a microphone is up to the director.

Example

SARAH: (off) Gregg, this is the second time I called. Can't you hear me?
GREGG: (shouting) I'll be with you as soon as I get this car fixed!

Although the example shows that Sarah is (off), only the director can decide how *far* off her voice should be. The actors at the microphone are often unable to judge the proper distance they should be from the microphone. The director, standing at the far end of the room (or listening in the studio control room), has the opportunity to act as if his ears are that of the listening audience and is best able to judge how far or close the actors (or sound effects) should be to create a sense of realism and movement. This can be done in a number of ways.

1. Falling from a great height can be accomplished by starting the scream on mike and slowly turning away from the mike and letting your voice fade out.
2. Walking away from the microphone fades your voice and gives the illusion of leaving the room. Longer distances should be done by sound effects.
3. Remaining in place but turning your head away from the microphone when you're talking gives the illusion of fading off.
4. Leaning your head back slowly sounds as if you're fading off.
5. Turning your back to the microphone and slowly turning to face the microphone gives the illusion of fading on mike from a greater distance.

One thing you must avoid is boring the audience by having the cast simply standing motionless and reading the scripts into a microphone. And yet, very often the audio theater is compelled to work in a small studio, or stage space. In reality, however, it isn't the size of the space that's important, it's the relationship and distance from the microphone that's most important. Even if the audio theater is done in the middle of Yankee Stadium, it couldn't have the actors' voices straying away from the all-important microphone. It is for that reason the director, prior to doing a show, should test the room for its acoustical properties so the audience are sure to hear every word and sound coming from the audio theater.

Importance of Sound Balancing

I've done hundreds of audio theater shows in hotel convention rooms, banquet rooms, on the stage, on radio and television; both with movie stars and the actors that did the scripts originally back on live radio. Everyone in the cast did an outstanding job with the shows. *The Lone Ranger* left a silver bullet and rode off into the sunset, and *Superman* did his usual super job, thanks to the actors, sound effects and music.

There was just one small mistake. Everyone in the audience had difficulty hearing the actors, sound effects and music! All because the person controlling the room's sound had set the wrong sound levels for the microphones and placed the speakers in the wrong locations. How could that happen? The director was too busy with the actors, sound effects and music and assumed the people controlling the mike and speaker levels were doing their jobs. The director should never assume anything as important as having their hard work not heard by the audience.

TESTING FOR THE PROPER SOUND

Directors should be familiar with the two ways of testing the microphones for the proper sound. One is to have the person doing your audio levels ride gain. "Riding gain" requires the audio person to move the sound volume gains according to the sound levels the actors, sound effects and music are sending him. If an actor suddenly speaks louder than he did in rehearsal, the audio person will lower the sound of his voice by moving the pot's (potentiometer) loudness level down.

This might be fine for a recording studio with their sophisticated sound equipment and controls, but at a remote location with a limited amount of audio equipment, such as in a school room, it might be asking too much for the amount of microphones that are being used at the same time.

The other method of having everyone heard at the proper level is to have all the microphones set at one maximum loudness level and left there. This means that the actors, sound effects, and music must never go beyond this maximum loudness level, and they all are responsible for being heard at the proper sound level.

All this technical testing should be done before the actors arrive. And the best way to do this is for the director to get on the mike and woof them. This is done by standing at a normal space from the mikes (normally one hand span) and making a voice test by saying "woof" in a normal speaking voice and holding the sound until the sound mixer sets the proper levels on all the actors' mikes. The same is done by the people doing the sound effects and music, only this time, the director is free to move around the room making certain that all the people in the audience will hear the show no matter where they are seated and listening.

ACOUSTICS

The science of absorption and reflection of sound is called acoustics. Most people with average hearing can fairly accurately tell the size of a room by its reverberation qualities. There can be no confusing the sound our voice makes in a gymnasium with a room with the dimension and reflective qualities of a bathroom. Because of the size of the gymnasium, the sound of our voice takes a longer time to return to us than it does in a smaller space, such as singing in the shower.

Another acoustical property of a room and one of great importance to the director is whether a room is "live" or "dead." A room is said to be "live" if it is lacking in absorbent materials, such as curtains, thick carpets, or stuffed furniture. This phenomenon can be readily observed when you paint a room. Removing these items allows the sound waves to bounce from wall to wall without anything absorbing the sound waves.

An effective way of determining whether a room is live or dead is by clapping your hands. If the resultant "slap" sound has some ring to the air, or echo, the room is live. If the sound is without any noticeable echo, the room may be considered dead. By repeating this clapping determination as you walk around the room, you will find that sections of the room vary in acoustical responses. It's important you know this when determining where to place the microphone to attain the best sound. Perhaps now, for no other reason, aren't you glad your audio theater allows you to work so closely together.

BODY MIKES

Because movement is so important to the audio theater, I don't recommend body mikes. As popular as they are to actors on the Broadway stage, audiences are able to watch every move the actors make without being dependant on where the sound of their voices are coming from. In fact, with these radio frequency mikes attached to the actors' bodies, audiences can hear every word sung or spoken no matter where they move in relation to the stage.

This is fine for the actors' stage movements, but not for the actors' movement in the audio theater. The sound of the actors' voices indicates where they are in relation to the action. And because an RF mike is attached to the actors' bodies, their voice levels remains the same no matter what head or body movements an actor makes.

The First Reading

The first reading takes place around a table where the show is being done. This is not a social hour for the actors. They need to use the same voices here that they will use on the air to become better prepared for the part. They also should listen carefully to the director's suggestions and ask any questions they may have about their characters. Although this reading is stop and go, it's being timed.

All that is needed to time a script properly is a watch that can be stopped and started without it affecting the overall timing. Although timing a show is only demanded if you are appearing on radio or television, I believe timing is an invaluable experience for anyone considering a professional career, or even if you aren't. Timing a script let's you know if you are lagging with the lines or rushing them, and makes you more aware of the emotions you put into your words.

THE IMPORTANCE OF TIME

Timing and editing a script are often two of the most difficult things that must be done in order for a script to time out properly. Therefore, no matter how much the director and actors love the lines, the timing of a show takes priority over music cues, sound effects cues and whatever the writer spent days creating. And because so many cast members in the audio theater are looking ahead to a professional career, aiming for self-improvement for their speaking habits, or just serious about having fun, an awareness of time gives the audio theater the ideal place to start realizing that the difference between being interesting or boring is just a matter of time.

Normally, a half-hour script is timed every thirty seconds. The shorter the script, the more frequent the timing intervals should be. Then when the script is on the air, the director has a good idea of whether the show is moving too slow or too fast. In either case, the director must be aware of these timings in order to make the actors either speed up their lines or slow them down. When a show has to end at a precise second, this information is extremely important to the success or failure of the show getting off the air on time.

Assistant directors are one step away from directing. If it's important that a script has to be timed, it's the assistant director who helps the director by taking that responsibility. They're also helpful in seeing that all the cast has the correct last-minute script changes and cuts, and for keeping an eye on the clock for the show's timing.

In doing a show that requires split-second timing, a director should never go on the air with a script that has already been timed as too long (too much show for your allotted time). Instead, always allow yourself at least five seconds cushion (extra time if needed) so that you can fill the time in case the show is in danger of finishing the show too short (finishing too early) by having the actors or sound effects stretching (lengthening their words or sounds).

Is a Timed Script Really Necessary?

It is, if you're seriously interested in having a professional sounding audio theater. Knowing that a script, a commercial, a speech, or even a sentence has to be done in a certain amount of time is competition you can measure with a clock.

Even if you are not reading for auditions, knowing how to shave (cut) three seconds off a piece of material shouldn't be frightening. Becoming aware of time in seconds is helpful in whatever your life ambitions might be. When you become aware of how critical time can be, it helps in making decisions with your writing, your acting, your speeches in business, and especially in directing in the audio theater. One thing you can't do, is confuse timing with pace.

Timing and Pace

Timing and pace complement one another. Pace sets the overall tempo of a script and timing provides the impetus that keeps the script's tempo from varying. Audiences like their stories to have order; not drag one moment and go too fast the next. And the best way to slow a story is to have too many words and too much talking. This is especially noticeable if you're doing comedy. Too many words spoil the comedy's pace and, more importantly, the audience's laughs.

The spoken timing of a word, or speech, is very often more important than the words themselves. Timing is knowing the precise moment when something is said, or done, that will bring the most success. If it's baseball, the hitter must know precisely when to swing a bat to make contact with the ball; if it's for an actor, it's knowing precisely when to speak or pause that will convey the most significance to the written or spoken words.

Pace or Speed?

Pacing your lines is speaking them in the natural flow of the script. When the director asks you to "watch your pacing of a certain speech," it doesn't mean how fast or slow you're reading your lines, it simply means your lines aren't being said with the overall pace of the show. Yes, it could mean you're doing your lines too fast or too slow, but that only means the problem is more with your *tempo* (a certain beat) rather than anything else. A "beat" can best be compared to music. Once the tempo or certain beat to a song has been established, you don't expect it to keep see-sawing all through the song. Once a tempo or scanning has been established, it should remain that way.

Keeping the overall beat of a scene, or even a script's lines, must be consistent with the overall purpose of the script you're doing. Whether it be a romantic story or comedy, once a tempo or pace of script is established, it must be maintained for continuity and success. And the best way to do it is to keep one eye on the script and the other on the director.

The Director's Hand Signals

In order to give the cast, sound effects and music the proper times to speak, do a sound, or play the music, the director uses hand signals. These hand movements by the director should be studied and remembered because, sooner or later, they'll give you the guidance you need, in the audio theater or a professional recording studio.

- To signal to an actor they are speaking too loud and to move back from the mike ... *move the palm of the hand away from the face.*
- To signal to an actor they are speaking too softly ... *draw the palm of your hand towards the face.*
- To indicate an actor or a scene is playing too fast ... *put all your fingers loosely on your thumbs and slowly draw your arms apart.*
- To warn someone, or the cast, there will be some last-minute changes ... *either point to an actor or wave to the cast and point to your eye in a "watch me" fashion.*
- To let the cast know that they are all doing fine ... *make a circular sign with your forefinger and thumb and extend the rest of your fingers.*

To let the cast know the script is on time ... *touch your nose with your forefinger, "on the nose."*

- If an actor or sound effect is too loud ... *lower your hand palm down.*
- To increase the pace of an actor ... *extend the forefinger and turn it clockwise according to how fast you want the actor to increase the pace.*
- To cue an actor to start talking, or sound effects or music to begin ... *point directly at them with your forefinger.*
- To cue to play the theme music ... *put your outstretched hand on top of an extended forefinger.*

Now that you're familiar with some of the basic requirements of an audio theater director, it's time to move up to the next step and make your audio theater even more creative, imaginative and exciting.

When both the actor and sound effects need a cue at the same time, it can be confusing if only a single index finger is pointed in the two directions. To make it simpler, the director's right hand may be used to cue the actors, and the left hand to cue sound effects.

Example: The Wanted Man Caper

> MARLOW: After two years of hunting down this Harry Gessner creep, this has got to be him. My answer is on the other side of the door.
> SFX: DOOR OPEN AND LOUD MACHINERY
> MARLOW: (Shouting to be heard) I'm looking for a Harry Gesner.
> HARRY: Who?
> MARLOW: Harry Gesner!
> HARRY: Never heard of him.... Now beat it ... I'm busy!!
> MARLOW: I just want to ask him a few questions about a murder that happened....
> HARRY: (Interrupting) I said I never heard of him!!
> MARLOW: Too bad, it's worth a thousand bucks to Gesner....
> SFX: MACHINERY SUDDENLY STOPS
> HARRY: (Normal voice) What's the question?

Notice in this scene no attempt has been made to simply fade the machinery sounds. Instead, the loudness of the machinery sets up the sudden silence at the end. Because of this, the timing has to be perfect for the sound effects, and Harry's line, "What's the question?" must be cued at the precise moment for it to get laughs.

Now that we're familiar with the importance of time and hand signals, the next step is the run-through, Although this will be done on the microphone for sound levels, this too will be timed. Actors may want to add a line, change a word, or cut a word. If any of these changes are to be made, the director must see to it that everyone in the cast is aware of the changes.

Dress Rehearsal

Although there are no costumes, makeup, props or scenery to look at, this is the last stop and final timing before air time. After taking a short break, everyone is assembled for the all-important dress rehearsal. This is where all the changes that were made are included, and timings are tested.

You may wonder why all the timings are so necessary. Because the audio theater could be perhaps your last stop before becoming a voice actor for Disney, or any number of cartoons, animations, narrations, commercials. Even business speeches should be properly timed to hold an audience's interest. Therefore, whether the time factor is minutes or seconds, there is no better place to start becoming conscious of time than in the audio theater.

One excellent way to do this is for the director to announce to your audience that you're going to pretend to go back in time to when all the radio shows were timed to the precise second so that the sponsors could always get in their commercials.

> DIRECTOR: We all know that time is money, but tonight you're going to hear and see time is money! Our show is timed to run (give time) give or take five seconds, and then ACE Hardware was kind enough to sponsor us for a 10-second commercial. And furthermore, just like the old days, unless we finish our show, give or take five seconds, we'll be cut off the air so that ACE Hardware gets in their all-important commercial! And to make it even more realistic, we're going to set this large clock where everyone can see the time and how close ACE gets in their commercial. We now have one minute to air, so if you have to go to the bathroom ... you can't! 5-4-3-2-1!

The "on the air" light flashes and the clock starts! Do you still want to know why becoming accustomed to the importance of time to your performances is so important?!

Summary

1. The director's job begins when the script arrives.

2. A "reading" is an informal first rehearsal for actors. Sound effects and music are not involved until the second rehearsal on mike.

3. Once on mike, a script is timed in 15-second intervals.

4. A script that has been timed as short in rehearsal should never go on the air.

5. Tempo and pace are the relative speed of the show.

6. Hand signals are the silent language of communication in the audio theater.

7. Actors, sound effects and music are all obliged to watch the director for these mimed instructions.

8. The assistant director times the show and sees that everyone has the right cuts and changes in the script. This experience is the next step to being a director.

9. The sound mixer is responsible in seeing the acting, sounds and music all come together in a pleasant, cohesive sound.

10. Microphones give all sounds equal consideration, whereas humans have the ability to focus on what they want to hear.

11. Perspective in the audio theater is where the sound information is in regards to the microphone.

12. The mixing of a show requires the talents of the audio engineer for technical acceptability and the director for dramatic impact. These two, working together, will determine the show's listening enjoyment to an audience.

8

Directing the Next Step Up

Putting What You Learned to Work

Inasmuch as Chapter Ten has a number of scenes and sketches you can use for rehearsals, or performances, this chapter will examine more closely the challenges the director will face doing a show live wherever your audio theater is asked to perform. Be it television, radio, the theater, or the stage, your audio theater is at home wherever it's being done.

No need for the actors to rehearse camera angles, or whether to be upstage or down stage. All these movements are done by their voices, sound effects and keeping their eyes on the director.

The All-Important Cues

One of the first concerns that actors, sound effects, or music have is knowing when the director wants them to speak, create a sound, or play the music. They also need to know if they're too loud, too soft, too fast, or too slow. And the only person they can depend on to know all the answers is the director. Since the shows are done live, the director can't very well holler what they want the cast to do; she must throw them a cue. If "throwing them a cue" reminds you of "throwing them a lifesaver," the two are very similar and both are done in a moment of need. It's as simple as that, or as complicated as that.

Some actors resent having to keep an eye on the director for a cue. They feel they're experienced enough to take the cue on their own. My advice is don't listen to them. Only the director is aware of the show's timing and pace, overall sound balance, and cueing the actors when to speak, when to stop, or if they're too soft or too loud. And this goes for the other important members of the cast, sound effects and music. Having said that, there are times when the cast members should take a cue on their own.

EXAMPLE

The next short scene is an example of what requires cueing and what doesn't need cueing to make the scene play smoothly.

> WOMAN: (frightened) John, you have to come home, and don't say it's my imagination! I know there's a storm but I'm hearing that noise again! That awful scratching sound like someone, or something, is trying to ... come through the wall!
> *CUE:* SFX: <u>SCRATCHING ON A WALL</u>
> *CUE:* Woman: There! There it is again ... it's getting louder and louder.... Can't you hear it?! You've got to come home ... you just ...
> *CUE:* SFX: <u>TELEPHONE HANGUP TONE</u>
> *CUE*: Woman: ... Hello ... Hello ... John! ... John!!!

The reason for the director cueing sound effects to do the scratching sounds is to cut the woman off in the middle of a speech. The rest of the line, "...come through the wall," is only added to give the actor something to say if the sound effect is a beat late and leaves her hanging, with nothing to say.

Supposing the actor playing the woman didn't want to be cued on air? And supposing the sound effect of the scratching is too soft and she doesn't know when to speak her line? Either sound effects would have to keep repeating the sounds, or the director would have to frantically signal the actor to speak. This might get the line finally spoken, but the pace and emotions of the scene would be lost.

To avoid all these complications, when an actor and sound effects are playing off one another (reacting to one another), to be on the safe side, the director is the one who should decide whether the scene needs a cue from him, or the actor and sound effects can take the cues on their own.

Cueing Tips

Although SFX cues are often written to be done after a line, the director might want to delay it for any number of reasons ... such as time purposes, or the all-important dramatic moments.

EXAMPLE

> CHUCK: You ain't got the guts to shoot that gun.
> SHIFTY: No?
> SFX: <u>GUNSHOT</u>

Does the gunshot sound happen right after the word "No?" or does the gunshot wait a beat (as long as it takes to say "Mississippi")? But supposing, in rehearsal, the actor playing Shifty did a short chuckle before the gunshot and the director liked it. Therefore the director would tell sound effects to wait for his cue. But what if the director forgot to cue and the actor forgot to chuckle? That would mean the gunshot would be a trifle late, but at least it would be there.

Be on the Safe Side

Prior to cueing SFX, actors, or music, the director should make sure she has their attention. This is done by holding her hand up and facing whoever is to be cued. The cue hand should never dart out like a karate punch. Instead, the arm should be lowered with the index finger extended and aimed at whoever is getting the cue. However, even with this prior cueing signal, there is a brief moment when the hand is pointed and when the recipient responds to the cue.

These moments of silence can affect the dramatic intensity of a scene, or ruin the timing of a comedy line. Therefore, there are a number of reasons when a director should allow the actors, sound effects, or music to react without waiting for a cue. This is especially true doing comedy, when timing is so important.

If there is any doubt about whether the director does the cueing or it's better for the cast members to take their cues on their own, this should all be discussed and settled in rehearsals. This is especially important when it comes to sound effects that have a familiar sound, such as the ringing of a wired telephone.

EXAMPLE

Sam is waiting for the results of a horse race. He's bet all his money, as well as a huge amount he borrowed from a mobster, on his horse to win ... make that *had* to win! To ease his anxiety he pours himself a drink.

SFX: <u>POURS DRINK ... GLASS DOWN</u>.
SAM: (Anxious) He said four rings meant I won and three I.... But it's gotta be four ... it's gotta be ... I can't lose ... I can't!
SFX: <u>SLAMS GLASS DOWN ON TABLE</u>
SAM : Ring ... will ya!... Get it over with!!
CUE: <u>SFX: PHONE STARTS RINGING</u>.

Because of the tension the phone rings are creating, the director will no doubt cue the first phone ring. But when? Wait a beat to build the suspense, or cut off part of Sam's speech for reality and to surprise the audience? After that cue is decided, instead of the second phone-ringing after a normal interval, the director may again want to go for the dramatic moments rather than reality. Therefore, rather than having the phone rings coming in a normal fashion, the director may want to take dramatic license and stretch the pauses between the rings. If this is the case, the succeeding phone rings will also be cued by the director for dramatic purposes.

The Board Fade Technically and Vocally

When the curtain comes down on the theatrical stage, or the lights are dimmed, audiences know that a particular scene is over. Then when it rises again, it's either a new scene or an interval of time has passed. Television and film cameras replace the stage's curtain by fading out a scene and fading in the new scene, or possibly a lapse of time. Often these "fades" are called dissolves. But what does the audio theater do? Does the director have to get on mike and yell to the audiences, "Hey, gang, that scene's over, but there's one coming right up, so sit tight!"

I'm afraid not. All that is needed to replicate the visual media that a scene is being changed is to do a board fade. The term "board" refers to a control panel that contains sound amplifiers for the microphones. Each mike has a pot (potentiometer), a term used to describe the volume control knob. If, for instance, you have four microphones being used by the actors and sound effects, and you want to fade them all out at once, you simply fade out the master pot that has the ability to control the sound volume of all the mikes plugged into that board.

A director and writer who have the knowledge of how and when to use the board fade will improve immeasurably the freedom the director will have in presenting an involved script requiring scene changes. Although the technical requirements of fading and increasing the sound from two mikes is the job of the audio mixer, it's the job of the director to determine how long the fades should last. This should be done with the director lowering his hand to indicate to the sound mixer to fade one mike's sound level down, while raising the other hand slowly up to indicate that the sound level on the second mike should be proportionately raised.

Think of the moves as similar to that of a see-saw. When one child goes down, the other comes up. How fast or slow this occurs is up to the director.

EXAMPLE

STUDENT: Professor, I'm still at a loss as to why my equation is faulty, and if you would just show me...

PROFESSOR: I thought I explained it very well, and I have an important meeting to attend.

STUDENT: It wouldn't take but a few minutes...

PROFESSOR: Young man, teaching at the college here hardly occupies all my time. I have a law practice that urgently needs my attention, (STARTING TO FADE OUT) *so if you'll excuse me, I must be going.*

The problem to avoid in doing board fades is to give the actor who is being faded out enough lines so the sound mixer has enough time to fade the actor out entirely without making it sound hurried. Therefore, never leave it up to the actor to ad lib something on their own! Some are good, while others are not. Instead of taking a chance with just "...so if you'll excuse me, I must be going," add some additional words, such as: "The traffic at this time of day is horrendous." When the professor's lines are completely faded out, the director takes a beat and cues whatever is next, an actor, sound effects, music, or a scene.

A word of caution. Warn the person doing the audio as to what is important to be heard and that the rest is fill (filling time), otherwise the person doing audio will fade it out when the entire sentence, including the fill, is heard.

Example

PROFESSOR: Young man, teaching at the college here hardly occupies all my time. I have a law practice that urgently needs my attention, (STARTING TO FADE OUT) so if you'll excuse me, I must be going because ... *the traffic at this time of day is horrendous.*

SECOND STUDENT: (FADING UP) You mean he just walked out? Wow. I agree. I think it's unfair to have a professor who devotes so much time to his law practice that he doesn't have time to prepare us to compete in our competitive field of law. Am I right?

SFX: <u>RAUCOUS APPLAUSE FROM STUDENTS</u>

In the event you don't have the equipment for doing a board fade technically, or you're rehearsing where it isn't practical to have a technical setup, a board fade can be accomplished with the same two actors vocally. All the director has to do is hand-signal the first actor to slowly back away from the microphone so her voice fades off, while cueing the second actor to move from a distance towards the mike so that his voice slowly replaces the other actor's voice.

The Cross Fade

The cross fade is a cousin of the "board fade" and can be very effective, only a little trickier when used with sound effects.

Example

> SFX: <u>INTERIOR OF JET</u>
> NANCY: (thinking) In just another half-hour we'll be landing and I can't wait to see that new sports car Bill just bought. (start fading) He certainly worked hard enough for it....
> SFX: <u>CROSS FADE JET FADING WITH CAR ENGINE FADING UP FULL</u>.
> TOMMY: Buying this baby was the best thing I ever did ... I can't wait for Nancy to see it!

Cross-fading from one scene to another is basically the same cueing motions from the director, whether it's to be done technically or with the actors and sound effects. Technically, the director points to the sound mixer and begins lowering one arm, then raising the other. Doing it live is a little trickier. He must first get the actors' and sound effects' attention so they both fade out Mary's lines and the jet plane sounds; then the director cues Bob and the car sounds to start cross-fading their sounds. The actual length of time these two cross-fades take depends on the director keeping them in time with the show's pace.

Example

> SFX: <u>WIND AND FOOTSTEPS IN THE SNOW</u>
> JOHN: Will that wind ever stop blowing?
> BUD: It's better than the heat and mosquitoes of the Amazon River.
> JOHN: I guess you're right.... It's this wind ... day and night ... night and day....
> SFX: <u>CROSS-FADE TO RIVER PADDLING</u>
> PHIL: As bad as these river mosquitoes are, at least we aren't freezing our butts off!

Tip

If the director wanted to get really creative, he would cue the sound of the canoe paddling in the rhythm of the way John is saying: "night and day ... night and day."

SEGUES

A segue is the cross-fade's short cut. It's also the movie's "cut to the chase!" When you want to go from one scene to another, the segue gets you there without a pause, or change of sound levels. This is why two similar-sounding sound effects are excellent for this type of transitioning.

Example

> SFX: <u>CLAP OF THUNDER</u>
> MOTHER: (worried) Listen to that awful thunder! And all Mary's wearing is her skimpy cheerleader's outfit! She must be having an awful time!

SFX: CLAP OF THUNDER SEGUES TO BOOM OF BASS DRUM FOL-
LOWED BY A CHEERING CROWD.
MARY: Another touchdown! What a night! What a night.... What a beautiful
night! (megaphone) Let's hear it for our Nyack Giants!

Tip

Notice that the Mother refers to Mary and the writer refers to the character's name as "Mary," but the audience can't read it, they just hear a girl's
voice. Is this Mary's voice? In order to make certain the audience is aware
that the voice is that of Mary, you must include some information that was
already given. In this case, the Mother refers to the "cheerleader's outfit," and
in the following scene, Mary supports this by using a megaphone and leading a cheer.

Cross-fades and segues are just two tools you can use along with sound
effects to make your scripts a more visual and exciting way of expressing your
ideas and avoid the bugaboo that all writers have about running out of ideas.

Stream of Consciousness

Although the stream of consciousness is somewhat narrative in form, the
content is focused on what the character is thinking at the moment. This
becomes even more effective when one actor's thoughts are heard, while the
other actor's words are faintly heard in the background. In the following
example, Temple is close on mike, while his wife talks more rapidly off mike.

To avoid confusion, and to keep reminding the actress that her voice is
an angry, audible stream of consciousness, the writer split the husband and
wife's speeches in this unusual manner.

EXAMPLE

TEMPLE: Why ... why does she have to torment me so.... Couldn't she see what
she was doing? Even when she kept laughing and daring ... encouraging me
to do something ... something ... anything ... and I listened.... But not anymore ... I picked up the knife ... gripped it tightly.... What I wouldn't give to
see the expression on her taunting, evil face.... Oh, what I wouldn't give!!
WIFE: Why are you looking at me like that? Why I ever married you I'll never
know ... Look at you with that dumb look on your face. Now, that's a good
boy ... Pick up the knife ... I know what you'd like to do with it ... if you had
the guts.... You with guts?... Don't make me laugh! Give me the damn knife,
stupid, before the pizza gets cold! Give it ... Do I have to beg, stupid?! Give
it!!! (gurgling scream)
MUSIC: MATCHES SCREAM

What's difficult doing this type of stream of consciousness is that the lines from the actors have to overlap with different emotional levels. Temple should be on mike, talking in an agonizing voice, while his wife should be off, speaking in an unemotional, nagging manner until the very end, when she is stabbed. Then the director cues an agonizing scream and, before it ends, he cues the music that has the same screaming sound. Another example of a stream of consciousness can be done in a more normal atmosphere.

EXAMPLE

SOUND: <u>HUM OF JET PLANE</u>
STEWARDESS: Can I get you anything, sir? A comfy blanket and pillow...?
VETERAN: I'm fine.
STEWARDESS: There are a few other World War II veterans going to some reunion.... You want me to change your seat?
VETERAN: I'm fine.
STEWARDESS: They were in some airplane squadron.... Was that...?
VETERAN: (firm) I'm fine!
STEWARDESS: Well ... (fading off) Just buzz me if I can be of any help....
SOUND: <u>JET HUM UP AND FADES UNDER</u>
VETERAN: (remembering) Why am I going there?... Who do you expect is still alive from that old *Smilin' Jack*? Red? Hal? Bob? And what was that gunner's name from Brooklyn...?
SOUND: <u>CROSS FADE B-52 BOMBER PLANE SOUNDS</u>
VETERAN: (over the noise and younger voice) What's wrong with that new gunner from Brooklyn...? He should have gotten that plane! Was he too scared to pull the damned trigger?!
LIEUTENANT: No, captain ... he was too damned dead!

Having the stewardess' voice fade slightly off and raising the level of the jet plane sound briefly and then lowering it indicates the stewardess has left and the veteran is alone. Then as the veteran begins remembering, the director should cue sound effects to start fading the jet sounds and cross-fading the bomber sounds very slowly so that by the time the veteran starts thinking of the flight crew's names, we're back in World War II finding out what is making this short-tempered veteran want to go to the reunion.

TIP

Writing for audio theater is not like reading a book. It is therefore the director's job to make certain that every word a writer puts in his script is clear to the audience. Smilin' Jack might be the realistic nickname the crew in World War II have named their bomber plane, but to a younger audience not familiar with the custom, the director should see that something more definitive, such as flight crew, is substituted. The same is true for adding "tail" to just "gunner." Then by changing "Brooklyn" to "afraid of heights" makes the old veteran's line: "...too scared to pull the damned trigger?!" more meaningful.

EXAMPLE

VETERAN: (remembering) Why am I going there? Who do you expect is still alive from my old flight crew? Red? Hal? Bob? And what was that tail gunner's name who was afraid of heights?

In making the cross-fade back to World War II, the elderly veteran's voice should have a younger sound. In addition to doing dialects and crying like a baby, an audio actor should practice giving their voice as many different sounds as possible. Keep in mind, the audio theater's director might have another actor do the sound of the younger man's voice, but the director in the big money professional world might start thinking if your voice can't sound younger, what other voices can't you do? Not a good way to be remembered by a director in a competitive profession that demands versatile voices.

From Camera to Microphone

The title of this hour-long production was *The Velvet Touch,* an adaptation of the movie that also starred Rosalind Russell. This is an excellent example of how a script written for film can so successfully be done in an audio-only media. The same is true for theatrical plays done on the Broadway stage. No other media has your audio theater's ability to create pictures in the mind's eye of a listening-only audience, or be so entertaining to a live audience watching the creativeness being done for their listening *and* watching pleasure.

The Appeal of the Audio Theater

I've included a number of pages from the original script to give you an idea of why a Hollywood film star was so anxious to be heard on dramatic radio. For one reason, she would reach a larger audience on radio in one night than her movie would do over weeks, months, or even ever. Second, once she did the show on live radio, it was over in one hour. No early calls for makeup and costumes; no shooting the scene over and over for the cameras and no waiting to see how all these scenes were put together. She knew how all this was accomplished and over in one thrilling hour. Now, is there little wonder why movie stars today are so anxious to do animations and cartoons where they are never seen, only heard?

So the next time you're in the same company as a friendly movie, television, or Broadway star, and you're doing a national convention, say you have a starring role in your audio theater for them. Don't be surprised if they accept your invitation for the unique, voice-only acting experience!

And now, Rosalind Russell, starring in the radio version of the film *The Velvet Touch,* but of course first we have a commercial.

WALLING: (NORMAL) THIS IS THE "SCREEN DIRECTOR'S PLAYHOUSE"—ONE OF THE WEEKLY FEATURES ON NBC'S "ALL-STAR FESTIVAL" OF COMEDY, MUSIC THEATER AND DRAMA ... BROUGHT TO YOU BY: THE MAKERS OF ANACIN ... FOR THE FAST RELIEF FROM THE PAIN OF HEADACHE, NEURITIS AND NEURALGIA! RCA VICTOR ... WORLD LEADER IN RADIO ... FIRST IN RECORDED MUSIC ... FIRST IN TELEVISION! AND BY CHESTERFIELD CIGARETTES ... ALWAYS MILDER — BETTER TASTING — COOLER SMOKING — PLUS NO UNPLEASANT AFTERTASTE. AND THAT'S THE BIGGEST PLUS IN CIGARETTE HISTORY.

MUSIC: SD-3 SCREEN DIRECTORS' ORCHESTRA FILLER

ANNOUNCER: NOW, THE FIRST ACT OF THE SCREEN DIRECTOR'S PLAYHOUSE PRESENTATION OF "THE VELVET TOUCH," STARRING ROSALIND RUSSELL IN HER ORIGINAL ROLE OF VALERIE STANTON.

MUSIC: SOMBER CURTAIN-RAISER-UP, DOWN AND BEHIND

1   VAL: (A NERVOUS CALL, CLOSE ON MIKE) Gordon?... Gordon!

2   ... (SHRILL BLEAT) Gordon!

MUSIC: UP BRIEFLY AND FADE COMPLETELY OUT FOR:

3   VAL: (STREAM OF CONSCIOUSNESS-NEUROTIC) He's dead. No ...

4   it's not true. It's a play. I'm acting. Gordon is the director ... my director.

5   But Gordon's dead. I killed him. Black hair on the blue rug. Gray at

6   the temples. (HORRIFIED) *Red* at the temples. Blood. Blood on a blue rug.

7   SOUND: SUDDEN LOUD TICKING OF CLOCK. FADE TO NORMAL BACKGROUND

8   VAL: (AS BEFORE) The clock. Gordon's clock. Time. How can it

9   go on? Why doesn't it stop? The blood runs over the rug from

1   his forehead, where I struck him with a statuette. (BEGGING) Why did

2   he have to die? I only wanted to be free to love Michael. I'll always

3   remember this place. I'll always remember the things I'm feeling now.

4   Gordon's office. The theater downstairs.

1   SOUND: SUDDEN BACKGROUND OF BROADWAY TRAFFIC NOISES — FADE TO NORMAL LEVEL UNDER

5   VAL: Broadway outside, I never knew what it was like to be afraid. Street

6   ... crowds ... people ... the people who pay to see me on stage.

7   SOUND: TAP ON THE DOOR

8   ERNIE: (OFF, MUFFLED) Mr. Dunning?

9 VAL: (GASP OF TERROR)

10 Ernie: (OFF, MUFFLED) You in there, Mr. Dunning?

11 SOUND: OFF, MUFFLED FOOTSTEPS FADE AWAY

12 VAL: (BEAT) (EXHALES BREATH IN RELIEF) Ernie ... the stage

13 manager. What if he'd seen me crouching over Gordon's

14 body? I'd explain ... accident. Didn't want to kill him.

15 Why doesn't the blood stop? Red ... blue rug. (SHARPLY)

16 Have to get out of here!... Get away! Theatre downstairs. Last

17 night. They'll be striking the sets. Saying good-bye. I'll have

18 to go downstairs. Have to act ... be calm. Valerie Stanton's

19 finest performance. Act ... smile ... walk to the door...

20 SOUND: STEPS OVER RUG

21 VAL: Open the door ... No. Fingerprints. Use *my* handkerchief.

22 SOUND: BAG SNAPS OPEN. RUMMAGE, CLOSES

23 VAL: Now open the door and close the door.

1 SOUND: DOOR OPENS, CLOSES ... SHUT OUT PREVIOUS SOUND
   PATTERN.

2 NOW WE HEAR DISTANT STAGE CREW SOUNDS — HAMMERING,

3 MOVING FURNITURE ... STRIKING SETS. (WORKING AD LIBS OFF)

4 Ernie: (UP AND WAY OFF) Put that wild wall on the truck, Mac.

5 Easy on the mirror, it has to go back to Fryfields. Joe, grab the

6 other end of that piano...

7 VAL: (CONTINUING FROM THE CLOSED DOOR)

8 Nobody can see me. They're working on the stage. I'm trembling.

9 Stop it. Swallow. (SWALLOWS) Take a breath. (BREATHES)

10 Leave the room behind ... and Gordon ... and the blood. Walk down

11 the stairs ... quietly and softly into the lobby.

12 SOUND: PADDED FOOTSTEPS SLOWLY DESCEND STAIRS

13 VAL: Why doesn't the world stop? Why doesn't it stand still — now — like

14 this. I'll never have to face anybody again ... never have to tell...

15 Barney: (WHISTLING ...

16 SOUND: HIS FOOTSTEPS FADE FROM OFF, PASSED STAIRS

17 AND FADES OFF AGAIN

18 VAL: (FEAR) Barney Soper! The janitor ... didn't see me. Sweeping the

19 ticket stubs at the end of the lobby. Better go back. No, too late. Have to
   go on

20 quietly. Maybe he won't look up. Walk quietly down the final two steps...

21 SOUND: FOUR MORE STEPS

22 VAL: There ... stand straight ... now walk easily. Bottom of the steps. Now

23 ... down the theater aisle ... he doesn't see me...

ENG: SLOWLY FADE ON STAGE CREW SOUNDS AND BUSINESS

Now that you've seen how suspenseful your audio theater can be adapting what was originally a movie, the cue above to the "*ENG*" is one of the reasons that makes it possible. The abbreviation "ENG" refers to the sound engineer. Not the person doing sound effects, but the person doing the overall sound mixing.

If for instance a show needs three microphones for the actors and two microphones for sound effects, the loudness levels for the microphones may be, and often are, set at different levels. In the case of the cue above for *The Velvet Touch,* a few of the actors go over and say their ad libs (non-scripted words) along with the sound effects on the sound effects' mikes. In this way the sound engineer can keep the actor's mike at the normal level and fade in the sound effects mikes to whatever sound level is needed.

Reviewing the Cuts and Changes

On page 1 of the script, after the music has faded under, the story starts with a teaser to arouse the listening audience's interest.

EXAMPLE

VAL: (A NERVOUS CALL, CLOSE ON MIKE) Gordon?... (PANIC) Gordon!... (SHRILL BLEAT) Gordon!!

Right away the audience knows something is wrong ... but what? I can't think of a better or quicker way to start a story and grab an audience. After the music comes up briefly and fades out, the director cues Val to begin her stream of consciousness that will unravel the story from her neurotic point of view.

Compare the edited script with the original script and decide which is more appropriate for a listening theater audience. But don't just take my word for the changes; how would you have edited it if you were the director? Or perhaps you would have left it as it is. You'll have an opportunity to decide when you read how my edited version looks with the adds and deletions in the next few pages.

EXAMPLE

(I've put all my suggestion for changes in ***bold and italic*** letters.)

*SOUND: **SUDDEN LOUD** TICKING OF CLOCK, FADE TO NORMAL BACK-GROUND*

Isn't the "loudness" of the ticking clock dependent upon Val's hysteria? Shouldn't it meet her voice's sound level and then fade to normal background? This is an excellent use of sound effects. No gunshots, car crashes, or explosion noises here! Just a subtle use of a clock while Val is still (HORRIFIED) thinking about the killing, and the clock sounds should be at that level of loudness.

SOUND: *TAP ON DOOR*

Although it wasn't indicated in the original script, I'm certain that the director gave a note to sound effects to wait for her cue. Not only for a timing purpose, but how long or short, loud or soft she wanted it to sound.

**SOUND: SUDDEN BACKGROUND OF BROADWAY TRAFFIC NOISES —
FADE TO NORMAL**
VAL: *Broadway's outside. I never knew what it was like to be afraid. Street ...
crowds ... people...the people who pay to see me on the stage.*

COMMENT

Why do we need the traffic noises? Doesn't that interrupt her stream of consciousness? And because they came in so suddenly from out of the blue, what is their purpose other than to emphasize "Broadway outside?" Wouldn't it be better if Ernie's knock was sudden and firm enough to snap Val back to reality? If so, wouldn't Ernie's voice have to reflect what the knocking sound suggests?

SOUND: TAP ON THE DOOR
ERNIE: Mr. Dunning....
VAL: (GASP OF TERROR)
ERNIE: You in there, Mr. Dunning?
SOUND: (CUE) FIRMER TAP AND CUE THE FOOTSTEPS OFF

If the director felt in reading the writer's script that Ernie leaves awfully abruptly, she might want to cue a firmer tap and then cue the footsteps off. That's the beauty of hand signals, all the director has to do for a knocking and walking cue is make the knocking motion and walking motion with her hands. But neither will be effective if the actors don't keep one eye on their scripts and the other on the director.

VAL: (BEAT) (EXHALES BREATH IN RELIEF)

Although the writer indicates a "beat" before Val "exhales breath in relief," it most likely was a cue from the director. She may have wanted to wait until the footsteps were completely gone before Val began speaking. This is worth remembering. Whenever a sound effect fades in, or out, it's always wise for the director to cue the actor to speak.

VAL: *(BEAT) (EXHALES BREATH IN RELIEF) Ernie ... the stage manager. What
if he'd seen me crouching over Gordon's body? I'd explain ... accident. Didn't want*

to kill him. Why doesn't the blood stop? Red ... blue rug. (SHARPLY) Have to get out of here!... Get away. Theater downstairs. Last night. They'll be striking the sets. Saying good-bye. I'll have to go downstairs. Have to act ... be calm. Valerie Stanton's finest performance. Act ... smile ... walk to the door...

(If part of the speech goes on the next page like this one did, either the writer or actor should write the word "more" in parentheses on the previous page.)

SOUND: STEPS OVER RUG
VAL: *Open the door.... No. Fingerprints. Use a handkerchief.*

Inasmuch as the audience doesn't know how far Val is from the door, why do we need *STEPS OVER RUG*? And since the steps would be muffled anyway, why not just wait a beat and blend her last line with the next line.

VAL: *Open the door.... No. Fingerprints. Use* "your *handkerchief."*
SOUND: BAG SNAPS OPEN, RUMMAGE ... CLOSES

Instead of having to slow the scene down with the cue of pocketbook being opened and rummaged through, since the sound effect isn't mentioned by Val, a simple "your handkerchief" describes the action and doesn't slow the scene's pace.

VAL: *Now ... open the door.*
SOUND: DOOR OPENS AND CLOSES ... SHUT OUT PREVIOUS SOUND PATTERN. NOW WE HEAR STAGE CREW HAMMERING, MOVING FURNITURE, STRIKING SETS.

The previous *sound pattern* refers to a series of sound effects done one after another. In this case, the sound effects done with the pocketbook. When the door opens is when the stage noises should come in and only then does the door close.

BIZ: (Short for "business") WORKING AD LIBS OFF
ERNIE: *(UP AND WAY OFF) Put that wild wall on the truck, Mac. Easy on the mirror, has to go to Fryfield's. Joe, grab the other end of that piano...*
VAL: *(CONTINUING FROM DOOR CLOSE) Nobody can see me. They're working on the stage. I'm trembling. Stop it. Swallow. (SWALLOWS) Take a breath. (BREATHES) Leave the room behind ... and Gordon ... and the blood. Walk down the stairs* (quietly) *into the lobby.*
SOUND: PADDED FOOTSTEPS SLOWLY DESCEND STAIRS.

Wouldn't Val normally say the word "quietly" and not let the whistling sound replace the footsteps?

VAL: *(FEAR) Barney Soper! The janitor ... sweeping the ticket stubs at the end of the lobby. Better go back. No, too late. Have to go on ... quietly. Maybe* he won't look (**cut "up" and "walk down the stairs" and replace with the following line**)

VAL: Maybe he won't look this way...or hear me on these carpeted stairs.

SOUND: FOUR MORE STEPS (CUT THESE STEP SOUNDS)

VAL: There ... stand straight ... walk easily. *"Bottom of the steps."* Now ... down the theatre aisle.... He didn't see me....

ENGINEER: SLOWLY FADE ON STAGE CREW SOUNDS AND BUSINESS

If you were directing this scene, what changes would you have made? Before you read all the changes that I made in my final edited scene, you do your own changes and make a comparison. Remember there is no right or wrong way, just your way.

MY FINAL EDITED SCENE

MUSIC: SOMBRE CURTAIN-RAISER — UP, DOWN AND UNDER

VAL: (A nervous call, close on mike) Gordon? ... (PANIC) Gordon! ... (SHRILL BLEAT) Gordon!!

MUSIC: UP BRIEFLY AND FADE COMPLETELY OUT FOR:

VAL: (STREAM OF CONSCIOUSNESS — NEUROTIC) He's dead. No ... it's not true. It's a play. I'm acting. Gordon is the director ... my director. But Gordon's dead. I killed him. Black hair on the blue rug. Gray at the temples. (HORRIFIED) *Red* at the temples. Blood. Blood on a blue rug.

SOUND: TICKING OF CLOCK IS HEARD AND FADED UNDER

VAL: The clock. Gordon's clock. Time. How can it go on? Why doesn't it stop? The blood runs over the rug from his forehead, where I struck him with the statuette. (BEGGING) Why did he have to die? I only wanted to be free to love Michael. I'll always remember this place. I'll always remember this place. I'll always remember the things I'm feeling now. Gordon's office ... the theatre downstairs ... Broadway outside. I never knew what it was like to be afraid. Streets ... crowds ... people ... the people who pay to see me on the stage.

SOUND: KNOCK ... CLOCK SOUNDS OUT

ERNIE: (off, muffled) Mr. Dunning?

VAL: (gasp of terror)

ERNIE: You in there, Mr. Dunning?

SOUND: FOOTSTEPS FADE OFF

VAL: (BEAT) (EXHALES BREATH IN RELIEF) Ernie ... the stage manager. What if he'd seen me crouching over Gordon's body? I'd explain ... accident. Didn't want to kill him. Why doesn't the blood stop? Red ... blue rug. (sharply) Have to get out of here!... Get away. Theater downstairs. Last night. They'll be striking the sets. Saying good-bye. I'll have to go downstairs and act like nothing ever happened ... it'll be difficult ... but isn't that what acting is all about?

Still believe a director's job in your audio theater isn't much more than making some acting suggestions and throwing a few cues? Proper directing can be the difference between an exciting, imaginative performance, or one with a line of actors just reading their parts. Having read just a few pages of such a great play as *The Velvet Touch*, which option would make you the proudest?

And yes, if Hollywood can adapt an involved movie script to a voice-only theater before a live audience, what is stopping you from adapting scripts from other media?

(Please note: There wasn't room for the entire script, therefore, to find out how *The Velvet Touch* ended, see this chapter's Summary.)

Many of the shows, such as Screen Director's Playhouse, that starred Hollywood stars doing brilliant plays are available for a small rental price from SPERDVAC (www.sperdvac.org).

Summary

1. Experience in the vocal theater, because of its intensive focus on sound, gives anyone entering film or television an added dimension of creative expression. It was perhaps Orson Welles' experience in radio that resulted in his later critically acclaimed, innovative use of sound in films.

2. Although the audio theater frees the writer from visual restraints, it must never be forgotten that the audio theater audience can "see" only what it hears. It's up to the director to make certain that the writer's words and the sound artist's effects are best used for that purpose.

3. Establishing sounds at the beginning of a scene indicates to the audience where and when the action is taking place. Once the actors begin speaking, the sounds may be gradually faded down so as not to interfere with the dialogue. It is then up to the director to keep the sounds in the background, or to lose (take out) them.

4. Sound effects are the actors movements; and they must act as one when called upon.

5. The first indication of a script's playing time is its number of pages. If a writer wants the director to read their script, they must figure each page takes approximately a minute of time.

6. Directors must be aware of sneaky actors with a series of long speeches. By withholding the pace they intend to do only on air, they jeopardize the show's timing.

7. Sound effects in the audio theater are like the special effects in films. A director needs to use them wisely.

8. The mixing of a show requires the talents of the audio engineer for technical acceptability and the director for dramatic impact. These two, working together, will determine the show's listening enjoyment for an audience.

9. Reality has no place on a comedy show. Doors rarely open, they only close. And they rarely just "close"; they are slammed!

10. Whether you actually broadcast your show over local radio or television, or do it in a theater, or even whether you do it live in these venues, the most exciting and beneficial way of doing your show or your exercises is to time them. Whether it be a 20-second spot announcement or a half-hour (29:30) dramatic show, the practice and discipline of being forced to comply with responsibility is invaluable ... and the most fun.

11. A board fade is accomplished by the sound mixer decreasing the sound of one actor's voice down to zero. If it is done live by the actor, it's done by the actor slowly backing away from the mike.

12. A cross-fade involves two microphones. As one actor's voice (or sound) fades on one mike, the actor's voice (or sound) is introduced and increases in volume to replace the voice or sound that has faded out.

13. The term segue (seg-way) refers to two separate elements, such as recorded music, being joined without the sound level first being faded in and out as in cross-fading. For instance, the theme music comes to a close, and the opening bridge immediately begins playing.

14. A stream of consciousness is seeing the inside of a character's emotional behavior. It's accomplished by the actor speaking their words very close to the mike.

15. When cross-fading one scene to another, allow the actors enough words to cover the transition.

The Ending to the Velvet Touch

It's the closing night of Val's play. The scene calls for Val to commit suicide by going into a small enclosed room on stage and killing herself with a handgun. As she walks slowly towards the small room, the detective who has been investigating the case arrives and learns from the prop man that Val took a real, not a prop, gun out on stage! Moments later the gunshot is heard. And as the curtain falls, Val steps from the room, bows to the applauding audience and is arrested for her crime. When the detective was questioned later as to why he didn't arrest Val before she went on stage and risked her killing herself, he shrugged and said, "She already confessed to her crime and begged me to allow her to find out just how good of an actress she really was to play such a heartbreaking and real-life role."

Chapter 9

Comparing Audio Theater
with Other Media

The Advantages of Audio Theater

Writing is writing, and acting is acting, it's only where it's being done that is different. If audio theater had a curtain, setting, furniture and spotlight, it would be a play. If it had locations and a camera, it would be a movie. Whether your goals are to write, act, or create sounds in other media, there is no better place to start than the audio theater. Where else can you acquire experience without first having experience?

Unlike other media that demand years of experience in order for your voice to be heard professionally, or even dramatically improved, audio theater gives you that opportunity now, as well as the fun, excitement and challenges of creating entertainment that appeals not just to the audience's eyes and ears, but to something much more personal and private; their imagination.

This is what is so important about audio theater. What is learned and practiced in the audio theater takes you out of the "wannabe" class and gives you the experience that is so important for wherever your talents may take you. If it's acting, the audio theater will give you the opportunity to use your voice for a variety of characters and sounds, all of which are demanded in whatever media you may choose.

Being asked to do the voice of a bashful lobster, crying like a baby, sizzz-zling like a snake, or giving an important business or political speech for the first time can be frightening. But not when your voice already has had experience doing those roles, and dozens more, all in front of an audience ... a live, responsive audience!

That is what the audio theater is all about. Adapting your voices and writings and getting valuable experience so you're comfortable in any other media you choose to pursue. Therefore, in showing how dissimilar the scripts might be for different media, writers and actors will have an opportunity to see how similar, or different, they are to the audio theater versions.

In addition, you will soon learn that how you start out your different careers are not always the way you'll attain your goals. Take for instance the art of performing pantomimes!

Writing Pantomimes?

The first comparison to another art form is one you would never expect. How can the audio theater, which depends on sounds and words, be compared with another art form that never makes a sound or says a word, like pantomimes? Yes, pantomimes!

Having started out writing for radio and doing some sound effects in college for our weekly radio broadcasts, I was asked by a television comedian to write a pantomime. The trouble was, the only mime artist I had ever seen was from France, named Marcel Marceau. And because he was rarely seen in this country in person, or on television, I only knew he was a mime artist that did all the classic moves in a graceful, nonverbal manner. And that's what confused me; the person who asked me to write the pantomime was neither graceful nor traditional ... he was a standup comedian!

The few times I saw Marceau, I appreciated all the moves he created, but never thought he was funny. Then I remembered him tripping over something imaginary in one of his performances, and I began supposing this imaginary "thing" made a noise. After all, just because Marceau was a traditional mime artist, what was to keep someone without his great talents silently reacting to the sound effects accompanying his moves? So that's what I did, as I connected what I learned about radio writing and sound effects and applied it to writing pantomimes. Only instead of using words, I used movements and accompanying sounds.

Evidently my idea worked. After writing pantomimes for Dick Van Dyke for a number of years, I received a call to write the same type of pantomimes for Red Skelton's weekly television show.

Foleying in the Audio Theater?

You betcha! Normally, Foleying adds sound effects in post production to "sweeten" or improve what is already on film, or tape. In the audio theater, Foleying is motivated by the manner in which the actor says the words.

Why Foley the sound effects? It better describes movement without writing words. Therefore, instead of just speaking the words that suggest movement, the actor actually mimes the movement without ever leaving the microphone!

Doesn't it make sense that if Foleying improves physical action, these same physical movements would be reflected in the sound of our voices? After all, the sound of our voices does not always come from just our mouths, sometimes it comes from our feet. So when the script calls for you to be saying your lines while you're supposedly walking, what's to keep you from taking your shoes off and moving your feet in sync with the walking sounds coming from the sound effects? After all, when you actually walk does your voice sound the same as when you're seated comfortably in a chair?

Walking on a treadmill will never move you from place to place, but doesn't that leg movement affect the sound of your voice? Most actors during radio's glory days thought so.

When Agnes Moorehead did Lucille Fletcher's "Sorry, Wrong Number" on *Suspense*, the night of May 25, 1943, when the phone rang, Moorehead's hand moved in sync with the sound effect of the phone being taken off the receiver. And when the script indicated she was to slam down the phone in frustration, sound effects may have slammed down the phone, but it was the sound of Moorehead's voice that matched the sound effect's frustration and anger. And more importantly, the frightened listeners at home heard two sounds; the phone being hung up, and Moorehead's fear of what she just overheard.

Having the actors and sound effects working so closely together will not only improve the sound of the script, it will entertain and often surprise an audience that is watching. Therefore, in order to make audio theater unique, it isn't just a media of words being spoken, it must have movement for the imagination.

Adapting Scripts from the Stage Theater

If you have written a play for the stage, or have read a play you'd like to adapt to your audio theater, I've included a few pages to show what similarities and differences there are between the audio theater's format and that of the stage play. The first problem is, how do you go about adapting what was seen and heard to just being heard?

As the curtain rises, before a word is spoken, audiences have already read their play bills for information regarding what they are going to see. Then when the curtain rises, they can make further opinions simply by what they can see on the stage: What sort of furniture is in the room, or pictures on the wall. Is the room homey and friendly, or simply practical without much thought for comfort? All this must be described in detail by the author for all the crafts involved.

<u>ACT I</u>

The living room of Jeff Winston's duplex East Side, it just missing being on the upper East Side, still, it's more money than Jeff's struggling advertising agency can afford. And that's what keeps Jeff running. However, when you're a single parent with a lot of guilt — your four young daughters in a private school, in a good neighborhood — it's worth the running and struggling. Especially if you're trying to be a perfect single parent. This is reflected in everything that Jeff does ... right down to the warm, cozy, homey look he hopes he's achieved with the early–American furniture and a fireplace located in the upstage center rear wall. Over the mantle hangs a carved eagle with a flag in its claws, with the encouraging words "Don't Give Up the Ship." Stage left a balcony with a row of bedroom and bathroom doors. Jeff's office is stage left of the stairs. The dining area is stage right with a nearby swinging door that leads to the kitchen. The main entrance to the apartment is in the stage right wall.

Everything the writer wants seen by the theater's stage audience must be included for the various crafts; the actors, directors, stage hands, prop people, lighting director, costume designers and makeup people. Whereas none of this descriptive writing is needed for the audio theater. What is needed are the spoken words, sounds, or music that best describe the scene to the audio theater's imagination.

Secondly, you'll notice the difference between the audio theater's script format and that of the stage. Whereas the sentences in the stage's script are single-spaced lines, those in the audio theater are double-spaced. The reason being the length of time between the rehearsal time and the play actually being done on stage for the public. Whatever changes made needn't be scribbled in a hurry between sentences for an on-air, live deadline; they can take weeks to be resolved. And inasmuch as the normal length of a stage play is 81 pages, if all the lines were double-spaced the amount of pages would be a whopping 160 pages!

The Stage Play's Script

TIME: The present ... late afternoon.

AT CURTAIN: Soft, sensuous MUSIC that increases in volume as the curtain rises. Then, an unseen male, husky voice is heard from the sofa.

MAN: Oh, darling ... darling.... Say you love me ... please say you love me!

(A glimpse of red hair appears above back of sofa. With it, a small pillow drops to the floor. Then a voice, presumably from the sofa, moans sexily.)

WOMAN: Oh ... quick, sweetheart.... Do you have something?

(Lauren, age seven, gets up from the sofa and angrily turns the television off.)

LAUREN: What do you want, stupid ... a hamburger? So much for afternoon television! What a day I picked to get sick!

(At the tender age of seven, it's hard to tell whether Lauren will grow up to be a ravishing beauty, attractive, or stay as she is. She has red hair, a plain face and glasses. But just as nature compensates animals for any protective deficiencies ... the porcupine its quills ... Lauren has a haughty manner and glib tongue. At the moment, her eclectic taste in clothes includes: pin leotards, tap shoes, a yellow karate belt and a sequined tiara. As she rises from the sofa she fantasizes.)

LAUREN: All right, Shane McLoughlin! You better not try and kiss me like that! Because I'm a Taekwondo yellow-belted karate expert! (Does karate hand-chopping move and yell!) I'm sorry, Shane, you're all dead and bleeding. But next time, you'll know better than to mess with ... Lauren Winston! (Another vocal fanfare.) (SHE then goes to the sofa, puts on the pink tutu, and hums a tune as She exits tap dancing into the kitchen stage right.)

SOUND: DOOR CHIMES.

(Lauren reappears with can of soda and tap dances over to get a footstool)

LAUREN: I'm coming ... I'm coming...

(Lauren gets footstool and places it in front of the door. Takes off glasses and peers out.)

LAUREN: Face the little peephole so I can see who you are.

GAY: (Lyrically) We're here to see Jeff Winston, dearie. Is he home?

LAUREN: (cautious) Maybe he is, and maybe he isn't.... Who are you?

GAY: His reason for drinking.

LAUREN: Drinking what?

GAY: Will you just open the door ... please?

LAUREN: Jeff Winston is my father and he doesn't want me to let in strangers.

GAY: Your father is perfectly right, dearie. Now will you open the door?

(Lauren pauses thoughtfully, then shrugs.)

LAUREN: Who'd hurt a little kid like me?

(Lauren does the business of opening bolts. As she opens the door, Gay sweeps past her. He's dressed in a black, shiny silk suit that sets off his braided, blond hair.)

LAUREN: (Trying to impress) I'm Lauren Winston, and I have a yellow belt! (Lifts tutu to show karate belt.) See?

GAY: Adorable ... but not with that hideous colored pink tutu!

In reading *The Gingerbread Man,* you can see the stage settings keep a theater audience informed and entertained simply by what they were seeing on stage. In adapting *The Gingerbread Man* to the audio theater, this all requires being pictured in the audience's imagination with voices, sounds and music.

Although the script format is basically the same, the spaces between the sentences are not. Inasmuch as time isn't a factor with a stage play, there is no need for last-minute changes. All this can be done in the weeks of rehearsals and the tryouts before the play reaches Broadway.

What is important in adapting a stage play to the audio theater is cutting every word that doesn't offer information the audience needs for their imagination.

EXAMPLE

<u>ANNOUNCER</u>: Our story opens in an apartment just off Fifth Avenue ... make that just far enough off Fifth Avenue to be affordable for Jeff Winston, the single parent of four daughters. As the story opens, Lauren, the youngest of Jeff's daughters, has stayed home from school for another imagined illness and is having a difficult time deciding whether to do her math homework or watch her favorite daytime soap on television.
<u>MUSIC: ROMANTIC</u>
MAN: (TV VOICE FILTER) Oh, darling ... darling, I can't live without you.... Just say you love me ... please ... say it.... Say you love me!
WOMAN: Oh, quick, sweetheart, do you have something?
LAUREN: What do you want, stupid ... a hamburger?
<u>SOUND: CLICKS MUSIC OUT</u>
LAUREN: So much for afternoon television. What a day I picked to get sick. Dumb soap operas and dumber math homework! (LOFTY) But when I'm a fashion model I won't *have* to know how to do math ... just be tall and skinny!

In reading the audio theater version of the stage play, the words are basically the same, but the pace has increased considerably. Even the long description of the stage's setting has been described by the audio theater's announcer in a few words. All the "sight gags" (things that look funny without words) or "business" (movements the actors do without words) are cut. In short, anything an audience can't see simply by hearing the audio actors' spoken words are cut. The same is true of the screen play's script.

The Film Script

A film script is the story that a writer puts down on paper; a "shooting script" is what the director uses to get the story down on film. We saw how *The Velvet Touch* was adapted to the audio theater. What about adapting *Friday the 13th Part VI: Jason Lives* to the audio theater?

A FILM'S SHOOTING SCRIPT

In reading the following shooting script, you can see how much information is dependent on what the movie or television audiences are able to see. This requires not only cameras and sound equipment, but a "shooting" film script indicating all the camera angles the director needs to have in order for the film to be shot efficiently and smoothly.

Tom McLoughlin, a prominent screenwriter/director, was kind enough to give me a few pages from a shooting script he directed titled *Friday the 13th Part VI: Jason Lives*. Because Tom was such a successful director, I couldn't help asking him how important he felt audio theater was for getting started in a field as competitive as films? He simply answered, "Anything that lets you use your imagination, whether it's writing, acting, or directing, and especially in front of a live, critical audience, is extremely important for whatever you do, and not just films."

He then smiled and said, "It's rare that anybody ever starts out directing a high budget film. I started by studying and performing pantomimes and then became the lead singer for the rock group TNT. I even had a small part acting in a Woody Allen movie. But I always wanted to be a writer and director. After getting a stack of rejections, I finally got what I wanted by writing and directing a horror film I wrote, *One Dark Night*. This didn't happen overnight, but you know something, I've never regretted all the experience it took getting to the place I always dreamed about."

Isn't that what the audio theater does by giving you valuable experience for where you eventually want to be? And to prove it, see how a movie as visual and difficult as *Friday the 13th* can be adapted to the audio theater. First the film's shooting script.

Example — Friday the 13th Part VI: Jason Lives

LOW ANGLE — ON TOMMY
He struggles to pull the spear out. It's apparently driven into the bottom of the coffin as well. Hawes leans down into the grave.
HAWES: Let's just get the hell out of here! My heart can't take any more of this!
CLOSE ON JASON'S FACE
Jason's wicked eyes glare at Tommy.
RESUME ON TOMMY
The boy, of course, does not see what's about to occur. He finally yanks the spear out, and throws it into the grass. Slowly he removes his gloves and tosses them to Hawes. He starts to climb out. JASON SPRINGS UP FROM BEHIND AND GRABS HIM.
CLOSE ON HAWES SCREAMING
He goes crazy with hysteria and starts to run.
ANGLE DOWN ON GRAVE
Tommy fights for his life as Jason tries to pull him down into his grave. He manages to kick Jason back down long enough to climb out.
TOMMY scrambles for the gas can as the STORM CLOUDS DETONATE ABOVE. He gets it open, turns around, and starts throwing it on the rising corpse of Jason.

ANGLE ON JASON
The gas splashes all over him as he keeps coming!
REVERSE ON TOMMY
He backs up as Jason stalks him. Knowing there's enough gas on his predator, he drops the can.
TIGHTER — ON JASON
He's coming closer!
TIGHTER ON TOMMY
Panicking, he searches his pockets for his matches. He finds them. As he pulls them out, the STORM CLOUDS ERUPT WITH AN INCREDIBLE DOWN-POUR OF WATER!
JASON
Stops as the rain drenches him. Maggots start to wash off him as he stares at his helpless victim.
RESUME TOMMY
He tries desperately to light a match in this pouring rain.
TOMMY'S HANDS
Struggling with the soaked matches.
JASON
Starts to close in. Suddenly HAWES EMERGES FROM BEHIND HOLDING UP A SHOVEL. HE HOLLERS AS HE SWINGS IT!
ANGLE ON HAWES
He WHACKS the back of Jason's head as hard as he can. It doesn't even faze this undead super killer!
JASON WHIPS AROUND ON HAWES
His arm lunges forcefully at Hawes' chest.
ANGLE ON HAWES' BACK
JASON'S HAND CLUTCHES HAWES' HEART. BURSTS OUT HAWES' BACK!
ANGLE ON GRAVE
Hawes' body falls back into Jason's grave.
TIGHT ON COFFIN
As Hawes lands in coffin, the lid shuts over him.
ANGLE ON TOMMY
Horrified and weaponless, he runs like hell!

There you have some pages of a shooting script. What isn't on these script pages are all the notations written for the camera angles. The next time this movie is on television you can see how the camera shot all these written words.

ADAPTING *FRIDAY THE 13TH* TO THE AUDIO THEATER

Having just read the shooting script, did you notice how much information had to be compressed for the director into so few words? This is not like writing a composition for an English class, the words for a film's shooting script must inform in the least amount of time and space.

TOMMY (struggling grunts)
The lightning rod is too hot and it's even driven into the coffin!
SOUND: FOLLOW ALL ACTIONS
HAWES: (panic) Leave it in and get up out of the grave before that corpse....
TOMMY: (screaming) It's got me! His clammy fingers are pulling at me...
HAWES: Give me your hand!! And kick his face and pull up ... up!! One more
   ... pull!! (final grunt) Now let's get out of here!
TOMMY: No, give me the gas can!... This gasoline will stop him!
(SOUND: POURING GAS)
HAWES: No. It isn't, it isn't stopping him.... He keeps coming up out of the
   grave!
(CLAP OF THUNDER AND RAIN)
TOMMY: I'm gonna set fire to that gasoline.... That'll stop him!
SOUND (STRIKING SOUNDS)
HAWES: Just hurry and do it !! (effort) while I get this grave-digging shovel!
TOMMY: They're not lighting ... the rain soaked them!
HAWES: This shovel will stop him!
POUNDING ON BODY WITH METAL SHOVEL
TOMMY: It isn't.... All it's doing is knocking the maggots off his face! Run ...
   run!!!
HAWES: (horrified effort) I can't ... he's choking me and dragging me to the
   grave ... (breathless) He's going to throw me down to die in his coffin!!! Don't
   ... I beg of you ... (voice trails off in a scream as Hawes falls into the grave!)
MUSIC

In comparing the different media, the one may want to depend on words
and pictures, while audio theater on imagination and movement. If there
wasn't movement in the audio theater's adaptation of the film, there would
simply be two actors yelling words at one another without sounds helping
their audience visualize the action.

During radio's golden age, adapting this film would basically be done
the same way for an audience of millions of radio listeners in the safety of
their homes. Today the audio theater listeners have a choice. Because audio
theater is normally done in front of a live audience, those in the audience
have the choice of closing their eyes and simply listening and letting their
mind's eye picture the story, or listening and watching the performance.

And there's plenty to watch! Something that can't be done in any other
media. It's one thing hearing and seeing a body being torn in half on television and film, it's another to hear, as well as watch, how the sound of the
body being torn in half is being created!

The Soap Opera

This genre offers a huge change of pace. Try doing this scene in your
audio theater. Not only is it nostalgic for some old-time radio fans in the audi-

ence, many movie actors in those early radio days started their careers on soaps. Therefore, I warn you that doing a soap in the audio theater requires excellent acting with a story line that is often redundant and boring. But I can't think of another type of writing that will stretch your acting ability, not only giving your voice a good workout as much as it will keep you, as an actor, from not making fun of the material that millions of devoted TV and radio fans watched, and often fretted over, year after year. Are they all bored house-wives? Not on your life. Here's a hint. What do you think many of the major league sports figures watch when they're out of town and have a night game?

Soaps have varied, and loyal fans have kept soaps on the air five days a week, fifty-two weeks a year, year after year. Helen Trent, for example, was on the radio for 27 years! And the show's star, Virginia Clark, remained the same 35 years old for 11 years!

You have to believe nothing lasts that long without dedication; and that's what the actors had, day in and day out. Without it, how could Helen Trent stay on the air if she, along with her fans, didn't believe with all their hearts there was romance after the age of 35!

Soap operas started out as 15-minute shows on radio, and because they were sponsored by soap products, their name quickly went from "daytime seri-als" to simply "soaps," but the serial part remained. Writing for soaps on radio was a five-day-, fifty-two-week job that needed the type of story lines that kept the busy home audiences tuning in day after day, week after week and year after year.

Don't be fooled. Experienced soap actors could not only make what the authors wrote interesting and appealing, it kept these actors in demand.

This included the all-important announcers, whose voice not only read the commercials, they sold what they said, which oftentimes required the skills of an actor.

EXAMPLE: WAVE

ANNOUNCER

(Acting) *When the fabulously wealthy widow Agatha Murchfield, and her weak-willed son Rodney, and a shady stranger who claims to be Agatha's long-lost son Caldwell, whom she can't recall having because of the many things going on at the country club back then, face one another, was this really her long-forgotten son or simply someone after the Murchfield millions? We'll soon find out today.*

(Announcing) But first, if you can't make a choice as to what soap to use on your laundry, let Wave come to the rescue! And always remember, when dirt's in ... wave it goodbye with WAVE."

(Acting) *It's a sunny day in Nyack-on-the-Hudson and Ma Hanson had just baked up a batch of donuts when her good neighbor, Hank Ernest, smelled the aroma and came calling with some disquieting news.*

EXAMPLE: HANK KNOWS HIS DONUTS

SOUND: CUP DOWN ON SAUCER.

MA: More coffee, Hank?

HANK: Nope, two's my limit, Ma ... unless of course you throw in one of them cinnamon donuts I've been sniffing since I came in here.

MA: I think that can be arranged.

SOUND: SCRAPE OF CHAIR AND STEPS.

MA: Got some in the oven. You be thinking about what's so urgent you came to tell me.

HANK: Now I don't want you to go to any trouble, Ma.

MA: I'm just flattered you like them. Now what is it you called to tell me that is so urgent, Hank?

SOUND: PHONE RING OFF.

MA: Now who do you suppose that can be at this hour?

SOUND: CHAIR SCRAPE.

HANK: Probably just a salesman. But while you're finding out.... I'll just help myself.

SOUND: PHONE RING OFF.

MA: I'm coming ... coming.

SOUND: FOOTSTEPS ON ... PHONE RING OFF.

MA: I'm coming, land's sake.... Hold your horses...

SOUND: PHONE RING FADES ON TO MATCH THE STEPS. PHONE OFF CRADLE.

MA: Hello?... Hello?

SOUND: JIGGLES CRADLE.

MA: Hello?

SOUND: PHONE BACK ON CRADLE. SOUND: STEPS ON

MA: (mumbling) Oh dear, they hung up. This is the second call I missed this month. I'm just gonna have to move this phone from the parlor to the kitchen.

SOUND: STEPS. AS MA WALKS TO KITCHEN, HANK'S VOICE BECOMES LOUDER

HANK: Another missed call, Ma? You're just gonna have to stop doin' all that walkin' and move that phone from the parlor to the kitchen.

SOUND: STEPS STOP

MA: (smiling) Now why didn't I think of that, Hank? Have yourself another donut. Now what is it that's so important you wanted to tell me?

HANK: Oh, that! It's darn important too! I wrote it down on a piece of paper so I'd be sure to remember them exact words.... Now where did I put it...? (sound patting clothes) It ain't in my vest. Maybe in my overalls.... Nope, drat it ... I KNOW! I left it out on my pump when I got water for my dog, Speedy. I'll go get it now, Ma.... Mind if I take a donut to my dog? He'd bite me if I didn't.

MA: No, Hank ... take two, the rest are going to the hospital where I'm volunteering.

HANK: But what about what I wrote to remember?

MA: I'll bake another batch of donuts for tomorrow.... You can tell me then. I

just pray it isn't about my late mortgage payments.... If it is, I just don't know where the money is coming from.
MUSIC: THEME
ANNOUNCER: Tune in tomorrow and see if Ma can wave away her troubles the way you can WAVE away your washing problems!
MUSIC: UP AND OUT

I warned you! But before you make fun of those golden days of soaps, the actors or writers didn't. Soaps in those early days were restricted by what the sponsors and the Federal Communications Commission considered appropriate for the listeners to hear. No violence, and definitely no sexual story lines. What was left took excellent actors to make the stories appealing and interesting.

The few times I did the sounds on *Ma Perkins*, the actress who played the part of Ma, Virginia Paine, not only played the part of Ma Perkins, she *became* Ma Perkins. Virginia Paine received the role of the 60-year-old Ma Perkins at the ripe old age of 23! And never missed a performance in 27 years! How serious did she take the role? The moment Virginia entered the studio for rehearsals, she became Ma Perkins. Her voice changed, her attitude changed, the cast even referred to Virginia as "Ma."

I once asked an actor how he jumped from doing soaps to becoming a Hollywood star. He just shrugged and said, "You'd be surprised what will happen if you just give everything you got to whatever you're given."

The Versatility of the Audio Theater

From a horror movie to an old time soap, can you think of any other media so versatile as the audio theater? Which proves a good, imaginative story doesn't need cameras, costumes, or elaborate stage settings, just as long as the story from another media appeals to the imagination of the audio theater's audience.

Summary

1. In adapting a story from another media, the most important thing to remember is that today's stories are done primarily for visual media, whereas audio theater is basically imaginative.

2. Because audio theater is most often done in front of a live audience, the actors must not stand like sticks reading their lines. They must act them!

3. No matter how tempting it is to put on a Stetson hat when you're doing a Western story ... resist it!

4. Practice creating different voices by watching cartoons and muting the audio. Then record your voice in sync with the characters and play it back with the cartoon's voices still muted. How did your voice compare with those on the cartoon?

5. A good way of acquiring new-sounding voices is not to pay attention to how people look, but how they sound. Also watch their mouth movements and posture if you find someone with an interesting and unusual sounding voice.

6. Don't be afraid to Foley your body along with sound effects. This gives stage movement, and your voice a more realistic sound.

7. Never forget that many of the live, dramatic radio shows that kept a nation entertained at home just listening were being done in a theater on stage. This meant that radio often had two audiences; those at home and those in the theater. This was especially true if the stories were high-budgeted radio dramas starring the actors who were seen in the films. These scripts were never just written for listening, but watching as well. And for a good reason; sponsors demanded their products be seen in theaters and associated with Hollywood's most important stars.

8. This is true today in your audio theater. There are hundreds of opportunities for an audio theater to do shows. Some on radio, television, fund-raisers, schools and popular old-time radio conventions. Don't forget to invite movie or television stars who, in addition to selling and autographing their books, are more than willing to appear and experience what it's like to act with their voices and sound effects.

9. Once your audio theater becomes up and running, have the scripts you do most often recorded to CDs and available for your audiences ... for a price.

10. I can't tell you how exciting and valuable the audio theater can be for anyone who is interested in a professional career, improving their speaking voice for business, or just as a hobby. Remember what President Reagan said: "I owe my success to my voice."

10

The Warm-Up

The Warm-Up

They do it in Las Vegas, or at your favorite television comedy series before they start taping, and now you'll be doing it in your audio theater, a warm-up. Whoever you select to do the warm-up, usually the announcer or director, starts off by welcoming the audience and asking them if they have ever seen audio theater done in person, or listened to Jack Benny, Red Skelton, or Fibber McGee and Molly on tapes or CDs. If they have, or even if they haven't, you can tell them they can either watch and listen to the show, or close their eyes and imagine what they're hearing. Just promise the audience that while their eyes are closed it won't be like cable television ... you won't be taking off your clothes!

Next you can ask the audience if they've met one another. Then have them turn around and shake hands with one another. (Then as they do, they'll find the person in back of them has done the same and there's nothing to shake hands with but their backs.)

> MC: Now that we're all friends, how many in the audience know what sound effects are? (Selects someone for an answer.) Now that we know what "sound effects" are, what is "Foleying"? (Selects someone for an answer.)

As you can see, both sound effects and Foleying are the same ... but a whole lot different. At one time both radio and films called it sound effects. But then a movie sound effects man named Jack Foley did a sound effect without resorting to the use of filmed sounds, but simply and quickly with manual effects, and the appreciative director was so impressed and pleased that he called what Foley did "Foleying." But rather than just tell you all about this very technical subject, how about selecting some volunteers from the audience to demonstrate the differences between simply doing the sound effects and Foleying the sound effects?

SFX NEEDED:

1. Some small leafy branches.
2. Tray of water large enough to get some paper towels sopping wet.
3. Plastic tray with water.
4. Potato chips in a soft Ziploc bag.
5. Ziploc bag of corn starch.
6. Small tap bell for judges.

(After two volunteers have been selected ... a male and a female ... we find out a little bit about them and then set the scene.)

> MC: The scene is a hiker walking up a steep hill and encountering different types of walking surfaces. All the sounds needed are laid out on a table and the person who does the sound effects for audio theater will show you the proper way to create each sound. (After an intro, the sound person demonstrates each sound effect.) (When that is done, the MC explains the contestants will do the sounds two ways ... the way it was done during the golden age of dramatic radio, and the Foley method that is so popular in films.) First, the way sound effects were originally done. But if you hear this bell (hits tap bell) you'll know you made a mistake. And the contestant that makes the least mistakes with doing the sound effects, both the audio theater way and Foleying, will get a signed copy of *The Audio Theater Guide*. (Passes out the scripts.)
>
> MC: "I had no idea the hill was so steep and covered with bushes when I started walking in the woods. But I hadn't taken more than a few steps when I stepped into some potato chips someone had dropped along the trail. I kicked the bag aside and kept walking until I got to a wooden bridge. The bridge was short and I hadn't taken too many steps when I had to stop. The ground next to the bridge was covered with snow, so I found myself walking in snow ... slower and slower and then faster and faster until I went up the stairs of the porch to my hotel, stamped the snow off my shoes, and sat down in a chair too fast and ripped open my pants!"
>
> MC: Now contestant number one, are you ready? Now we're going to hear this same story done with sound effects. And don't forget each mistake you make gets a tap on the mistake bell by our sound man. Here we go with the story. "I had no idea the hill was so steep and covered with bushes when I started walking in the woods (branches and leaves). I hadn't taken more than a few steps when I stepped into some potato chips (crunching) someone had dropped along the trail. I kicked the bag aside (kicking bag) and kept walking faster (branches and leaves) until I got to a stream of water. There was no bridge and so I had to walk in the water (steps in water) one step at a time. The stream was narrow ... but when I got out of the water (water sound) on the other side, I found myself walking in snow (corn starch) step after step after step until I finally reached a wooden bench and stopped. I was so tired from walking, I sat down on a wooden bench too fast ... much too fast ... and ripped the seat of my pants! (pants ripped)

The second sketch is done as if it were a cartoon, or a film. Now the contestants have to do the sound effects in sync with the MC's body movements. If the MC takes five steps, the contestant must make the same amount of steps done in sync with the MC's leg movements. The same is true with the other sounds. At the conclusion of the contests, because both contestants did so well, each of them receives a signed copy of *The Audio Theater Guide*. And now that the audience is in a good mood, the MC thanks the audience and the regular show begins for an audience that is ready and willing to be entertained.

The Comedy Warm-Up

MC: (friendly) How many people have heard the sound of a gunshot? Well tonight, in one of the sketches, there's going to be one and we'd just like you to know how loud it's going to sound. First of all, let me introduce our sound effects man. (Does intro)

MC: Now audience, put your fingers to your ears and our sound effects specialist will demonstrate just how loud this gunshot is going to be. (MC puts fingers in his ears and the sound man puts one finger in his ear and pulls the trigger. No gunshot, keeps pulling trigger)

MC: What happened to the gunshot?

SFX: I don't know...

MC: Can't you check and find out?

(SFX: CLICKS A FEW MORE TIMES IN THE AIR AND fiNALLY LOOKS DOWN THE BARREL AND GIVES IT ONE MORE CLICK AND WE HEAR A LOUD GUNSHOT OFF STAGE)

SFX: I knew there was nothing wrong!

(APPLAUSE)

THE AUDIENCE AUDITION

MC: (looking at watch) Was the traffic that bad getting here? This next sketch requires kind of a difficult introduction and the announcer isn't here. I suppose I could do it ... but you've heard enough of me, haven't you? (fast) Don't answer that please! So I won't do this. But if any of you aspiring announcers are in the audience, now is an opportunity to step up to the plate and announce the introduction to this next sketch we're going to do. Don't be shy, this may be the big show business break you've always wanted!

(After the MC gets some volunteers, he passes out the introductions and gives them five minutes to silently rehearse. During that five minute break, he answers questions from the audience. When the five minutes are up, he selects the first contestant to read the intro to the private eye thriller.)

CONTESTANT

And now sit back and relax and listen to another thrilling episode from the files of ... not Sam Spade, or Richard Diamond, of not even

Donald Trump, but Herbie Trump. Or as his friends in Brooklyn call
him, *Hoibie* Trump. (wait for laugh) Trump is the private eye of last
resort, and tonight he calls this little caper:
  "WHAT DO THE BIG BLEACHED BLONDE FROM BROOK-
LYN AND HER BROKEN-DOWN, BEADY-EYED BOYFRIEND
FROM BOSTON HAVE IN COMMON? — CAPER."

After all the contestants have auditioned, the audience picks out a winner
who is presented with a signed book on audio theater, while the other contestants are given a CD recording of a previous Herbie Trump's show done
by the audio theater.

The Importance of the Warm-Up

Yes, it's to have fun ... and yes, it's to relax the audience ... but most of
all, it's to prepare an audience for an experience they may never have had
before ... being entertained in a unique theater ... a theater that doesn't depend
on what the audience sees, but only on what is so rare today ... the power of
imagination.

Summary

1. Never ever make anyone in the audience feel uncomfortable.
2. A warm-up is done simply and only to put audiences in a spirit of
fun.
3. Treat your audiences as you would guests in your home.
4. Treat every audience as if it's an audition for the next step up in your
career.
5. If you can leave an audience wishing for more of what they just heard
and imagined, you know you can't do any better than that.

11

The Comedy Theater

Of all the different types of shows you can do in your audio theater, the one I would suggest that is most challenging is comedy. No funny hats, or any visual means of support, just the ability to create pictures in the minds of the audience, and the immediate reaction you receive. As one comedian put it, "Comedy is the fast food of entertainment." Which is true; there's no long wait as to whether the audience likes what you're doing, or not.

I'm not suggesting comedy simply because of the laughs you'll hopefully receive, but for the precise timing that comedy demands. But is it realistic to say that just the words and sounds of the audio theater can compete with the scenery, props, and special effects that television and the movies provide? You betcha! And to prove it, Gene Perret, one of television's most successful comedy writers, with Emmys to prove it, made this comparison between television and radio comedies.

"When I was writing for *The Carol Burnett Show*, I was stunned one day when two of the younger writers asked, 'What was radio like?' It had never occurred to me that there are people in the world, especially in the industry, who had never known radio.

"Although I had never worked in radio, it had a profound influence on me and my writing. I grew up with radio. Bob Hope, Red Skelton, Jack Benny, Burns and Allen, Edgar Bergen and Charlie McCarthy, Fibber McGee and Molly ... these were the characters I laughed at as a youngster. They were the ones who influenced my sense of humor.

"With comedy writing now being my craft, I now began to feel that radio was superior to television for a couple of reasons. First, radio was constantly changing. Each year, the same shows would change in subtle ways, and the reason for that being that each listener supplied the cast, the sets; almost everything except the dialogue.

"When I heard Fibber McGee talk, I pictured how he looked. It probably wasn't how he actually looked, but in my mind, he appeared any way I wanted to see him. When he opened his closet and all the paraphernalia spilled out, I saw it in my head. His living room existed only in my mind. Jack Benny's vault with all the security around it looked any way I imagined it to look. Next year, I might redesign all the sets. I can't do that with television ... but on radio I could."

So said one of television's most talented comedy writers.

Doing Comedy in the Audio Theater

Once again, the name of the comedy genius Jack Benny is mentioned. For those readers who are not that familiar with Jack, or haven't read about his style of comedy in some of my other books, Jack Benny truly understood the advantage imagination held over the more visual "things."

One of the most popular comedic effects in radio was the miserly Jack Benny's frequent trips to visit his money in a subterranean depository in his basement, referred to as the "vault." To get there, Benny was accompanied by numerous sounds on echo, including footsteps down stone stairs, clanging chains, metal doors squeaking open and banging closed, alarm bells, sirens, klaxon horns, and very often, sounds as sudden and unanticipated as a duck frantically quacking! Why a "duck quacking"? To get more unexpected, outlandish laughs ... period.

Jack or his writers never gave a thought as to why a duck quacking would be funny, or were afraid it would not be funny; the writers wrote, sound effects did it, and Jack Benny got the laughs. Why? Not because the material would be that funny to anyone else, but because Jack Benny's character was so well written and recognized by his audience as being the crown prince of penny-pinching, that all the writers had to do was exaggerate just how penny-pinching he really was.

The second rule of comedy is not to be afraid to be as funny as you can be. Of course what added to the illusion of these sounds was Jack Benny's flawless timing. Where did Jack get this flawless timing? Was he born with it? Did he pay someone to teach it to him? No, he worked hard for it in theaters filled with critical audiences. It was there that he learned the most important road to success was not what you said or did, but how you said it, and how you did it with one important word ... timing.

Timing for Laughs

It isn't always what you say that is funny, or even how you say it that is funny, it's *when* you say it.

Mel Blanc, in addition to doing all sorts of vocal effects, did numerous dialects. One of which was the taciturn Little Mexican, who rarely ever spoke more than a single word.

EXAMPLE—SCENE: TRAIN STATION

JACK: Pardon me, are you waiting for a train?
MEL: Si.
JACK: Are you meeting someone?
MEL: Si.
JACK: A relative?
MEL: Si.
JACK: What's your name?
MEL: Sy.
JACK: Sy?
MEL: Si.
JACK: This relative you're waiting for — is it a woman?
MEL: Si.
JACK: What's her name?
MEL: Sue.
JACK: Sue?
MEL: Si.
JACK: Does she work?
MEL: Si.
JACK: What does she do?
MEL: Sew.
JACK: Sew?
MEL: Si.
SOUND: TRAIN WHISTLE
JACK: Is that your train?
MEL: No, I missed it talking to you!
MUSIC: PLAYOFF

This short comedy sketch, written by George Balzer, depended entirely on timing. Knowing just the proper moment to talk, and not to talk, is the best example I can give you for the art of timing.

Benny's Trip to His Money

Jack Benny succeeded in impressing on both his listening and theater audience that he was never older than 39, and he was cheap. Cheap enough not to trust a bank and have his money down in his cellar in a vault guarded by an armed guard.

Interestingly enough, when this highly successful vault routine was tried on Benny's television series, it was a disappointing failure. Not even the duck quacking got a snicker. Why? The reality of seeing the vault setting lacked the playful fun that audiences imagined. The Benny writers tried everything, even a moat around the safe with live alligators protecting it, with no success. All because the television director felt that now he had the visual advantage of showing Benny's audience what, for so many years, they could only imagine; and just how much "funnier" the television cameras were, as opposed to the radio listener's imagination. A big mistake, and the sketch was buried, just as deeply as Benny's Maxwell car was junked. Both were victims of the power of imagination.

EXAMPLE

SOUND: TRAFFIC AND CAR RUNNING
JACK: Ah, there's nothing like an auto ride on a day like this.... Gosh, how time flies.... Here it is, 1936, and I bought this car in 1924 ... and it was only ten years old when I bought it.... Yes, sir!
SOUND: AUTO HORN
JACK: I understand the model after this one had the crank in the front.... Gosh, what they won't think of next. Well, I guess I'll step on the gas and let her out a little.
SOUND: LOUSY MOTOR UP ... COUGHS ... COUPLE OF GUNSHOTS ... MORE COUGHING AND SPUTTERING ... MOTOR DIES WITH A DUCK CALL.
JACK: Hmmmm ... it's missing a little.... Might as well get out and crank it.
SOUND: CREAK OF CAR AS JACK GETS OUT ... SOUND OF CRANKING ... MOTOR STARTS UP ... COUGHS AND SPUTTERING ... TWO GUNSHOTS ... MOTOR DIES AND DUCK CALL.

To milk as many laughs out of this sketch from the theater audience, the writers knew the sketch's success depended on how the sound effects were done. If it was done only with sound effect recordings, the sounds might be the same to the listening audiences at home, but how did that entertain the listening and watching audience in the theater?

This is why the vocal effects genius Mel Blanc was so valuable to the show. Now, instead of the studio audience watching a sound effects man putting a needle on a record, they could watch and listen to Mel creating the old, rickety, Maxwell car engine sounds with his voice ... right down to the car's coughing, sputtering and duck quacking! But again, as funny as this was to the listener's imagination, it died on television. Couldn't the television's special effects department create an old car as funny looking as the radio audience could imagine? No, because seeing a car fall apart is a technical experience, while hearing a car fall apart is an imaginary one. If it was at all possible to have a picture of what everyone in the home audience imagined, no two cars would have looked exactly the same.

Couldn't this sketch have been done in the privacy of a studio without an audience? Of course. Were there not many comedians in those days doing comedy routines and selling them on records? There was just one thing they all had in common that was so necessary. Both the radio comedians and the comedians on records all had audiences present, and not just for the laughs, but for the all-important timing.

Yet timing isn't about any specified number of words as much as it's about the reactions that the words have on the listener. In short, too little, or too much, of anything in comedy is what is referred to as timing.

Ladies' Red Bloomers in Audio Theater?

Ladies' red bloomers in audio theater? Bloomers, even ladies' bloomers, don't make noises! No, but the audience in the audio theater can see these sight gags (things not dependent on words) and how they help the overall sound of a closet crashing, the laughter and, most importantly, the spirit of fun. But, just in case anyone in the audience was offended by this risqué sight, the bloomers should be large enough to fit any medium-sized, modest elephant.

The Spirit of Fun

The "spirit of fun" began in infancy with your toes — "This little piggie went to market" — and by the time the nursery rhyme got to the littlest toe, you caught on this was some kind of innocent fun and you giggled. Not just because you thought your little toe was any funnier than the other four, but you were now in the spirit of fun and giggled at your first exposure to benign comedy that had a beginning, a middle and a funny little toe for an ending.

Getting Laughs

The ability to get laughs is not a funny thing; it's serious business. People who express sadness feel they are on pretty safe grounds. When attending a funeral, for instance, you never hear anyone asking, or even whispering, "Why is everyone crying?" Whereas, how many times have you laughed at something, or even anything, you thought was hysterical and someone gave you a quizzical look and responded, "What's so funny?" Then, if you have to think about why you're laughing, you have taken yourself out of the "spirit of fun," and there is no quicker way to stop laughing than to start analyzing why you feel like laughing.

There have been as many definitions in books as to why we laugh as there are comedians, and comedy writers, but they never pin it down and say what we should laugh at. Experts such as Freud may say, "We laugh at what we feel superior to," but did Freud ever get off the couch and try out his theory in front of a *Tonight Show* audience?

What makes comedy difficult is that it's so personal. It's your judgment as perceived by an audience. I can't think of any other art form that gives you a quicker and more decisive reaction of what the verdict might be. It's either laughter, or it's not. It's as if an art critic took a look at the picture you painted and walked away holding his nose.

COMEDY ESSENTIALS

Having done both writing and sound effects for comedy, I can only give you what I feel are the two most essential comedic demands: timing and the element of surprise. Timing is that particular instant when all conditions are working together to bring about the most desired results. Think of it in terms of musical lyrics. One word too many throws the rhythm of the song off and the song doesn't flow smoothly. The other is the element of surprise.

Audiences don't just watch and listen. They also think and even try and outthink what the comedians are saying. Therefore, a comedian has to say the very last thing that an audience is logically thinking in order to get and keep getting the desired response ... laughs.

GETTING STARTED

To get you started in doing comedy in your audio theater I have written a number of scenes and scripts for practicing and performing throughout the book. But since we have started discussing one of the most popular radio comedy programs, *Fibber McGee and Molly*, the similarity between that comedy and those you'll be doing in audio theater are too familiar to be ignored. It's an excellent example of the importance of the three different skills needed for a comedy to be successful ... writing, acting and sound effects working together in harmony.

THE SETUP

First the audience must know what is expected of them. And the best way to do that is with a setup. The setup is a joke's foundation. It gets the audience's mind thinking in a specific direction and then suddenly (timing) ... tricking those expectations with the element of surprise that justifies a comedic action. Because the "McGee Closet Crash" was the highlight of every show, these "setups" were needed to make Fibber have to go to their over-stuffed hall closet, open the door and have the mother of all crashes come tumbling out.

But what made this closet crash funnier than any of the other comedy crashes? To begin with, it was plausible. Everyone in the audience was familiar with having a cluttered closet. Therefore, it wasn't the surprise of having a few items fall out of the closet that made it funny, it was the surprise of the enormity of things and sounds that came cascading endlessly out of the closet!

EXAMPLE

MOLLY: Can't you remember where you put your fishing hat?
FIBBER: Of course I can, Molly. I remember wearing it when we went to Maine in August last year ... or was it in September? What a vacation that was! All except for that leaky boat, and that thunderstorm. We have to go back there sometime just the same ... even though I didn't catch any fish and got a flat tire and forgot to bring a spare tire! That's it, by golly, I left it over there in the hall closet!
MOLLY: Your hat?
FIBBER: No, Molly, my spare tire!

What is wrong with the pace of the above short scene? To begin with, it's a comedy. And nothing kills the fun of a comedy more than words that detract from the scene's pace, especially when the fans of the show have been alerted to the fact that McGee stuffs everything in the hall closet. Why not his fishing hat? Doesn't this mean they'll be hearing the famous closet crash sounds any second?

In alerting the audience's expectation that the famous closet comedy crash is soon going to happen begins when Fibber can't remember where he put his fishing hat. After that, the main purpose of the lines between Fibber and Molly are to create a tension of expectation as to when the crash is going to happen. Therefore, let's see how we can make the setup a little tighter.

EXAMPLE

MOLLY: Can't you remember where you put your fishing cap?
FIBBER: Of course I can, Molly. I remember wearing it when we went fishing in Maine last August, or was it September? What a great vacation that was! All except for that leaky boat, that thunderstorm, that flat tire, and I forgot to bring a spare tire and I didn't catch any fish!

To start with, the pace of a sketch, especially a comedy sketch, is normally affected by either too many words or the length of the words. As Fibber begins listing the problems, we start off by cutting "last August, or was it September?" What has that got to do with getting to the all-important closet crash? Next comes changing "*that* leaky boat, *that* thunderstorm, *that* flat tire" to the simpler and shorter "**the** leaky boat, **the** thunderstorm, **the** flat tire."

The word *that* is a more specific and demanding word and asks the audience to respond with a question of what boat you're referring to. Whereas "the" boat, "the" thunderstorm and "the" flat tire refer to all boats, thunderstorms and flat tires in general and is shorter and quicker to say than "that." Remember, rhythm and pace should have priority in all comedy. Pace being the overall mood of a script, and timing, or rhythm, being how the lines are read that will best maintain that mood.

A comedy line that reads improperly, or slows down the beat of the words, may not only kill a laugh, it can destroy an audience's spirit of fun. Therefore a director should never forget there are no words in the dictionary, nor sentences, however brilliantly written, that are worth using if they slow or destroy the rhythm and pace of the comedy, and this includes *where* the words are placed in the sentence.

Comedy lines should have a rhythm similar to the beat of words in a song. A comedy line should only contain the words that pertain to the joke. They should never be simply conversational.

Even the placement of words in a comedy line are important. Their only reason for being is an indication where an audience should laugh. Therefore the most important word should always comes last.

A rule of thumb in comedy is surprising the audience. Therefore, by saving the best for last you keep the audience in suspense. Inasmuch as the whole reason for Fibber going to Maine was to catch fish, that should be his last and biggest disappointment. Why else would Fibber want to endure or ignore all his problems by returning to Maine? Certainly not to get a "flat tire." Keep in mind, all these words are spoken as a lead-in to the much-awaited closet crash and should be as short and informative as possible.

EXAMPLE

MOLLY: Can't you remember where you put your fishing hat, Fibber?
FIBBER: It's got to be somewhere. I wore it on our fishing trip ... and what a great vacation that was ... except for the leaky boat, the thunder-storm, the flat tire, no spare tire and I didn't catch any fish!
MOLLY: I know I shouldn't ask but ... did you look in the hall closet?
FIBBER: That's it, Molly.... It's in the hall closet!

MOLLY: Your hat?
FIBBER: No, Molly ... my spare tire!
MOLLY: Oh, heavenly days!
SOUND EFFECTS: CLOSET CRASH

As you can see, the closet crash was the main focus of the dialogue and always got the big laughs from the audience. If that's the case, why delay the closet crash with Molly's line, "Oh, heavenly days!"?

Why is that necessary? It isn't even funny, so why was it always said prior to the awaited closet crash?

Over the years that line became the cue words for the closet crash, and when the audience heard it, they knew the waiting was over. That may have been one reason, but more importantly, the writers added Molly's line for timing purposes. By Molly saying those three words, "Oh, heavenly days," it gave the audience time to start smiling a beat before the big laugh. Without that line the crash would come too abruptly.

The Two Different Types of Comedy Sounds

Doing comedy often requires two different types of sounds; those that are done on non-visual media such as radio, and those that are seen by an audience in the audio theater, on stage, at conventions, or on television.

Crashes come in all shapes, sizes and contents ... even red bloomers. A large cardboard box filled with an assortment of junk can be shaken for a closet crash. But if it's done to get laughs, it's important how and what makes the crash look as well as sound funny. If you're thinking that bloomers, no matter what their colors are, aren't noted for the sounds they make, so why are they included with the crash sounds? Because despite the fact the crash sounds were primarily heard on radios in homes, the audiences in the theater both heard and saw the crash. And it was their laughter that the show's producers were after. And because the laughs done with a machine didn't become popular until television, live comedy shows in radio often depended on sight gags (something funny that doesn't need words). And what could be a more unexpected and innocuous item than red, oversized, bloomers, or a bedpan tumbling out of a hall closet for getting laughs? Unless, of course, it's a teeny, tiny, tinkle bell.

It Ain't Over Until You Hear the Tinkle

Baseball may have its last-ditch hope that a game isn't over until the fat lady sings, but early sound effects artists always believed "it ain't over until the tinkle bell rings!" This was particularly important for a laugh almost as big as the huge one Fibber's crash had just gotten. The sound effects artists always managed to squeeze another big laugh by waiting until the laughter from the huge closet crash began to subside and then either gently shaking a small tinkle bell, or dropping and clinking a small spoon on a slab of marble.

Why do you suppose either the bell or the spoon got these big laughs after a crash? Is it because the tiny sounds are just another type of a straw that broke the camel's back? Or is it because even the bell and spoon sounds didn't want to be left out of the noisier crash? Couldn't an empty can falling be just as funny. Not if it made too much noise. Then it might be considered part of the original crash that was late falling and making the noise. No, the final payoff sound has to be something tiny-sounding and done when it is least expected, as if to say, "Hey, you haven't heard me yet!" The photograph below shows Monty Fraser getting the last, and often the biggest, laugh with the tiny, tinkle bell, which has always posed the question, "Was it the bell sound, or the timing it took to know just the proper moment to do the tinkling?"

After a huge crash in a *Fibber McGee and Molly* episode, Monty Fraser gets one last audience laugh by ringing a small bell after the louder sounds have faded.

Amos 'n' Andy

Although the *Amos 'n' Andy* show didn't have any closet crashes, a vault in the basement, a Maxwell car, or red bloomers, it got this country through the Great Depression with its homey type of humor. How funny was it? It had a nightly listening audience that surpassed Johnny's Carson's *Tonight Show* audience. Theaters stopped their films so their audiences could hear the *Amos 'n' Andy* radio program on the speakers.

Amos 'n' Andy was a situation comedy based on two lovable characters that was first heard on radio in a nightly series from 1928 until 1943. As funny as these two characters were, and the other characters' voices they did, audiences at home never heard any studio laughter. This was because Gosden and Correll, the show's creators, felt that if a studio audience saw that all the voices they heard were coming from two white men sitting across from one another at a table, it would spoil how the audience's imagination pictured the show's homey characters and humor. And as long as this show was on the air, listeners never referred to the characters as "black" or "colored," it was always just "Amos 'n' Andy," the voices that understood what the nation was going through during the Great Depression.

The following scene is typical of what you might have listened to on the *Amos 'n' Andy* radio show back during when this country desperately needed cheering up. Andy Brown has just returned from a wedding he attended and is describing it to his good friend, Amos Jones.

EXAMPLE: THE WEDDING FLOWERS

ANDY: (Expansive) Oh, yeah, Amos ... you ain't nevuh seen nuthin like it. They didn't spare no expenses on this here wedding ... no, suh.

AMOS: Didn't, huh?

ANDY: Oh, no, Amos. They even had a bunch of red roses piled all up and down the aisle for the bride and groom to walk on.

AMOS: A pile of fresh, red roses in the aisle in January? Uh, uh. Ain't that sumpin.

ANDY: Oh, yeah, money was no objection. But it woulda cost even more if them red roses had been real.

AMOS: They weren't, huh? What were they ... tulips?

ANDY: No ... potato chips.

AMOS: Potato chips?

ANDY: Not them broken kind you gets in a bag, these was the big, crispy, dunkin' kind.

AMOS: But didn't they still look like potato chips?

ANDY: They would have if they hadn't been painted a rosy pink.

AMOS: Rosy pink potato chips?

ANDY: The only thing different between them and the real roses was these rose petals crunched.

AMOS: Roses that crunches?

ANDY: Especially when the bride and groom started walking down the aisle. Sometimes the chips got to crunching so loud they drowned out the organ playing "Here Comes the Bride."

AMOS: That loud, huh?

ANDY: That wasn't as bad as the smell ... it kind of filled the air with a greasy aroma that set off a wave of stomach growls.

AMOS: What did the preacher do?

ANDY: What could he do? Between the crunching and the growling, the preacher had to call off the wedding.

AMOS: For good?

ANDY: No ... to go across the street for hamburgers!

MUSIC:

Not bad for two men who wrote and did all the voices on a 15-minute radio show every evening! They even did their own sound effects. If Andy took off his shoes, he'd grunt with relief. If he asked Amos for a cigar, Amos would pass him a pencil, and when they were eating, the audience heard dishes rattling supplied by the sound effects department, but not done by a sound effects artist.

Even back in those early days of radio, long before Jack Foley, Gosden and Correll knew the importance of helping the sounds of their voices by actually doing the physical requirements asked for in the script.

Getting Ideas in Hard Times

Amos 'n' Andy was on the air five days a week during one of this country's most difficult times, the Great Depression. Where did they get their ideas to try and cheer up their listeners? They certainly didn't sit and wait day in and day out for inspiring thoughts to strike. If they did they'd have been off the air in a week. Therefore, in addition to reading newspapers and magazines and listening to the radio to learn what was most troubling Americans, they learned to be observant.

You have probably eaten a mountain of potato chips and never thought they resembled roses, and particularly red roses. If you did, you never associated them with a wedding. But then again, most likely Gosden and Correll didn't either. That isn't the way ideas work. Most likely it started with one of them noticing how a certain large chip resembled a flower petal. You've done it, I've done it; but we just smile at the similarity and let it go at that. We aren't someone who has to put on a 15-minute radio show five nights a week either. When you are, you learn to put to work any and all ideas that come to your mind, even if they're as common as potato chips.

Once you notice the similarity between a potato chip and a flower petal, what do you do? Then you ask yourself, where would substituting salty potato chips for flowers be most inappropriate and surprising? Why, of course, a wedding! And the rest is just writing the words to make an audience see how potato chips painted red could be mistaken for rose petals at a wedding!

UPDATING THE SAME IDEA

We saw how Gosden and Correll took a simple idea and worked it into a comedy sketch. Supposing a writer in your audio theater wanted to use the same basic idea and update it so that two women could use it in a similar sketch? Would the same premise still hold up today?

HANNAH: Sarah ... am I glad I ran into you!

SARAH: Where have you been keeping yourself, Hannah?

HANNAH: You'll never believe it! You know all those fancy weddings these celebrities are always having that cost in the millions? My friend Frieda's didn't cost anything near that.

SARAH: How near?

HANNAH: Seventy-eight dollars and change.

SARAH: Where was the wedding ... on the Internet?

HANNAH: Wait'll you hear! She even had a bunch of red roses piled all up and down the aisle for the bride and groom to walk on.

SARAH: A pile of fresh red roses in the aisle.... Didn't that take up all the money?

HANNAH: I suppose they would have if the roses were real....

SARAH: They weren't real roses?... What were they, paper roses?

HANNAH: No, potato chips.

SARAH: Potato chips?

HANNAH: You know how thoughtful Frank is.

SARAH: I would never guess.

HANNAH: You know how Frieda hates the hay fever she gets around flowers, especially roses? So Frank just put two and two together.

SARAH: And came up with potato chips? Couldn't the guests see that they weren't real, honest-to-goodness red roses?

HANNAH: Of course not. Frank spray-painted them a rosy pink.

SARAH: Rosy pink-painted potato chips?

HANNAH: The only thing different between them and real roses was that these rose petals did sound effects.

SARAH: Sound effects?

HANNAH: When you stepped on them they crunched.

SARAH: They crunched?

HANNAH: That was the only drawback. Although Frieda and Frank both tried tip-toeing down the aisle, they still out-crunched the organ's *Here Comes the Bride.*

SARAH: Didn't the guests start to get suspicious about those rose-painted potato chips?

HANNAH: Nope! ... But their stomachs did. The roses' greasy smell began setting off a wave of stomachs growling.

SARAH: What did the preacher do?

HANNAH: What could he do? ... Between the smelly crunching and the stomach growling noises, he called off the wedding.

SARAH: For good?

HANNAH: No ... to go across the street for hamburgers!

MUSIC: PLAY OFF

This is another example of the advantages that audio theater has over visual media. Although the original *Amos 'n' Andy* sketch was written and played by two white men, Freeman Gosden and Charles Correll, neither the black nor white listeners ever gave a thought to their color. They were just Amos and Andy, the only bright light in the darkness of the country's Great Depression. Never, in all the years *Amos 'n' Andy* was on radio, did I ever hear anyone say, "Hey, did you hear the two black guys last night?" It was always Amos and Andy for the entire time they were on the air.

(More on the careers of Freeman Gosden and Charles Correll can be found in two other of my books: *Radio Sound Effects: Who Did It, and How, in the Era of Live Broadcasting* or *Radio Live! Television Live!: Those Golden Days When Horses Were Coconuts*.)

Given a Choice, Go for the Laughs

To get you started doing comedy in your audio theater I have written a number of scenes and scripts for practicing and performing throughout the book that will illustrate the importance of the three different skills, writing, acting and sound effects working together as a team.

In doing the sound effects on a comedy show you must always do what is funniest, not what is most realistic. I once wrote a pantomime for Dick Van Dyke in which he played the part of a cat, Tabby the Cat, to be exact. In the sketch, Tabby becomes bored and wants some excitement by ripping his mistress' new silk curtains, but first, he needs to sharpen his nails by rapidly striking the nails of his front two paws together rapidly like a butcher sharpening his knives. I even wrote the following sound effects cue to go with nail-sharpening moves.

Remember this was a sketch done in pantomime. And although the comedian made the moves with his hands in cat-like fashion, I never heard the sound effects I wrote to match the action. When I questioned why I didn't hear the sound effects of "TWO BAYONETS CLASHING TOGETHER," the person doing the sound effects testily explained, "I have two cats and neither one of them makes the sound of bayonets clashing together when they sharpen *their* nails!"

Although the sound man may have been excellent on dramatic shows, he didn't realize the most important part of comedy depends upon an audience being in a state of playfulness; a playfulness that welcomes relief from reality by laughing at the unexpected, or the exaggerated.

This doesn't mean the actors doing comedy should be in a playful mood. Acting for laughs is probably the most difficult challenge an actor can have, and they must never play it as if they know what they're doing is funny. Make that never, ever!

Never Let Audiences Know You're Doing Comedy

Perhaps the best comedic actors are serious actors with a sense of humor. They never treat their material as if it is funny. They leave that up to the audience. This is a lesson all members of your audio theater must learn ... treating your comedy material seriously. Yes, the material must be funny, but it's how the actors react to it that allows the audience to judge if they agree.

Never forget audiences don't have buttons you can push to get laughs. They've come to be entertained. That doesn't mean they have stopped thinking. If you're setting up a joke, they're often trying to come up with the punch line. This doesn't make an audience hostile towards your entertainment, it just makes it challenging. An audience is there to laugh and you're there to make them. You can't ask them, or beg them, to laugh, or even pay them to laugh, you have to *make* them laugh, in a very nice way of course. Besides, where in this chapter did I say doing comedy was easy?

Summary

1. Comedy requires a playful mood from the audience.
2. If given a choice between realism or laughter ... take laughs.
3. Know your audience.
4. Be brief and obvious.
5. Save the word that the joke relies on until last.
6. If it comes to a long joke, make it a funnier short joke.
7. Nothing hates clutter more than comedy.
8. When you get your audience in a spirit of fun, you're halfway there to getting laughs.

9. Being in fun shifts our sense of values.

10. Being sufficiently concerned about something kills the laughter.

11. Getting laughs from SFX demands the utmost in timing.

12. Making it clear what the joke is all about is the first step to getting laughs.

13. The proper pause is often funnier than the improper word.

14. What makes doing comedy more difficult than drama is that audiences laugh in so many ways and cry in so few.

15. Never try to have fun with a subject an audience feels too serious about.

16. Finally, the comical quality of your written material, or sound effects, is what makes an audience give their approval ... they laugh.

12

Scenes, Comedy Sketches, Commercials, and More

To get you started, I've written some more commercials, comedies, narrations, scenes and sketches both for practice and performing in your audio theater. Whether your reason is professional, or simply improving whatever your speaking ability needs may be, there is no better place to start getting this valuable experience than everyone working together in front of live audiences in your audio theater.

Timing Your Timings

In doing these next scenes, commercials and sketches, get in the habit of timing your work. You'll find that these clock timings will often vary from your previous readings. To avoid this, rehearse each script until you're satisfied with what you hear. Then challenge yourself in rehearsals, and on your shows, by attempting to keep within those timings. When this is done to the point where you can come within a matter of seconds of your original timing, you'll soon find out how more professional sounding your audio theater will be.

The Announcer-Actor

Since all programs in the audio theater are started with an introduction from the announcer, what better way to start this chapter than with the all-important announcer. Although announcers, actors and vocal effects specialists are often interchangeable, there are important differences. In addition to having a pleasant, enthusiastic and sincere sounding voice, announcers must enunciate (pronounce words clearly), not have a regional accent, and be able to read the commercial in the allotted (allowed) time. The importance of all this should be obvious, and that is, the sponsors pay to have every second heard, whether it's on radio or television.

Commercials are often referred to as being "read" in a certain time; but if the announcer simply "reads" or "recites" the words for timing purposes, his career as an announcer would be very short. Commercials are another form of acting. You may never have tasted an Alka-Seltzer, but if that is reflected in your voice, your announcing career will be very short.

Commercials are another form of acting. Your words must be clearly spoken, with all the right emphases on the words. More importantly, it's how you say the words that matters most. You must have your audiences in mind and say your words directly to them in a friendly, informative manner while still keeping within the allotted time.

I've selected some commercials that were done during the golden age of radio. See how convincing you can be with this thirty-second Alka-Seltzer commercial that was once heard on the popular radio program *One Man's Family*.

In reading the commercial, take note of all the different time changes from the different rehearsals. If you've never thought about what a difference one second can make in your busy life, notice how the timing seconds change at the various parts in the commercial. Although this is a sneaky commercial done with actors, they were not fooling around with the timings. Because one of the Alka-Seltzer advertising agency people would also be carefully checking the time to see they were getting what they paid for. Figure 12-1 is the original copy of the way the commercial was done on August 23, 1951.

ONE MAN'S FAMILY
THURSDAY, AUGUST 23, 1951   ANNOUNCEMENT #2

ANNOUNCER: Overheard in Mr. Smithers' Drug Store in Mountain View ...
MAN: Are you Mr. Smithers?
MR. S: Yes.... What can I do for you?
MAN: I'm looking for Sam Holbert's place. I was told if I had any trouble I could just stop at the drug store and you'd be able to help me.
MR. S: Of course! You take the highway right through town. At the end of Main Street there's a filling station on the right hand side, and just beyond that the road forks. You keep to the right, and Holbert's place is the second one on the left.
MAN: Thanks. I think I've got it. (STARTS TO LEAVE) Oh, say ... I need a package of ALKA-SELTZER. I've been doing some steady driving and my muscles are beginning to "feel" it! You know how they get ... sore and aching?
ANNOUNCER: Yes ... long hours behind the wheel *can* make muscles sore and aching, all right! And when that happens, friends ... there's nothing quite like ALKA-SELTZER for soothing, comforting relief! ALKA-SELTZER'S pleasant and easy to take, and the way it can ease sore, aching muscles is really

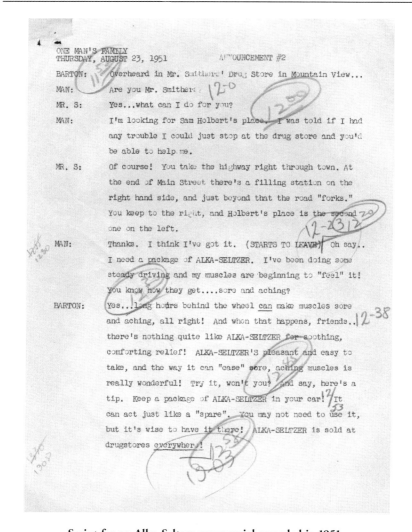

Script for an Alka-Seltzer commercial recorded in 1951.

wonderful! Try it, won't you? And say, here's a tip. Keep a package of ALKA-SELTZER in your car! It can act just like a "spare." You may not need to use it, but it's wise to have it there! ALKA-SELTZER is sold at drugstores *everywhere!*

Did you notice how little commercials have changed over the years? It's the same now as it was then, selling things in a certain amount of time. This is why striving to get a "feeling" for time is so necessary. As you can see by all the different time changes from the different rehearsals, an announcer has to be very adaptable with their voice in order to be successful.

This next commercial demands a younger, more persuasive voice that will appeal to children. Try acting, not just "reading" it in 15 seconds.

EXAMPLE

Hey, kids! Want to do better in school? Get Alpha-Boy! Alpha-Boy is electronically programmed to know all the answers. Do you know how to spell "egregious"? Alpha-Boy does! Get Alpha-Boy today!!

In the beginning you will most likely keep referring to your watch to see if you're doing your commercials in exactly 15 seconds, but if you keep working at it, you'll soon be surprised to find you no longer need a watch on your wrist. You'll have a "feeling" in your head as to just how long, or short, 15 seconds really is.

Before you tried doing that Alpha-Boy commercial in 15 seconds, did you give yourself all the advantages of being successful? If the director has given you any special readings he wants emphasized, mark them in your script. And be certain you have a dictionary handy for any words you need to refer to for their meaning or pronunciation.

Although reading this commercial in 15 seconds is a comfortable amount of time, we're living in a "ten-second" time period of life. Commercials, especially television commercials, are done in ten-second increments. Therefore, go back and read the Alpha-Boy commercial in ten seconds and make it fly in its believability!

EXAMPLE

ANNOUNCER
"Hey, *kids!* Want to do better in school? *Get Alpha-Boy!* Alpha-Boy is electronically programmed to know *all* the answers!!! Do you know how to spell *"e-gre'-gious"*?? *Alpha-Boy* does! *Get Alpha-Boy today!*

If you're recording your voice and practicing doing commercials, try and see how different your voice will sound between the two commercials. Although they call the person that does all these different types of singular readings an "announcer," they require just as much acting as the more conventional actors. And wasn't that what was required for the Alka-Seltzer commercial?

More Announcing-Acting Work

In addition to doing commercials, billboards, introductions and narrations, the announcer is responsible for doing the lead-ins (introductions) to the various sketches, acting as a straight man and doing narrations. All these various roles require both acting and versatile voices, and everyone in the audio theater should have the opportunity to rotate their skills, and experience just how creative and challenging it is being an announcer-narrator-actor in the audio theater.

Inasmuch as the audio theater doesn't need scenery or props, doing a series of short scenes rapidly, one after another, can be an added option to your audio theater. All that is needed is musical playoff to separate the sketches.

This type of program works best when done with a more serious story. It also offers an opportunity for audiences to witness a greater number of actors doing a wider variety of scenes in a shorter amount of time.

This is especially true if you're called upon to do a narrative introduction to stories similar to those once heard on the live and creepy days of *Inner Sanctum*. As a writing and acting project, I have given you the introductions and it's now up to your audio theater to write the stories that best fit this spooky format.

In reading *Tales from the Grave*'s introduction you can see how the actor's voice, sound effects, and music all blend together to create a mood that is consistent with the nature of the show.

Although the thunder and wind sounds should be done with tapes or CDs, the screeches from the cat should be done vocally. It's never a good idea for the sound effects to be done electronically in front of a live audience. Having the cat effects done vocally is important for the audience to see and sets radio theater apart from visual media.

The selection of an actor to do the cat sounds is dependent upon their ability. After that concern is satisfied, select the actor who will most surprise the audience's imagination. A teenage girl?

The part of the host can be the announcer, or any actor wanting to become familiar with the requirements needed to do narrative acting. Although this narrative piece, *Tales from the Grave,* was written for its vocal challenges, it may be edited to whatever length is appropriate for a script written by someone in the audio theater with this spooky-type format.

TALES FROM THE GRAVE

SFX: WIND ESTAB AND BG

HOST: Good evening ... midnight ... the hour when it's quiet and peaceful, when all the visitors have left their flowers, mumbled a few words of sorrow and left ... left for the next holiday, or when it's convenient ... to visit their loved one's lonely graves.

SFX: WIND UP: Hear that ... to some it sounds like tormented souls, moaning in pain and crying out from the cramped, coldness of their coffins.

SFX WIND TO SYNC WITH WORD:

HellllllllllllllP ... hellllllllllllllllP ... hellllllllllllllllllllllllP

<u>SFX: WIND FADES TO BG</u>: These poor tormented souls put up this fuss whenever visitors leave ... they seem so desperate ... they don't seem to realize they're ... you know ... out of it ... *dead* out of it! (sinister chuckle)

    Have you seen any witches yet? No? How strange. But perhaps you haven't been looking in the right places. I'm sure you'll have better luck here ... amongst the shadows and gloom of my cemetery.

<u>ORGAN: UP AND UNDER</u>

(MOCK SURPRISE)

    Of course in my cemetery. And do I have a dilly of a frightening story for you tonight. Surprised? You shouldn't be ... after all, you're the one that asked to hear another, "*Tale from the Grave.*" (LAUGHS)

<u>MUSIC: UP AND UNDER</u>

<u>SFX: SLIGHT RUSTLE OF FOOTSTEPS IN GRASS</u>: Be careful to walk right behind me ... I wouldn't want you falling in a freshly dug grave.

<u>SFX: SUDDEN SCREECH OF CAT</u>: There, didn't I tell you? Now that we found the black cat ... can a witch be far behind? (playful) Perhaps hiding over there in the shadows of that gravestone ... or over there ... or there! (pauses) Or perhaps in your very own home! (chuckles) How about in that seldom-used closet ... or when was the last time you looked under your bed? Hmmmmm? Of course it's ridiculous! And just to prove it, I dare you to turn out all the lights and listen to my tale in complete darkness! I double dare you!

<u>MUSIC: MYSTERIOSO</u>

    But I must warn you ... of all the stories that lie brooding in this graveyard, none is stranger nor more bizarre than the tale you're about to hear. So if any of you ... scaredy cats want to turn back, now is the time. And advise anyone with a weak heart do so at once!

<u>SFX: CLAP OF THUNDER</u>: The burial place we are looking for is unusual. The man had a terrifying fear of being buried alive, of awakening in a dark coffin, beneath tons of dirt, unable to get out, gasping for air and crying out in vain. He therefore requested to be interned above ground in a mausoleum. You say there is nothing unusual about interment in mausoleums? Perhaps not. But would you grant me that it's a trifle odd to have a coffin with a locked lid that opens from the inside?

<u>SFX: RUMBLE OF THUNDER</u>: Here, I'll have the door to the mausoleum open in a moment ... or should we knock first? Hmmmm?

<u>SFX: KEY IN LOCK AND DOOR SQUEAKING OPEN</u>: Well, come in, come in and don't forget to wipe your feet. Here, hold the flashlight while I read the inscription on the coffin. (reading)

    "Thomas Treborn, born on Halloween and died on Halloween with little to be proud of in-between."

<u>MUSIC: SNEAK IT IN</u>

    Here then is his strange and eerie story ... the story of The Man Without a Face.

<u>MUSIC: UP INTO COMMERCIAL</u>

More Scenes, Commercials and Sketches

Inasmuch as the audio theater doesn't need scenery or props, only musical playoffs to separate the sketches, a number of these short comedy scenes and sketches can be done along with your normal program. This will be especially helpful if you want to do a major story that requires only a few actors and little action.

THE QUARRELSOMES

ANNOUNCER: Welcome to another episode of the Quarrelsomes, brought to you by Quick, the easy and beneficial way of having breakfast. No cooking, or coming out of a box, you simply unwrap it, pop it in your mouth and you'll feel satisfied.... Quick! (15 seconds)

> (Friendly and intimate) Tonight's episode finds Nancy and Ken Quarrelsome at home. And while Ken is busy balancing their checkbook, Nancy seems to have come across something far less serious in a magazine. (10 seconds).

NANCY: (On cue, Nancy tries to suppress a giggle but after a beat she's back to giggling.)

TOM: (annoyed) Do you have to, Nancy?

NANCY: (Giggling) I'm sorry, Tom. But this cartoon is hysterical. Just take a look at it.

TOM: It can't be as funny as your checkbook. Especially the check to Saks Fifth Avenue!

NANCY: If this doesn't make you laugh ... I'll give you all my credit cards.

TOM: Is that a promise?

NANCY: Yes, it's a promise.

TOM: Hand it over.

SFX: MAGAZINE SOUND.

NANCY: (Giggling) Well...?

TOM: This is what's funny?

NANCY: (trying to control herself) Are you on the right page?

TOM: Yes ... and you owe me all your credit cards! Now *that's* funny!

NANCY: No, Ken ... that's dreaming!

THE LONE RANGER'S GREAT-GREAT-GRANDDAUGHTER

MUSIC: WILLIAM TELL OVERTURE

ANNOUNCER: Hear that, audience?... What hero of the West does that remind you of?

AUDIENCE: (shouting) The Lone Ranger!

ANNOUNCER: Who?

AUDIENCE: THE LONE RANGER!

ANNOUNCER: And who can forget him? That masked hero on his great horse Silver coming to the aid of those in need and leaving behind a silver bullet to....

RUBY: (in audience) Hold it right there, motor mouth!

ANNOUNCER: (slightly offended) Me ... motor mouth? We're doing a show. Who are you? (woman comes out of the audience)

RUBY: Doesn't my ten-gallon hat, chaps, spurs and two six-guns give you any hint?

ANNOUNCER: No...

RUBY: Same old story! Without the mask I look like every other woman in (name city).

ANNOUNCER: Mask? Who are you?... No, it can't be ... you don't mean?

RUBY: I'm the great-great-granddaughter of that famous masked man.

ANNOUNCER: You don't mean you're the great-great-granddaughter of *The Lone Ranger*?

RUBY: How many women do you know running around saying they're the great-great-granddaughter of a masked man?

ANNOUNCER: But, *The Lone Ranger*! (DUMB) I never even heard he dated.

RUBY: No, but you heard about how he rode off into the sunset leaving behind bullets made out of silver.

ANNOUNCER: But that was only for the people in serious need of help!

RUBY: And just why do you think all those people were in need of serious help?

ANNOUNCER: You don't mean ... because of the silver bullets...?

RUBY: I had to ask Congress to bail me out.

ANNOUNCER: Is there anything these fans of *The Lone Ranger* can do to help?

RUBY: (holds up script page) I thought you'd never ask. For anyone who wants an autographed 8-by-10 glossy of *The Lone Ranger* on his wedding night without his mask on ... raise your hand with a credit in it ... but you must be eighteen or older....

MUSIC: WILLIAM TELL OVERTURE DROWNS THEM BOTH OUT

APPLAUSE

Acting and Interacting with Sound Effects

These next two sketches require acting and interacting with sound effects. You may change the lines or sound effects to suit your audio theater. If you do, put into practice what works for your theater. And most of all, don't be afraid to change sound effects, make cuts, or improve lines, just make sure you turn the serious business of creating ... into the fun of what it's like to imagine.

THE QUIBBLETONS

ANNOUNCER: As we listen in on another episode of the Quibbletons, we find Homer standing in the garage, cold and shivering from his accidental fall into an icy stream while fly fishing. As he tries to make it into the house and get his wet clothes off ... he has one big obstacle to overcome ... his wife. (20 seconds)

HOMER: (shivering) So far so good. I opened the garage door and got the car in without Harriett hearing me ... now if I can just get these ... wet ... boots ... off ... and...

SOUND EFFECTS: CAUTIOUS SLOSHING BOOT SOUNDS IN SYNC

HARRIETT: (Fading in and overlapping) ... and don't even think of coming in the house with those wet, smelly boots!

SOUND EFFECTS: STEPS STOP

HOMER: Oh, hi, darling.

HARRIETT: Don't darling me, those boots are soaking wet!

HOMER: But only on the inside. Look, honey, I'll tell you all about it after a hot shower.

SOUND EFFECTS: TAKES TWO SLOSHING STEPS

HARRIETT: Hold it right there, sloshy! You're not taking another step unless you can jump over my expensive ten-foot Oriental rug!

HOMER: (Sneezes) By the time I have these boots off I'll have pneumonia!

HARRIETT: Pneumonia they have shots for, Oriental rugs don't even have health insurance! Now take them smelly boots off!!

HOMER: They're not that smelly!

HARRIETT: (screams) There's a black widow spider in your ear!

HOMER: Oh, that's nothing. Help me with my boots.

HARRIETT: Nothing!? A poisonous spider in your ear is nothing?

HOMER: It would be if it was real ... it's one of my trout flies.

HARRIETT: Then how do you catch a fish ... sticking your ear in the water?

HOMER: (Sneezes) Will you stop with the jokes and help me with the boots!?

SFX: STRUGGLING WITH BOOT AND WET SUCTION SOUNDS.

HARRIETT: (Grunting and struggling) These aren't boots ... they're indoor swimming pools.

HOMER: (Effort) Will you stop it ... maybe they're a little damp...

SFX: SUCTION SOUND OF BOOT COMING OFF.

HARRIETT: There!... They're off! Now we'll see just how "damp" the inside of this boot really is!

SFX: LONG POURING OF WATER. SOUND FINALLY STOPS.

HOMER: All right, so a little water seeped in. If you find another drop, I'll drink it!

SFX: BOOT BEING SHAKEN.

HARRIETT: How about eating it?

HOMER: Eating what?

SFX: FROG CROAKING.

HARRIETT: Fried or sautéed frog legs!

MUSIC: PLAYOFF

Here's another example of the announcer setting up the sketch. Only this time, instead of just announcing the sketch, the announcer can be one of the actors in the sketch. This commercial can be given prior to any sketch in this chapter, or to a sketch written by someone in the audio theater.

NATURE'S WAY COMMERCIAL

MUSIC: WILLIAM TELL OVERTURE

ANNOUNCER: Audience! Who does that music remind you of?

AUDIENCE: The Lone Ranger!

ANNOUNCER: The Lone who...?

AUDIENCE: The Lone Ranger!

ANNOUNCER: Exactly! And who can forget: (hand cupped to ear) "A fiery horse with the speed of light, a cloud of dust and a hearty hi yo, Silver!?" That western hero on his great white horse, Silver, and his faithful companion, Tonto, riding out of the west looking for adventures to solve and fair maidens to save (voice change) ... but not tonight! No ... our thrilling Western adventure tonight is not about The Lone Ranger ... but one that is just as thrilling, or even more thrilling. The hero is not a familiar one but one to remember. Despite her courageousness and modesty, she was known simply as: (BEAT) the sweet, sassy, scintillating, sometimes sexy-singer-this side-of-Salt-Lake-City-by-way-of- Sheboygan Sunbonnet Sue! But first ... a word from our sponsor.

ANNOUNCER: Tonight's program is brought to you by ... Nature's Way, the only product that promises you ... really promises you ... the sensible and gently way of getting back to your old self again. (intimate) Very often when we become grouchy and irritable it's simply a matter of getting ... well, you know ... regular again. But when we can't and need a little help ... reach for Nature's Way. Then perhaps next time this next scene won't happen to you.

MUSIC: LIGHT AND DOMESTIC

SFX: DOOR CLOSE

HUSBAND: Hi, honey.... I'm home!

WIFE: (abrasive) So whatta ya want, a million bucks!?

HUSBAND: I just thought...

WIFE: That "Hi, honey, I'm home. Hi, honey, I'm home" doesn't get old after twenty years? Just once can't you come up with something original like, "Hi, honey, we won the lottery! Hi, honey, we're going to Hawaii! Hi, honey, we're getting a new car."?

HUSBAND: (gently interrupting the above) Dear? Dear? Dear? What's the matter? You don't sound like your old ... well, you know ... your old regular self. Is that why you're so irritable, sluggish and out of sorts?

WIFE: (melting) I suppose so. But how do you always know?

HUSBAND: (gently) Because, dear, your wig is on inside out.

ANNOUNCER: (friendly) Sound familiar? It doesn't have to be. Just one teaspoon of "Nature's Way" at night and you'll be feeling like this "Nature's Way" user in the morning.

MUSIC BRIGHT

HUSBAND: (yawning ... then suddenly awake) Look at the time! My alarm didn't go off!

WIFE: (purring sexily) I know, darling ... but it will ... it will...

HUSBAND: (gives various readings) ... Honey?... Honey?... Why are you looking at me like that? Honey? (sighing) Oh, honey...!

ANNOUNCER: And if you want an "Oh, honey" kind of morning ... every morning ... take gentle, soothing "Nature's Way" every night!

APPLAUSE

SUNBONNET SUE

MUSIC: "HIGH NOON" TYPE MUSIC

ANNOUNCER: Our story begins with the sheriff having his eye on the clock and his hand on his gun. He sits alone in his office waiting for the train from

Dodge City to bring a hired gun who swore to kill him ... the notorious Kid! We call this story simply ... THE — SNEAKIEST-SIDEWINDING-SINISTER-SIX-GUN SHOOTING-SON-OF-A-GUN from SIOUX CITY!

MUSIC: FADES UNDER AND OUT.

SFX: TICKING OF CLOCK.

SHERIFF: Yeah, I'm the sheriff. Hear that clock ticking?

SFX: CLOCK TICKING UP SLIGHTLY

SHERIFF: It means I'm soon gonna be up against the quickest gunfighter in all the West and all I got until payday is four bullets. Four bullets against the notorious Kid ... also known as ... THE SNEAKIEST-SIDEWINDING-SIN-ISTER-SIX-GUN SHOOTING-SON-OF-A-GUN from SIOUX CITY! And his train is due in at three-thirty and the clock on the wall says one o'clock.

SFX: CUCKOO TWO TIMES. (VOCAL EFFECT)

SHERIFF: (Correcting himself.) Two o'clock.

SFX: CUCKOO

SHERIFF: Three o'clock.

SFX: HALF A CUCKOO SOUND.

SHERIFF: Three-fifteen.

SFX: CUCKOO START TO MAKE SOUND.

SHERIFF: Aw, shut up!

SFX: GUNSHOT.

SFX: CUCKOO COUGHING ... ANOTHER GUNSHOT ... CUCKOO DIES.

SFX: FRANTIC DOOR KNOCK.

SHERIFF: Come in!

SUE: Oh, sheriff, sheriff, sheriff! I heard the shooting and why, oh, why does there always have to be shootings and killings in the valley ... and why is it so dark in here?

SHERIFF: 'Cause yore sun bonnet's on backwards!

SUE: No wonder my lipstick isn't on straight!

SHERIFF: What's yore name, gal?

SUE: Sue.

SHERIFF: Sue?

SUE: Si.

SHERIFF: Sue-Si ... like in seesaw?

SUE: No, like *Sunbonnet* Sue...

SHERIFF: Sunbonnet Sue?

SUE: (Overlapping sheriff's line) I ain't finished ... more like, SUNBONNET SUE, the SWEET- AND-SASSY- SCINTILLATING-SINGER-FROM-SALT-LAKE-CITY-BY-WAY-OF-SHEBOYGAN SINGER OF SENTIMENTAL AND SEXY SALOON SONGS!

SFX: DISTANT TRAIN WHISTLE

SHERIFF: Ya better leave, Sunbonnet Sue, the sweet and sassy, scintillating —

SUE: Aw, shut up! What was that train whistle?

SHERIFF: There's gonna be a killing and somebody's blood is gonna git splattered all over the place!!

SUE: Oh, why must there be such silly, six-gun–blood-spattered shootings simply 'cause nobody's invented cable television?

SFX: DOOR KNOCK.

GABBY: Sheriff ... Sheriff!!! The train's acoming with you-know-who on it!

SHERIFF: I know ... the Kid!

SAL: The Kid?!! You mean ... THE SNEAKY-AND-SINISTER-SIDE-WIND-ING-SIX-GUN-SHOOTER-FROM-SIOUX-CITY?

SHERIFF: No. That's just his nickname. His real name is: BIG-BAD-BILL-THE-BODACIOUS-BLACK-BEARDED-BADLAND'S-BANK-BANDIT!

GABBY: Then why do they call him the Kid?

SHERIFF: 'Cause he's short ... real short. When he ain't got something to stand on, the folks he shoots get shot in their knees.

SOUND: TRAIN WHISTLE

SUE: (Singing.) "Do you hear that whistle down the line...?"

SHERIFF: Aw, shut up, Sue!! Ya gotta help me, old-timer!

GABBY: I would, sheriff ... but not for a gunfight with the Kid!

SHERIFF: Why ... cause yore a thin-skinned, yeller belly!??

GABBY: No, cause I got the popcorn concession! So long, sheriff!

SFX: DOOR SLAM.

SHERIFF: You don't have an extra gun, do ya, Sue?

SUE: Where's yore six-shooter, sheriff?!

SHERIFF: All I got is a three-shooter.

SUE: A three-shooter?

SHERIFF: Town cut my budget in half! And I already used them up killing the cuckoo clock. (THOUGHT) I know I got some extra bullets someplace. But where did I put them ... in the desk? In my other pants? No. I know!... I'll bet they're in the hall closet!

SUE: Oh, heavenly days, sheriff ... not in the hall closet!

SHERIFF: I'll just open it up...

SFX: FIBBER McGEE AND MOLLY CLOSET CRASH

(AFTER THE CRASH A SMALL BELL RINGING)

SHERIFF: I gotta clean that out one of these days.

SUE: Well, good luck, sheriff!

SHERIFF: Where are you going?

SUE: I've got to get my bet down on the Kid!

SFX: DOOR SLAM.

SHERIFF: Suddenly a horse stopped outside!

SFX: HOOFBEATS STOPPING FOLLOWED BY A CAR SKID AND WHIN-NEY.

SHERIFF: It was the Kid driving a horse-mobile! And I only had one bullet left! He opened the door ... (door opens) and stood there sneering. Wow, was he short! I got down on my knees, aimed as low as I could and fired my last bullet...

SFX: GUNSHOT AND METAL SOUND.

... and hit the spittoon. Then it ricocheted off and hit my whisky bottle!

SFX: GLASS CRASH.

... then under my bed's pee pot...

SFX: POT SOUND.

... and finished off the cuckoo clock!

SFX: COUGHING (Vocal effect)

SHERIFF: Then the Kid took out his tiny gun and aimed it at my kneecaps ...

but before he could pull the tiny little trigger ... he suddenly fell to the floor in a heap ... a very small heap ... but a heap just the same. And there, standing in the doorway with a smug look on her face, was Sunbonnet Sue, singer of sentimental saloon songs!

SUE: (sexy) You left out sexy ... blue eyes!

SHERIFF: But how did you kill the most notorious killer ... granted not the *tallest* killer in the West ... but how did you do it, Sue?

SUE: Before he came in, I sang him a sultry, sexy song men simply die for ... so you men put your hands over your ears, and hit it, professor!

PIANO: MELANCHOLY BABY

SUE: (SINGS TUNE TO MELANCHOLY BABY) "So smile, my honey dear ... while I kiss away each tear ... or you'll be pushing up daisies tooooooo!"

ANNOUNCER: (OVER APPLAUSE) Playing the part of the courageous and sometimes crap-shooting, card shark from Cucamonga, California, sheriff was ... (actor's name)

Co-starring was that sweet, sassy, scintillating, sometimes sexiest-singer-this side-of-Salt-Lake-City-by-way-of-Sheboygan, Sunbonnet Sue! (actor's name) and playing that grubby Gabby was: (actor's name)

And saying all these sibilant, sweet-sounding-soothsayer-sounds was me — (actor's name). Now ... everybody join in and sing!!

MUSIC: UP INTO APPLAUSE

Although this sketch only involves a small cast, I would suggest it has three people doing sound effects and is an excellent example of the importance of interaction between the actors and sound effects.

HERBIE TRUMP, PRIVATE EYE

ANNOUNCER: (to audience) How many of you in the audience are fans of the old private eye series that you hear on old-time radio?... Raise your hands. Great. you're all in for a treat. Because tonight we're going to pay tribute to all those private eyes of the golden age of radio, like Richard Diamond, Sam Spade, Herbie Trump...

VOICE: Herbie who?

ANNOUNCER: Herbie Trump

VOICE: Never heard of him. How long was his show on the air?

ANNOUNCER: Once.

VOICE: What year was it?

ANNOUNCER: Tonight! This is it! So stand by, and no coughing, please. If you have to cough, do it now. The sponsor doesn't allow any coughing once we're on the air. You have five seconds! Five ... four ... three ... two ... one...

MUSIC: THEME UP AND UNDER

ANNOUNCER: (Big smile) Herbie Trump ... private eye! Brought to you by *Camel Cigarettes!* The only cigarette that promises you, really promises you, not a cough in a carload! (change) And now for some more thrilling adventures from the files of ... Herbie Trump, private eye.

MUSIC: UP AND UNDER

ANNOUNCER: In tonight's exciting episode, Trump faces death everywhere he turns in a caper he simply calls: "The big-bleached-blonde's-big-bad-beady-eyed-boyfriend's-revenge!"

MUSIC: UP AND UNDER

SFX: FOGHORN AND UNDER

ANNOUNCER: Herbie Trump, the private eye of last resort, is pacing nervously in his run-down, shabby office overlooking an even more run-down, shabbier waterfront. Trump has fallen on hard times ... real hard times ... only one thing will save him ... a phone call. An important phone call that will either give him some desperately needed money, or a not-so-needed taste of lead.

MUSIC: UP AND OUT

TRUMP: Yeah, my name is Trump, Herbie Trump, the guy you look for when you're in trouble. The trouble is, nobody's been looking except ... the mob ... and them I can do without.

SFX: FOGHORN

TRUMP: Hear that? That foghorn tells you I operate out of the city by the bay ... San Francisco. Only the bay I can afford isn't the one on post cards. Even though I'm on the twentieth floor, at high tide, I have to wear boots.

SFX: FOGHORN

TRUMP: And if that foghorn doesn't shut up, I'll go nuts!

TRUMP: It was late. I was still in my office waiting for that important phone call and the waiting was getting to me. Right now my nerves were strung tighter than a streetwalker's skirt. I needed a drink bad. I got out the bottle ... put the bottle on the table....

SFX BOTTLE BREAKING

Then I remembered I didn't have a table! I hocked it to buy the bottle! Like I say, I was broke ... real broke! Just then the phone rang.

SFX: SICK PHONE RING

TRUMP: It was a lousy-sounding phone ring ... but it was all I could afford. I picked it up...

SFX: PHONE OFF HOOK

TRUMP: ...and could tell by the sound of her voice it was a blonde ... a bleached blonde. She was having trouble with Black Bart ... her beady-eyed-boyfriend-from-Brooklyn. I quoted her a fat figure and hung up.

SFX: PHONE ON CRADLE

TRUMP: I was probably a sucker taking on a killer like Black Bart ... the big bleached blonde's big bad beady-eyed boyfriend ... but like I said, I was broke and needed the money. I leaned back in my chair and, just as I put my feet up on the desk, I remembered something very important...

SFX: TUB CRASH

I didn't have a desk ... I hocked it. Like I say, I was broke ... real broke. Suddenly I heard someone at the door! I dug my hand into my shoulder holster for my hair-triggered pistol!

SFX: GUNSHOT

TRUMP: ...and almost shot off my nose! That's the trouble with triggers made of hairs! Suddenly there was a pounding at the door. And I only had one bullet left!

SFX: POUNDING

TRUMP: But supposing it wasn't any good? Supposing my gun misfired! I had to be sure my last and only bullet was good!

SFX: GUNSHOT

TRUMP: Thank goodness it is ... was! Stupid!! Now I can only hope he'll fall for the old trick of making a gunshot sound vocally! BANG! BANG! BANG! But before I had a chance to rehearse, they tried to crash down my iron-reinforced door!! I ran for my closet to hide! Then I just remembered, I hocked it!

SFX: DOOR CRASHING

TRUMP: But it wasn't Black Bart! It was the big, bleached blonde! Even without her hair being teased, she filled the doorway! I quickly told her what my fee was and she flashed a big teeth-whitened smile and lifted her skintight skirt...

SFX: RIP

...a little too high! She then dug into her slinky, silk stockings and pulled out my two-hundred-dollar fee ... in singles! That explained her lumpy legs and bowlegged walk. Suddenly, there was another knock!

SFX: POUNDING

TRUMP: This time it had to be Black Bart! I had to hide the big, bleached blonde! Her best chance was out on the street! I opened the window...

SFX: WINDOW OPENING

TRUMP: Then, as I helped the big, bleached blonde out the window ... I remembered something important!

Woman: WOMAN SCREAMING FADING

TRUMP: I was on the twentieth floor! She hit Lombard Street and bounced off a cable car! (matter of fact) But I had my own troubles.

SOUND: DOOR CRASHING

TRUMP: The door crashed open and I let Black Bart have it! BANG! BANG! BANG! Then he let me have it!

SOUND: LONG MACHINE GUN

TRUMP: Thank goodness he missed! I broke a chair over his head!

SFX: CHAIR BREAKING

TRUMP: And a bottle!

SFX: GLASS BREAKING

TRUMP: Then he broke a chair over my head!

SFX: CHAIR BREAKING

TRUMP: And a bottle!

SFX: GLASS BREAKING

TRUMP: (gagging) Then he had me by the throat ... then

SFX: STRUGGLING

TRUMP: Suddenly two shots rang out!!

SFX: ONE SHOT

TRUMP: More or less! I know I didn't shoot them, I was being choked, and Bart didn't do them, he had both hands around my neck ... then, suddenly, Bart let go of my throat and fell to the floor!

SFX: BODY FALL

TRUMP: And then, when the smoke cleared ... standing there ... holding the smoking gun was the big-bleached-bodacious-blonde!

MUSIC: THE STRIPPER FADE UNDER
TRUMP: I couldn't believe my eyes! Big-bleached-blonde?... How could you fall twenty floors, hit Lombard Street, bounce off a cable car and still manage to get back up twenty floors ... huh, how could you!?
BLONDE: (Brooklyn accent) What am I, stoopid? I took the elevator!
MUSIC: MUSIC UP TO APPLAUSE

Keep It Simple ... But Imaginative

Most of the sound effects needed for the various sketches can be done inexpensively and manually. Those that can't shouldn't be attempted to be done manually to the point where they sound ridiculous. Even doing a comedy, everything should be done as professionally as possible. The whole purpose of doing a comedy is to entertain the audience ... not the cast members. Therefore, when you come across a sound effect such as a foghorn, and it can't be done manually or vocally, unless it really sounds like a foghorn, change the joke to fit what you can do that will get a laugh. The point is, never sacrifice a good comedy, or story, simply because doing the effects manually are entertaining and creative looking for the audience. There are other reasons as well.

Sounds don't have to be just "difficult" to lay them down on a CD, they may be more convenient. If you're asked to travel to do a show for television, radio, conventions or whatever, it isn't always possible to carry the amount or size of the manual effects you normally use. Therefore, although I still recommend doing your sound effects in the most creative manner, never sacrifice a good show with a badly selected sound effect.

Therefore, if and when you need to lay down a difficult sound, you can either record it with a portable recorder, or get the sound from one of the commercial sound effects companies on the Internet. One I can recommend, because I often used this company when I was doing sound effects at NBC, is Sound Ideas. If they don't have the sound you need, no one does. (www.sound-ideas.com)

Summary

1. One of the most important reasons for being a part of audio theater is having your skills performed before a live audience.
2. The audio theater's live audience serves as the most valuable teacher

you've ever had. They don't give you homework, or grades, they just express themselves by the amount or lack of their laughs and applause.

3. If an audience loves what you do, let it go to your heart, not to your head. If an audience didn't care for what you did, don't let it discourage you ... make it encourage you to do better the next time.

4. In writing this summary I asked a number of comedians and comedy writers what their secret for success was. In addition to the usual answers of, "The importance of good comedy is timing," and "The right material," the most common answer given was just one word ... determination. It was what they wanted to do so badly it hurt! I couldn't agree with their honesty more.

13

The Most Asked for SFX
and How to Do Them

Today's audiences have heard every type of car crash, explosion or gunshot imaginable, but have they ever seen the way they are done? Even if that was possible, would it be very entertaining to watch? The majority of these sounds are sampled, synthesized and done with computers, with just touches of sounds that are Foleyed with manual effects in post production. Even there, the Foley artists have the luxury of having their effects recorded until a satisfactory sound is acceptable.

None of this is true in the audio theater. The acting, directing, music and sound effects are all done for audiences in real time. This must always be kept in mind by the writers so they do not write scripts that depend too heavily on effects that are not done manually. There is nothing imaginative or entertaining about someone pushing a button. Despite using non-manual effects on rare occasions, creating the sound of surf by gently tilting BBs back and fourth on a large bass drum, or in a cardboard box, will beat the surf heard mysteriously from a CD every time.

If creating the surf sound is imaginative and realistic enough for the audience, why do we need sounds on CDs? It all depends on how long the scene is and the type of script you're doing. If the scene is long, or it's impractical to transport a large amount of manual effects to a remote location, you would of course substitute CDs for the manual effects where necessary.

Having knowledge of the importance that both CD effects and manual effects play in giving a script balance is important, not just for the person doing the sound effects, but equally for the people writing the scripts, directing, and acting. That's why everyone in the audio theater should take advantage of the rare opportunity of trying their hand at writing, acting, directing and doing sound effects.

What's in a Name?

The most convenient way of identifying people is to give them names. We also know that one Mary isn't like the thousands of other Marys in this world. That's why it's often difficult to see one sound effect labeled GUN-SHOT and realize this same gunshot sound can be used for a car having a tire blow out. Or that a sound labeled BROOK can be used for adding a good "watery" sound to that of a driving rain.

This is fine for sounds that are similar sounding in nature, but what about the sound of a guillotine chopping off Queen Marie Antoinette's head? Yet if you were doing a story about the French Revolution, you'd learn it was a common occurrence, and in order for your story to be authentic, you would need the sound of a guillotine crashing down and beheading a hapless victim. Any ideas?

If the guillotine scene were for television or films, the cost of carpenters to build a guillotine from scratch would run into the tens of thousands of dollars and it would take weeks to construct. Next would come the special effects people to construct the actual guillotine, the makeup people to make the scene look gory, the camera people, the editors, Foley artists and post production personnel. All for a camera shot that may last a matter of seconds.

In the imaginative world of your audio theater, lopping off a head is far less complicated. All that is needed is a heavy piece of metal scraped smoothly and quickly down a metal pipe, hitting nothing more gory than a canvas bag filled with pebbles.

If it were done in the audio theater or a Foley film studio without an audience, this is the way it might be done if the director was only interested in the sound of the guillotine. But is it creative enough *looking* for an audience? This must always be taken in consideration when entertaining an audience. In addition to creating the proper sound, it should come as a surprise to the audience as to what uncommon materials were used.

For an audience I would suggest two people doing the guillotine effect. One would handle the large paper cutter and the other the beheading. As the one sound person gets ready to pull the handle down, the second sound person places a cantaloupe melon slightly hollowed out and filled with potato chips.

In doing this on air, the audience sees the normal items that can be used to fool our hearing when judging the ultimate sound. Then, too, when the audience wonders what is going to be used for the guillotine effect, the first person doing the guillotine blade effect uncovers the large paper cutter and the other would start filling the melon with the potato chips, once again, allowing the audience to see what makes audio theater so creative and unique.

Giving the audience a backstage look at what common items are used for sounds should be done in a working-like manner without any intention of "showing them off" to the audience.

There are any number of effects that can be used for a strange scratching sound on a hiker's camping tent during the night. The sound can be made by many things from a sheet of sandpaper to a more creative and surprising piece of burnt toast. How does the audience know for sure it's a piece of toast? The toast is taken out of a toaster that had been placed on the sound effects table. Not only does this produce an excellent soft scratching sound, it's also something the audience will have never associated with such a scary effect. And isn't that what entertainment is all about; exceeding the expectations of your audiences?

Early Foley Props

A number of different sounds have been heard since the beginning of time. Didn't oceans always make the sounds of waves? And wasn't there always the watery sound that rain makes? And didn't irate cave women who have caught their husbands looking at the woman in the next cave haul them off and give them a slap? Therefore, didn't the early sound effects people have to simulate these sounds for their audience without the convenience of the sounds being on records and tape machines, or CDs? Of course they did, and they still do in the modern Hollywood Foley studios.

Although these early vaudeville and silent film props seem to be too outdated for today's computerized sounds, they aren't. A Foley film studio is filled with them and looking for more. What if a film was shot in Paris and they needed the sound of a French taxi's bulb horn being squeezed by the driver? Rather than go to the expense, time and trouble of laying in a computerized sound, the Foley artist would simply get the horn and squeeze it in sync with what was showing on film. Not only would this way of making the sound be convenient, it's sound, unlike those from a computer, would be first generational. (A sound magnified only by a microphone).

Some of the Most Frequently Requested Sounds

This next list of sounds is by no means all the sounds you'll be asked to do. They are simply the most frequently asked for sounds. Familiarizing yourself with what makes two sounds different will give you enough information to tackle any sound a writer or director may request. Just remember, only resort to the sounds on CDs when a more entertaining and imaginative manual effect absolutely can't make the proper sound.

This will be especially true when working before an audience. Does a band perform on stage the same way as it does in a recording studio? Therefore, audiences are familiar with seeing actors saying their lines, but how many have seen how the sound of a guillotine is made removing some royal's head right before their eyes? Always remember, hearing a sound on CD is just informative, but watching how the sound is done is entertainment!

ARROW IN FLIGHT FROM BOW

Take one end of a ¼" dowel two feet long and swing it sharply across your body for the whooshing sound of an arrow in flight. (See also "Golf Swing.")

BELLS

All types of large bells ... fire alarm, school, church, fight gong ... can be had by taking a trip to an automobile junk yard and purchasing an old automobile brake drum. Lay the drum on it's back so the edges face towards you. Try hitting the drum with different size materials made of metal or wood for different tones.

BIRD FLYING

Bend a wire coat hanger in a circle and tie strips of cloth a foot long to the hoop. By shaking the wire hoop and rags in a rhythmic motion, you can simulate a bird's wings flapping in flight, or a boat's sails.

BOAT SAILS

If you haven't guessed, a bird's wings flap faster and more frequently than a boat's sails in a soft breeze. But just so there is no confusion as to which flap belongs to the sail, add the sounds of a large old bed sheet. (See "Parachute Opening" and "Tearing or Ripping.")

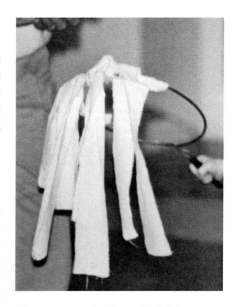

Apparatus to simulate a bird flying.

FAINTING OR FALLING

Although many directors insist that the sound effects people actually fall with their entire bodies on whatever surface the script called for—floors, dirt and even mud—there is another way that is much easier on the body and just as effective. This only involves your elbows and a firm table. Raise and fold both your arms towards you so that your elbows are pointing downward. Then relax your shoulders and arms and let your elbows fall, one slightly ahead of the other, to the table followed by your relaxed forearms falling loosely to the table on whatever surface is chosen. For dirt, use a gravel bag. For a muddy surface, soak a thick layer of wet paper towels.

BOILING BLOOD

Did you ever hear that expression: "Blood is thicker than water"? Well, it is. That's why you can't make the bubbling sound of blood with plain water. Try thickening the water first with a little cornstarch. (Let the audience see the cornstarch box as you put a small amount of cornstarch into the already thickened water.)

BOILING WATER

Blow bubbles gently into a container of water with a straw allowing a small amount of your breath to escape. The water makes the bubble sound, while your breath makes the sound of steam.

BOTTLE OPEN

For a wine bottle, wet a cork and insert it in the mouth of the bottle, making certain it isn't too tight or in too deep! On cue, twist the cork and pull the cork out at an angle for the popping sound. Try putting your right index finger in your mouth up against your left cheek. Just before the cue, tighten your cheek and quickly flip your finger out. Remember to clink the glass with the bottle to indicate you are doing the pouring.

BRAKE SCREECH

Hammer three large nails into a block of wood. Place your hand lightly on top of the wood and lightly push it slowly in the direction of the nails over a piece of glass. By varying the amount of pressure you apply, this prop can be used for numerous scratches and screeches, including the screech of a piece of chalk on a blackboard.

BREAKING BONES

Break the stalks of a fresh bunch of celery, or fresh carrots. For a more crushing effect, twist the bunch. For a small bone, break a very thin dowel stick, or a wooden matchstick.

BREAKING EGGS

Why not use a real egg? First of all they're messy, and secondly, there is no guarantee breaking a real egg will sound like a real egg. Try this instead: place a small piece of coarse sandpaper, five-inches square, in your hand and suddenly squeeze it.

BUSHES

Twist some dried leaves, along with their short, thin branches, in your hands according to how fast the person is walking, or running.

CHAMPAGNE

Break a small piece of an Alka-Seltzer tablet in water and hold the glass close to the microphone. If it's a fast cue, powder the Alka-Seltzer first.

CHATTERING MONKEY

Moisten the tip of a small cork with some turpentine and rub it vigorously along the side of a glass bottle, or a smooth glass surface.

CLANKY OLD CAR

Fill a large metal laundry tub with suitable metal objects and place the tub on a frying pan. By rhythmically rocking the tub back and forth, you will provide the noisy sounds of an old, comical, clanky car, or noisy, large engine. The secret is what you put in the tub, and what sort of rhythm you use for the effect.

CLICKS

Small light, camera clicks, etc., can be made by snapping the clasp on a ballpoint pen.

CLOCK SOUNDS

Use a metronome or a drummer's wood block for the ticking sound of a grandfather clock. For the ticking of an old-fashioned alarm clock, either find one at a garage sale, in the attic, or in a thrift shop. If you're not successful, try sharpening a pencil and tapping lightly on the face of an electric clock that has a glass or plastic face. For the alarm sound, use a door buzzer or bell.

COCKTAIL SHAKER

Shake some pieces of broken glass in a small amount of water in a metal coffee can.

COINS

Avoid nickels, dimes and pennies, instead, use large metal washers.

COMBINATION LOCK

Buy an inexpensive combination lock. In addition to the dialing sounds, clicking it open and closed makes an excellent sound for handcuffs being opened and closed, and for a rifle's bolt being closed.

CRACKING BONES OR KNUCKLES

Slowly crunch a walnut or peanut shell with a nut cracker or pair of pliers. Slowly twist a bunch of fresh celery agonizingly.

CRACKLING FIRE

Crinkle cellophane gently in your hands. To make the sound of a forest fire, hold the cellophane closer to the mike and add the sound of small sticks snapping. This is another example of a sound artist's nightmare ... having to make two different sounds from the same material. Barney Beck, the sound effects artist on the radio show *The Shadow* was once asked by Bud Collyer, the voice of radio's *Superman*, if he used cellophane for fire, what would he use if he had both a fire effect and unwrapping a Christmas present wrapped in cellophane in the same show? Barney's answer: "I always used two different colors."

CRASHES (TUB)

Fill a large plastic or metal tub with all the metal junk you can find, some for their hollow sound, like empty soda cans, other objects with more weight. (But not enough to hurt yourself!) By grasping the edge of the tub you can shake it with an intensity that best fits the crash you are trying to simulate.

The tub, or cardboard box, was often used by radio shows, or even the theater, because of its size and convenience for shows without either the time or budget for anything more complicated. This was never true on a comedy show.

There is no one method to do a comedy crash. It all has to do with what the crash is supposed to represent. It could be as simple as tripping over a bicycle or having an accumulation of junk in a hall closet come cascading out, as was made famous on the *Fibber McGee and Molly* show. Even then there were never two sound effects artists who would do that famous crash exactly the same.

You can make your crashes simply with a few empty soda cans, a couple of pieces of wood, a few more odds and ends, and put them all in a cardboard box. Then you can simulate a crash with the best of them. As with all sound effects, it isn't what you use ... it's how imaginative you use and sell them to the audience.

CREAKS

Rub an empty matchbook cover or medium-size paper picnic cup (not waxed) between your fingers. Or, the next time you're watching television, rub your fingers firmly over the channel changer for a good rubbing sound. For the sound of a squeaky door, what else? Find an old rusty hinge. If it isn't rusty enough, leave it out in the rain.

CROWD SOUNDS

Every large crowd has a different sound. A political convention can't be used for a sporting crowd, and a baseball crowd can't be used for a football crowd. Therefore you must use a vanilla type roar of a crowd rather than try and match it to the individual event. In radio we used recordings, but today, use a portable tape recorder, or a CD. For a smaller crowd the appropriate sound should come from the cast. (See "WallaWalla.")

CRUNCHING

The crunching sound of walking through leaves and bushes is not the same as rhythmic steps going to the fridge for a Pepsi. You'll have dried small branches tearing at your clothes and dried leaves to walk on. For the walking, twist the leaves, but be aware they should be slow and cautious, along with labored breathing from the actor.

DIGGING AND SHOVELING

Fill a medium-size wooden or cardboard box with as much dirt as the script calls for. Don't skimp. If you're doing the sounds for digging a grave, you don't want to hear cardboard sounds. To the dirt, add some stones to click your shovel against. Digging a grave isn't like digging sand at a beach.

DISH BREAKING

There are a number of ways of breaking glass, or dishes, some more elaborate than others. Just be certain you always wear gloves and safety glasses.

DOG SHAKING HIMSELF AFTER A BATH

Wet half a dozen non-inflated balloons and give them a vigorous shake.

DOG WALKING ON HARDWOOD FLOOR

Although a dog's paws are padded, we want to simulate the sound of the dog's nails. For that sound, use a pair of large gardener's cotton gloves and attach either staples or paper clips to the very ends of the glove's fingers. If the director doesn't want to hear the sound of the dog's nails, take two cloth napkins and ball them up tightly to the size of a golf ball. Lightly tapping the napkins on a wooden surface should give the required sound. But if she wants to play games and snottily demands, "But I want to hear the sound of the dog walking on a carpet," frown thoughtfully for a moment and reply, "Persian, or shag?"

DOORS

One of the earliest sound effects used in live radio to indicate movement was doors. People were either coming in or going out of a scene by way of a door opening or closing. It was radio's equivalent of the theater's going off stage or entrances. A sound effect as simple as a door opening and closing can indicate the pace of a show, or even emotions. A door opening too fast or too slow, too loud or too soft, can either punctuate a scene, or spoil it. Although you could find a full-size door at a garage sale or a building contractor that specializes in upgrading older homes, I would suggest you build, or have built, a much smaller door. If all your shows were done at one location, a normal-size door would be fine, but inasmuch as you'll be doing a great deal of traveling to different locations, a smaller door will fit your needs. Just one thing to be careful of, be sure that you use the same size thickness of the wood as a larger door, because it isn't always the size of your door, but its weight that determines its sound. If needed, put a five-pound dumbbell inside the door.

The size of this small door also comes in handy in attaching locking bolts, or even an old-fashioned telephone dialing prop.

A small door like this can simulate the sound of a full-size door.

When it comes time to break down a door, all that is needed is a paper-thin, wooden berry basket.

DRAWERS

Drag a short piece of 2 × 4 wood over a wooden surface that has been raised high enough to give the drawer a hollow sound.

DUELING SWORDS

Striking a bayonet against its scabbard, or using metallic kitchen utensils such as tongs and spatulas, may give you the clashing of metal sound, but for the *dueling* of swords, sounds come from your imagination.

The author uses a wooden berry basket for the sound of a door being broken down.

ECHO

Where no echo chamber is available but a piano is, place a microphone down near the piano's sounding board. With the top of the piano half open and a weight placed on the dampening pedal, the strings will be free to vibrate and give a sound or voice with a metallic, eerie effect.

ELECTRICAL SHORT CIRCUIT

Pour a small amount of water on a hot plate. If the short circuit lasts for any length of time, or requires an increase in volume, the sizzle-sputtering sound may need a second hot plate. As with all sound effects requiring dangerous props like a hot plate, extreme care must be taken. And definitely not for young children!

ELECTRIC SPARK

Wrap two pieces of rough sandpaper around two blackboard-size erasers. Rub them together in one fast sweeping motion.

ELEVATOR DOOR

Tilt a skateboard up so only two wheels are touching the surface.

EXPLOSIONS

Put some BBs in an inflated balloon and hold it close to a microphone. By punching the balloon you'll be surprised how realistic the explosion sounds.

FALLING INTO WATER

Sink a child's beach bucket in a large tub filled with water. Turn the bucket over so the bottom side is facing up. When cued, lift the bucket quickly out of the water.

FISHING

For the sound of catching a fish, make the sound that is most heard in nature films ... splashing water. Use a deep plastic dish tub, fill it with water and imagine you're a trout. Much can be learned from these nature films. The film may have been shot at a remote pond in Alaska surrounded by hundreds of circling silent birds, but only when the camera goes on a tight shot of a duck splashing in the water do we hear the one and only sound effect ... splashing water sounds. This is good to remember in doing any background sound effects; emphasize only the sounds that are most evident and needed.

FIZZING SOUND

Crush an Alka-Seltzer and drop it in a glass of water.

FOOTSTEPS ON WOOD

Although many people doing sound effects try to skimp on the size of the walking board, I've found the most efficient size was that at CBS. It was approximately five feet long and three feet wide. It was made of plywood three inches thick, with carpeting tacked on its entire reverse side. This was to absorb the wood's vibration and keep it from sounding like a "pickle barrel." Once again, for your audio theater's traveling needs, your walking board can be smaller in size as long as the thickness remains the same.

In order to do any footsteps on wood, pavement, marble, gravel, dirt or what have you, leather soles and heels are a must. Some sound people (yes, women Foley artists included) have metal slugs driven into the heels as opposed to having "taps" on the outside of the heels.

For a man's or woman's normal walking steps, you don't actually do any "walking," instead you stand in one place and move your shoes in place with what pace the script calls for ... running, jogging, walking slow, in a hurry or limping. For the steps of walking, place the emphasis on your heels rather than on the sole of the shoe. The most important thing to remember is to make your steps appropriate for the actor reading the lines. If the actor is a woman, make her steps lighter and slightly more hurried, as if she's encumbered by a tight skirt.

FOOTSTEPS FOR TWO PEOPLE

If you are doing a radio show alone and the script calls for two people walking at the same time, break up the rhythm of the steps by rocking up and down by hitting your heels hard and going over on your toe. Mix the cadence up by tapping twice with the toe of one shoe while coming down firmly on the heel of the other. By mixing your steps in this fashion, it will sound like two people walking and not soldiers marching in cadence.

One sound effect artist had difficulty doing this "two men walking" pattern and the director complained she could only hear one set of steps. The sound artist tried to placate her by replying, "One guy's barefoot."

Footsteps on Gravel

Although they can be done in a canvas sack of gravel, the gravel box comes in handy for any and all digging sounds, whether they're in gravel or dirt. If you don't have a gravel box, or don't have room for one, you can make the gravel steps with your hands by crunching the gravel in a canvas sack. By using the hand method, you can add to the effect by stepping on leaves.

Footsteps in Mud

Soak paper towels. To make it sound like deep mud, cook up a large bowl of Jell-O and make the slow "sucking" mud sounds by working the Jell-O with your hands. This same sound can be used for wild animals eating.

Footsteps Up the Stairs

By placing a small piece of wood under the walking board to give it a hollow stair-like sound, simple slide your soles on the wood in the rhythm of climbing stairs.

Footsteps Down the Stairs

Step heavily on the sole of your leather shoe and follow it lightly with the heel of the shoe.

Footsteps in Snow

Squeeze a soft leather pouch filled with cornstarch, or use a box of cornstarch that has been wrapped with duct tape.

Footsteps in Water

Two rubber suction cups (plumbers' helpers) in water can make all the walking water sounds you'll need. From wading, to sloshing, to trying to catch that elusive trout. These same plumbers' helpers make an excellent sound of horses' hooves on dirt or gravel.

Footsteps for Women

This is the way real men did ladies' footsteps. Lift your toes and rock back on your heels so that only the back edge of the heel is hitting the walking board. Make the steps shorter and, therefore, quicker because in radio, women were still confined in skirts.

FOOTSTEPS FOR CHILDREN

To reduce the weight of your body, have an old, extra pair of shoes and, by holding them in your hands and tapping them lightly against whatever surface is required, you can make a convincing walking or running sound. Or simply sit down when you do the steps for children.

FOOTSTEPS ON SIDEWALK

Do normal steps on pieces of slate, marble, flagstones, or any other stone-like material.

FOOTSTEPS BAREFOOTED

So that the listening audience makes no mistake that you're walking barefooted for a midnight snack, have the writer give you the word "OUCH," as if you stubbed your toe.

FRYING HAMBURGERS

Originally real hamburger meat was used. This was soon discarded when a program used that sound right before lunchtime. The agonized "oohs and aaahs" from the lunch-hungry audience so disrupted the live dramatic show that the sizzling sound of the frying hamburger meat soon became a non-fattening wet rag dropped on a hot plate.

GLACIER BREAKING UP

Rub a wet balloon close to the mike. If you have help, have them twist stalks of celery next to you in the same mike.

GLASS CRASH *see* DISH BREAKING

GOLD DUST

Fill a small cloth bag with BBs or sand.

GOLF SWING

Purchase a ¼" two foot long dowel stick and swoosh it through the air with a firm stroke (see "Arrow in Flight from Bow").

GOLF BALL HIT

A sudden whoosh of a dowel stick, followed by the flick of your forefinger against a small box of wooden or paper matches. (This is one of those simple sound effects that require two people.)

GUILLOTINE FALLING

Slide a hatchet down the length of a metal crowbar, or use an office cutter used to trim papers, and don't forget the gravel and potato chips.

GUNSHOTS

Even blank cartridges can put your eye out. Although this is a worried mother's frequent lament (and used often in the classic movie *A Christmas Story*), it's too true to be taken lightly. Even a pistol with blank shells is dangerous. When the pistol is fired, the paper wadding of a blank cartridge can become inflamed and travel quite a distance. This makes it especially dangerous doing a radio show with a group of people in close quarters. Instead use a leather, plastic, or canvas cushion and strike it sharply with a thin stick, such as a dowel purchased cheaply at a hardware store, or burst an inflated small paper bag or balloon.

HANDCUFFS

Long serrated bicycle lock. Slide the lock down the serrated metal for the closing sound and use door slide bolt for the closing of the handcuffs.

HARNESS SOUNDS

A stiff leather belt or pocketbook mixed with some short pieces of chain.

HEAD HIT

One of the best head hit "weapons" is a short piece of garden hose. For a head hit, strike a grapefruit sharply.

HORSES' HOOVES

"With thundering hoofbeats, the Lone Ranger rides again!" But only if you know how to take two coconut halves, or plumbers' helpers, and pound them convincingly in a tray filled with dirt. This is one of the reasons that drummers often made good sound effects artists. But to be honest, they were often guilty of doing three-legged horses. These are the easiest to do. You can practice with your hands by drumming your right two beats, followed by your left hand. Once you can do that, try speeding the movement up into a rhythm that might be mistaken for a galloping horse. Once you've got that down, try doing a four-legged horse. This is a lot trickier. This is two beats with your left hand, followed by two beats with your right hand. I told you it was tricky!

Have some stones in the dirt box for the sound of a horse walking on cobblestones. If a Western requires a horse going over a bridge, nail a small piece of board over the corner of your dirt tray. You might also have some gravel in the box for that effect as well. Just be certain before you use your dirt box for "thundering hoofbeats" that the dirt isn't so dry that the hoofbeats kick up a cloud of dust so you can't see your script! As a precaution, always slightly dampen the dirt with water from an old Windex bottle (see "Milking a Cow").

ICE CUBES

Small holiday light bulbs, or night-light bulbs.

ICE SKATING

Slide your fingernail against a thick spiral notebook.

JAIL DOOR OPENING AND CLOSING

Slide two pieces of flat and sturdy (½" thick) pieces of metal over a metallic base for the opening and closing sounds.

JAIL DOOR LOCKING

Using the same two pieces of metal you used for the opening and closings and clang them together. Slide one of the metal pieces against the other for the security bar dropping in place.

JAIL KEYS

Large keys suitable for opening a jail, or any large door, can be simulated by using several pairs of scissors and clinking them together.

JUNKY CAR

Fill the lid of a metal trash can with nuts, bolts and soda cans. By shaking the metal lid up and down, you can do a convincing sound of a car on its way to the junkyard.

KISSES FOR CARTOONS

Fold your arm and make the kissing sound at the bend.

LAVA

The bubbling sound for lava can be done by using water thickened with cornstarch, or by using oatmeal. In either case, in order for the sound to sound realistic, a microphone must be held close to the boiling mixture.

MACHINE GUN

Use a tubular empty oatmeal box and a large wooden cooking spoon. For the staccato effect of the gun, put the spoon inside the box and rapidly hit the box's side. Unless the script is a comedy, this is one of those times that the sounds should be recorded.

MACHINERY

For the continuous humming sound, use a hair dryer, shaver, vibrating toothbrush, muscle vibrator, or whatever else you may have. To vary the tone, place the object against different surfaces for the sounding board effect. Also try all the electronic toys that may be in a closet needing a battery, or purchased cheaply at garage sales or thrift shops. And when you buy an old fan for 50 cents and they tell you it's so cheap because it's missing the propeller, you tell them, "That's okay, I don't want it for cooling ... just the noise."

MARCHING FEET

Page 182 shows the versatility of the sound effects artists in the 1940s. While Ray Erlenborn toots a bulb horn and puts the needle down on a traffic record, he has a pistol on the table for gunshots, coconut halves for horses

Many sound effects could be made with these props. While Ray Erlenborn toots a bulb horn and puts the needle down on a traffic record, he has a pistol on the table for gunshots, coconut halves for horses' hooves, and a wood contraption for marching feet (courtesy Ray Erlenborn).

hooves, and a wood contraption for marching feet! Whew! The sound of marching feet is created by drumming the loosely strung pegs seen in the foreground on any suitable surface. For the sound of "Fall out!" simply flop the pegs down. To bring them back to attention, give the prop a sharp shake. And for "Forward march," start drumming again. The next time you see a vintage newsreel war film, see if the sound of the German soldiers marching was really on the film or was more recently Foleyed. For a closer view of how the soldiers look, see page 183.

Mechanical Sounds

A possible sound for a robot walking might be squeezing and releasing a three-hole paper punch. To get a little more creative, add an electronic humming sound to the mechanical sound?

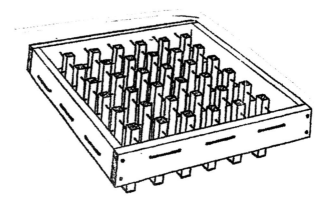

Peg box used to make the sound of marching feet.

MILKING A COW

Squirt water from a Windex-type dispenser or water pistol into a metal bucket. Just remember, you're not just squirting a water pistol into a metal bucket, you're rhythmically milking a cow. And if you have to pat ole bossy to excuse your cold hands, by all means make that sound by hitting your thighs. Gertrude Berg, star of *The Goldbergs* back in 1936, used to help out making the slapping sound by hitting her ample derriere.

MATCH STRIKE

How realistic do you want to be? A simple match striking sound can be made by brushing a pencil across a piece of sandpaper. For realism, use the wooden kitchen matches that come in a large cardboard box. Strike the match across the emery portion for the scratching sound, and then quickly hold the lit match close to the mike for the short igniting sound.

MUD

Place sopping wet newspapers or paper towels in a tray with a small amount of water. For the steps, use the same two rubber plungers used for the sound of walking in water.

OARS

Turn a doorknob in the rhythm of rowing.

PARACHUTE OPENING

You and your partner each hold the edges of a bed sheet loosely and, on cue, snap the sheet apart suddenly.

POURING A DRINK

Always touch the lip of the glass to the bottle of water before pouring. For a comedy effect, fill empty tennis ball cans, or pitchers, with water and keep pouring them until your sense of timing, or ears, tells you the laughs are just about to stop.

PUNCHES TO THE BODY

Hit your body accompanied by grunts and groans.

PUNCHES TO THE JAW

Punch a leather wallet with your fist, or wear a tight, thin leather glove and punch it with your bare hand. Although these were the accepted ways of doing "socks on the jaw," some directors insist on hearing something "different." If this should happen to you, don't do what Barney Beck, an excellent sound effects artist on such shows as *The Shadow,* did back in the glory days of radio.

This comes under the heading of a director's mantra of, "What else have you got?" No matter what Barney hit for the sound of a punch, nothing pleased the young woman director. Finally, he stood amongst the rubble of the director's rejections and began nursing his bruised fist. "I don't know what else I can give you. I've punched my wallet, a grapefruit, a bag of sand, a baseball catcher's mitt, the palms of my hands ... with and without gloves.... In fact, the only thing I haven't punched is you!" Despite Barney's smile when he said it, he was no longer requested to do the show.

Perhaps now would be a good time to graphically show you the difference between Foleying for a film and doing sound effects during the live days of radio and television.

Ken Dufva and David Lee Fein are excellent film Foley artists. Among the hundreds of films and television shows they have done, one is appropriate to illustrate Foleying and live sound effects. This is taken from my interview with them and is included in my book "Radio Live! Television Live!"

"For many of the punching sounds on *Rocky* and *Raging Bull,* we used boxing gloves and hit ourselves on the legs, arms and chests. Then we used the gloves to hit tires, a rubber mallet to smack a piece of 6 × 6 block of wood, and a baseball bat to pound an old leather saddle. After hitting all the sounds we had once and audio taping them, we would then start all over again and hit the various effects a number of different ways for variety. When we were finally satisfied with sounds we had made, we'd send them to Frank Warner, the sound effects editor. He would then play our sounds on one tape and add other taped sounds to our hits to give them a bigger sound. Some of the taped sounds he added to our punches were a piece of a clap of thunder, a lion roar, or a gunshot to make it sound like the director requested, a 'shattering' punch on the jaw."

One can only wonder if that radio director would have had the nerve to ask Ken and David, "What else have you got?"

RAIN

Rain is best done with a recorded sound. If that's not available try doing it the old-fashioned way. The equipment needed is: tissue paper, a supply of salt or sugar, some Scotch tape, a fine-meshed kitchen strainer and an empty shoebox and its cover. Place the shoebox on its end and tape the tissue paper down to the cover laying on the floor or table. Next place a microphone under the taut tissue paper and pour the salt or sugar into the strainer slowly with a picture of a gentle rainfall in your mind.

RATTLESNAKE

A baby's rattle. (Think snake.)

ROULETTE WHEEL

Place a marble in the bottom of a wooden salad bowl. Roll the ball around until the cue comes to stop it. For the sound of the ball stopping, drop a separate marble into a plastic shallow cup, or a coconut half used for the sound of horses' hooves.

RIFLE BOLT AND PISTOL

For the sound of loading a bolt-action rifle, use a large bolt used for doors. For loading a clip of ammunition into an automatic pistol, use the same door bolt as for the rifle.

RUBBING SOUNDS

A toy balloon makes a reliable and authentic rubbing sound. Use it for the sound of a boat rubbing against a dock. Another effect for an inflated toy balloon is that of an explosion (see explosions).

SAWING WOOD

Rub a piece of wood against sandpaper.

SCRAPING (CHAIR)

All you're interested in is the scraping sound of wood on wood, so you don't need a real chair. To make the sound, cover the bottom of a brick (for the chair's weight) with a flat piece of wood, hold the brick at an angle, and scrape against another piece of thick plywood.

SCREECHES

Hammer large nails into a small piece of wood and drag it across a thin, handkerchief-sized thin metal sheet.

SHUCKING AN EAR OF CORN

Buy an ear of corn and tear off the leaves. But like most props, it has many other uses. How about "turning a body inside out"? Once the leaves have been removed, break the raw corn in half for the sound of a bone being broken.

SHUFFLING PLAYING CARDS

Regular playing cards can be difficult to shuffle, especially when new. Try substituting the cards with a small pad of Post-it notes.

SIGNING PAPERS

Unwind a paper clip and scratch it against a script page. Don't forget the slight paper sounds.

SLAPSTICKS

Two thin and narrow pieces of hard wood joined together by a hinge three quarters of the way up the wood, allowing room for a handle. By holding the slapstick by the handle, opening the two pieces of wood and closing the top half of the wood strongly against the bottom half held in your hand, you create an excellent whip crack or face slap. Little wonder that comedians such as *The Three Stooges* called the prop a slapstick.

SLAPS WITH HANDS

Wet one hand and strike with the other hand. By wetting your hands it gives the slap a thinner, more feminine sounding slap. For a more masculine slap, hit your thigh.

SQUEAKY NOISES

There are any number of squeaky sounds that require their own specific sound. For the sound of a door hung with rusty hinges, you might try a large, real, rusty hinge that squeaks. By holding one side of the hinge in your left hand so the center pin is upright, press down on the right side so that it puts pressure on the vertical pin and produces a squeaky sound. The trick is to use the correct amount of pressure to give the desired sound. But is that the desired sound?

Remember, this is the squeaky sound of a door, not of an oarlock, or an old-fashioned pump handle pumping water, or of a room fan. Therefore, instead of just holding the hinge in the air, press or clamp it against a large object made of wood (a door?) so that it acts as a sounding board and produces a more realistic door sound.

When you need a spookier sound, the photograph below shows the best and most reliable wood squeak if you put some turpentine in hole where the wood handle is inserted. Next you work the handle back and forth until you get the appropriate squeak. But only do this right before you go on the air, not after the turpentine has had time to dry.

Device used for creating squeaks.

SQUEEGEE

Miscellaneous squeak sounds can be produced by rubbing the wet sole of a tennis or basketball shoe over a piece of old linoleum three-feet square. By varying the pressure your shoe applies to the linoleum, all sorts of squeaky sounds can be made ... even the sound of a squeegee cleaning a store window.

STABBING

Plunge a large knife into a large melon. Interestingly enough, the over-ripe pumpkin was banned from live radio after a number of home listeners complained about its frightening sound, proving that what sounds you can see are never as frightening as what your mind imagines.

SWINGING DOOR

With a door open, push it back and forth between the heels of your hand.

TEARING OR RIPPING

When green kitchen cloth shades were popular, they not only kept out the sun, they made the best tearing sounds. If you can find one of these old shades at a garage sale, or flea market, treasure it. If you can't, use an old and much-used cloth kitchen towel. But make some short rips in the towel before the cue comes to make certain the tearing sound has a dependable start.

TELEPHONE

For the ringing sound of an older telephone, simply get a two-bell door-bell at your hardware store. How good of a phone imitation are they? Before cell phones, these doorbells were often mistaken for the phone ringing.

For the best sounding effect you need a bread board (so called because before packaged sliced bread, a similar piece of flat wood was used for carving slices of bread). The board should be one-and-a-half-foot square and an inch thick. Next, you need to mount it on some insulating material such as a sponge rubber kneeling pad found in a hardware store. This keeps the bare wood from acting as a sounding board and making the bell tones too loud and resonant.

TELEPHONE BOOTH

Try and find an old metal roller skate. The metal wheels make not only the sound of a phone booth opening and closing or an elevator door opening and closing, but any metallic rolling sound. Even use one wheel alone for the turning of a safe's combination lock.

THUNDER

Shake a large piece of very thin metal according to the severity of the storm.

TRAINS

Although diesel trains are used today, they lack the "choo-choo" sound of a steam engine. So, in our audio theater, all trains are choo-choo trains.

The sound effect of a steam engine leaving the station can be done in a variety of ways as long as the rhythm is faithful to the actual engine sound. The most popular and long-lasting method was to punch small holes in a one-and-a-half-foot piece of thin tin. Screw or nail the tin to a wooden frame. To make the chugging sound, scrape a wire brush across the tin in sweeping motions to get the train started, then increase the frequency and shorten the strokes as the train picks up speed.

Some other methods include shaking BBs in an empty tennis ball can and scraping a stiff non-metal brush on a wide piece of coarse sandpaper. Whatever you use, ignore what the prop looks like and only listen to the sound.

WALKING *see* FOOTSTEPS

WALLAWALLA

During the live days of radio, the radio actor's union, the American Federation of Radio Artists (AFRA), had pay scales as to how many lines actors were allowed to speak. Over five lines was one category, under five lines was another category. There were also rulings as to how many parts you were allowed to play in one show. Therefore, if you were playing one part and given specific words to say in a crowd scene, they counted in the "under five lines" category and demanded payment. To avoid extra expense, or their budget wouldn't permit it, during a small crowd scene, directors would ask the cast for the nonsense words "WallaWalla" or "HubBub."

WATER SOUNDS

As with all the sounds listed, there are numerous ways of doing water effects. The simplest way is to get a container of water and make the water movement sounds with your hand.

Waves

Roll a drum head with some BBs on it in a rhythmic motion.

Whip Crack *see* Slapstick

Wind

Although many props have been made to simulate the sounds of wind, they are best used for dramatic demonstrations as an example of ingenuity prior to electronics. In order to produce the sound of wind, a sheet of smooth tarpaulin is placed over a barrel with a handle and, by turning the handle, the sound of the wind is changed in intensity by how fast or slow the handle is rotated.

Although this apparatus was often used in operas by the percussionists, and as far back as in Shakespeare's Globe Theater, it could also have been heard blowing up a storm on the early radio shows heard during the 1930s. And even today, if you go into a modern Foley studio, don't be surprised if there isn't one still being used for wind and other special effects.

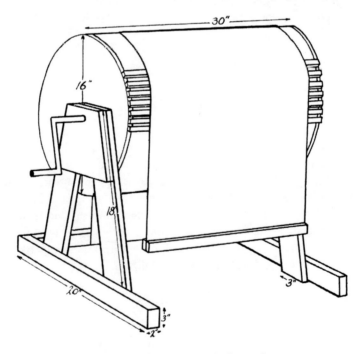

Apparatus for creating wind sounds.

WINDOWS

Slide a heavy piece of wood up, or down, an appropriate length of the prop you're using for your house door.

Summary

Now that you know how to do most of the sound effects I was requested to do, there were always a few that, at first, seemed impossible to do ... like the atomic bomb. But once you become familiar with the nine components of sound in the next chapter, you'll have a better understanding as to how it's possible to create any sound, from the roar of a dinosaur to the boom of the atom bomb.

14

Creating the More Impossible Sounds

The Atom Bomb?

During the time when this country was testing atomic bombs at French-man Flat, the networks sent television crews there to record the historic event. Although they were able to get a picture of the explosion, they were unable to record an acceptable sound. Not wanting to disappoint their curious view-ers that night on the CBS News, the director informed me that they needed the sound of an atom bomb detonating and I only had twenty minutes and three turntables to come up with the sound!

The turntables pictured operated on the same principal as today's disk jockeys. The difference being, if we scratched the needle across the record for an effect instead of placing the needle in a particular groove, our days in sound effects would be over. Records could be played with any of the six turntables' pickup arms. Each record could also be played at variable speeds other than its normal 78 rpms to produce different sounds. The slower the record's speed was set, the more dominant the bass became; the faster the record was played increased its treble sound.

Having only time to play three records, I had a choice, simply make the atom bomb loud and booming, or try and follow the picture on the screen. The first explosive sound was slow and mushroomed up and out before the larger detonation. In order to do this, my first sound had to be slower and more ominous. Therefore, my first sound of the atom bomb was a water-fall.

The fact that the waterfall record selected was the Mogambi Waterfalls had no influence on the ultimate roaring sound I needed ... it was the only waterfalls record in the CBS library! And by slowing the record down, it made a more convincing, slow, roaring sound that matched the seemingly deliber-

Three turntables used to create the sound of the explosion of an atom bomb.

ate amount of time it took for the bomb's detonation to reach its *peak*. At that point I added a huge explosive sound from dynamite and a building collapsing, again both at a slightly slower speed, for a bigger, more ominous impact. Then, as the mushroom cloud appeared to have reached its intensity and began to decay, I slowly faded my sounds with the picture on my monitor.

When the director went back to the newscaster, not a word was mentioned to the audience that the awesome sound they just heard was nothing more than three sound effects records played at different speeds. Although I never got a compliment for the sound I created, more importantly, the director never said, "What else have you got for the sound of the atom bomb?"

Although it's doubtful that you'll have to come up with the sound of an atom bomb, it's good to know just how a sound, no matter how unusual the sound may be, can be created. Although I've not listed how to create the sound of an atom bomb in my "Most Asked for SFX" chapter, it's a good idea to know just what goes into creating an unknown sound you may have to create.

Imitative Sounds

One of the basic methods used in creating a sound is to imitate it with another sound that is similar in physical properties. If you want the sound of footsteps walking in the snow, you might use a substance that has an appearance of snow, such as cornstarch. For the sound of a horse's hoofbeats, coconut shells come close to looking and sounding like the horse's hooves on a cobblestone road. Or the end of a plumber's plunger for walking on a softer surface such as dirt.

For the sound of "boiling blood" we've always heard that "blood is thicker than water" ... and it is. So instead of using water for the effects, cola syrup works very nicely. Just don't get syrup that is too thick because it will sound like a bubbling volcano. Therefore, in addition to a sound's appearance and size, the consistency of the object is equally important.

The Nine Important Components of Sound

There are nine components of sound that most influence how we perceive a sound effect. By modifying or eliminating any one, or a combination of these components, you either slightly change the sound or create a totally new sound. The nine components are: Pitch, Timbre, Harmonics, Loudness, Attack, Sustain, Decay, Speed and Rhythm.

PITCH

The pitch of a sound is determined by the frequency of the sound. While a sound's frequency depends on how many cycles of sound occur in one second, when we hear a sound, we rarely describe it as having a certain number of frequencies, we just say a sound has a certain pitch. Pitch refers to whether a sound is high (sometimes shrill), or low (bassy).

What makes a sound seem high and shrill to our ears is the large number of sound wave cycles (hertz) that occur per second. Conversely, a low or bassy sound has fewer hertz per second. Pitch also refers to the way we perceive frequency levels. Because our hearing is an entirely subjective matter, listening to a sound and hearing a sound are two entirely different matters.

A war veteran exposed to the loud noises of cannon and gunfire will not perceive sounds the same way as a teenager, unless of course the teenager exposes his ears to equally harmful loud noises as cannons and gunfire.

TIMBRE

The timbre of a sound is that unique quality that sets it apart from all other sounds. When you receive a phone call from a friend you haven't heard from in years, your ability to recognize her voice is due to the timbre in her voice. Timbre is a combination of fundamental frequencies, harmonics, and overtones that give each voice its unique coloring and character.

HARMONICS

When an object vibrates it propagates sound waves of a certain frequency. This frequency, in turn, sets in motion additional frequency waves called harmonics. Harmonics, or overtones, as they are sometimes called, are multiples of the basic frequency. The second harmonic of a frequency of 250 Hz is 500 Hz, and the fifth harmonic is 1,250 Hz. Each harmonic that is added is weaker than the one that preceded it. The combination of the basic frequency and its harmonics is what gives each musical instrument, and sound effect, its unique quality.

A concert violinist and a student just learning to play will produce two drastically different sounds. The beginner will simply drag the bow across the strings with little regard for fingering the strings with authority. As a result, the notes will sound uninteresting or even irritating to our ears.

Unlike the student, the concert violinist will use her experience and, instead of simply dragging the bow across the strings, she will attack the strings with the appropriate strength to produce the maximum amount of harmonics that we find so satisfying.

We've discussed poor technique in regards to playing a violin, but what about the quality of the violin? The wood and construction of the instrument acts as a sounding board to the vibrations caused by the musician's technique. If the violin is of poor quality, even a fine musician will have difficulty, or even be unable to produce a superior sound. This is true of any object's ability to produce sounds, even a drinking glass.

To determine whether a dinner glass is crystal, we strike the rim of the glass with our fingernail and listen for that pleasant "pinging" sound. We also know that it's impossible to attain this same sound from a jelly jar. The difference lies in the ability of each glass to vibrate when they are struck. It is therefore an object's ability to vibrate and set up harmonics that determines the pleasantness of the resultant tones. In respect to the two glasses, one is extremely thin and can generate a greater number of vibrations, while the other is too thick to vibrate properly.

LOUDNESS

The loudness of a sound depends on the intensity of the sound's stimulus. A dynamite explosion is louder than a cap pistol. Not because one is named "dynamite" and the other "cap pistol," but because of the greater number of air molecules the one is capable of displacing.

When we speak of something as being long or short, high or low, soft or loud, the words are meaningless unless we have a reference point. The measurement of a foot is long compared to an inch, but short compared to a yard. The sound of a gunshot may be deafening in a small room, but actually go unnoticed if the gun is fired in a subway station when a train comes roaring in and screeches to a stop. Loudness, as with everything else that is perceived, becomes meaningful only if we are able to compare it with something else.

Sound is caused by something vibrating. How many times it vibrates in one second is its frequency. In the case of air, it's not only how many times its molecules vibrate in one second, it's the amount of molecules compressed in a cycle that determines the amplitude (strength) of the sound's loudness.

If we turn the volume of our audio equipment up by three decibels, we have in effect doubled the level of loudness. If we turn up the level so that we can readily perceive that we have turned it up "twice" as loud, we have actually made the sound ten times louder. These figures are based on the fact that we hear sounds logarithmically and not linearly.

As you can see, the job of making your radio or television seem louder is more complicated than just cranking up the volume control.

Adding a woman's scream and a car's screech to thunder may sound like a stroke of creative genius to the average person, but now you know the scream and car screech are just two of the hundreds of other sounds you could have added to the thunder to increase its loudness. Because now that you are becoming more familiar with the nature of sound, your options for creating sound effects are only limited to your imagination. In searching for appropriate sounds, you must stop putting labels on sounds, such as "dynamite" or "cap pistol," and start thinking of their resultant sounds.

Must you use a stick of dynamite for the sound of dynamite? If so, how can we ever justify adding a woman's terrified scream to make the sound of dynamite seem louder? Or make the sound of the atom bomb sound so "realistic" by adding the roar of a waterfall?

ATTACK

An envelope of sound is composed of a sound's attack, sustain and decay. The way a sound is initiated is called its attack, while the time it takes to lose its intensity and become silent is its decay.

There are two types of attack: fast and slow. The closer the attack of a sound is to the peak of a sound, the faster the attack is. Such sounds as gunshots, slaps and door slams (especially on comedy shows) are a few examples.

Sounds that have a slow attack take longer to build to the sustain level. A dog's short warning growl prior to a vicious bark is one example. Stepping on a dried leaf while casually walking slowly, the slow tearing of a sheet of paper, or the slow, agonizing twisting of a bunch of celery to indicate bones being broken on a dungeon's torture rack are some of the sounds that have a slow attack.

SUSTAIN

Once a sound has reached its peak, the length of time the sound will *sustain* is dependent upon the energy from the source vibrations. Once the source sound stops, the sound will begin to decay.

DECAY

Decay time varies in direct relationship to the sustain time. If, however, this decay time is too long for the purpose it was meant for in the script, the sustain time may be hurried up by dampening (slowing the vibrations) of the object causing the sound.

This is especially true of objects such as cymbals and gongs that sometimes cause a ringing sound with a very slow decay. If you grasp a cymbal tightly, the sound will stop unrealistically fast. But by closing your fingers slowly on the cymbal, or gong, the sound will fade in a more realistic decaying manner.

SPEED

The measurable velocity of a sound determines its speed. By increasing or decreasing the speed of a sound, you can not only change the properties of one particular sound, but you have it in your power to change, as you saw, the sound of a waterfall into that of the detonation of that atom bomb!

RHYTHM

Rhythm is most identified with music. In that context it is also associated with such terms as cadence, meter and tempo. Therefore, rather than confuse the issue, for our purposes we will define rhythm as a recurring sound that alternates between strong and weak elements.

Sounding Boards

In a way, our mouth is a sounding board. Ordinary speech is caused by two things: the buzz or hum made in the throat by air passing the vocal cords, and the modification made to this air by how our mouth's palate, tongue, lips and teeth articulate these air passages into words.

Suppose instead of using your own air for your mouth to articulate into words it came from another source ... a train whistle, a foghorn? This was the basis for an amazing electronic device called a Sonovox, invented by Gilbert Wright while shaving with an electric razor.

The Sonovox was used extensively back in live radio for many interesting effects, especially on commercials. The sound effect of a train whistle was fed to an earphone-like device pressed against a woman's larynx. This woman was known as an "articulator." When feeding the sound of a train whistle to the lady articulator, she would mouth the words: *"Fight headaches three ways ... Bromo Seltzer, Bromo Seltzer, Bromo Seltzer."*

By only mouthing the formation of the words, and not speaking the words with her mouth, she literally was articulating the words from the sound being fed from the train recording! Now, in addition to her mouthing the words, her mouth also became a loudspeaker, giving the impression that a train whistle was rhythmically and eerily giving America spooky advice on how to get rid of a headache. Lucille Ball, in one of her earliest film appearances, demonstrated the Sonovox in a Pathe News film as far back as the 1930s.

In addition to commercials, the Sonovox was used in hundreds of different ways. It was truly a seemingly magical device ... but no more so than the human articulator.

Mixing and Matching

In this highly complicated and subjective business of reproducing existing sounds and creating new ones, you will very often have to implement all the components that we have discussed in order to create the desired effect. Very often one component will be so dominant that simply emphasizing that part of the sound, such as rhythm, will be sufficient.

One of the most popular manual effect is the one for marching feet, more familiarly known as "the wooden soldiers." Although simple in design, they are as popular today as a sound effect as they were in live dramatic radio. But is it the wooden pegs that makes it believable, or properly simulating the cadence, or rhythm, of marching feet that makes it so realistic?

The same is true with a car's windshield wiper. You can use just about any object you want for this effect, because it isn't what you use, but how you use it ... even your pointing finger. By lightly tapping your finger against just about any object you can simulate the windshield sound as long as you pay attention to one of the nine components. If you chose rhythm you made the right choice.

Both the windshield wiper and the marching feet demand a rhythmic beat. If you disregard the rhythm, you've only created wooden pegs and a finger making noise.

What Sound Do You Have for Dinosaurs?

The first question you should ask is ... is it for a comedy show, or is the sound to be straight (natural sounding)? After it's decided the sound should be as natural as possible, start wondering what sort of natural sound a dinosaur made? The only easy part is no one has ever heard what a dinosaur actually did sound like, so aren't you free to create any sound you want? Not on your life. Any sound you create, unless it's for comedy, must be believable.

In order to do that, don't be overwhelmed by the thought of creating a sound for something that has never been heard. The first thing you must do is look for clues in the script. As soon as you determine the sound isn't for comedy, you look for some help from what the writer has written. They will often prefix the sounds they want with descriptions such as "the huge beast let out an angry roar!"

Now you know that despite the reality of the actual sound, the writer wants *his* dinosaur to be a "*huge beast*" and it roared. It also meant that the writer, and most likely the director, both have preconceived ideas about what their dinosaur already sounds like. Which is fine for them, but not for you?

To avoid a great deal of lost time and motion, you better go with what the writer and director want, or look for another line of work. Perhaps you have a great idea for the way a dinosaur sounds, but as good as it may be, is it consistent with the story the writer has written?

The first step in creating a sound for this prehistoric beast is to go either to the library or your computer's Internet. There you'll find that the word dinosaur means terrible lizard. Next we learn there were all kinds of dinosaurs: there were carnivorous dinosaurs (Tyrannosaurus), herbivorous dinosaurs (Brontosaurus), some were armored (Stegosaurus), while some had horns (Triceratops), and they ranged in sizes from two-and-a-half feet to 90 feet, and they dated back to the Mesozoic Era! Swell. But what did they sound like? Although the writer and director wanted this dinosaur to roar, books only showed these huge beasts munching on grass, or wading in swamps and rooting in the water for weeds. Or perhaps these dinosaurs were truly ferocious beasts and they merely ate grasses and weeds as a salad ... their real snack food was early man and woman!

Most likely the sound they were after was the terrible fire-breathing dragon the writer and director remembered from their childhood books. If so, it's time to either create a sound from scratch, or imitate a sound from a creature that appears to resemble the mysterious creature you're after.

To Create or Imitate?

In creating a difficult sound such as a prehistoric beast, you can either create a sound, or imitate it. If for instance you wanted to create a sound for an extinct saber-toothed tiger, the similarities between the saber-toothed tiger and the present day tiger are such that it wouldn't take too much of an imagination stretch to use the current tiger sound and work from there.

The one thing you don't want to do is create a sound that is so foreign to the present-day animal that it makes it either not believable, or simply silly. Having a saber-toothed tiger open its jaws and make a meowing squeal might be termed creative, but only if it was in keeping with a story that called for such a bizarre, comedic sound.

Sound effects is a highly creative art. A pig grunting is one sound; mix that sound with the sound of a woman crying hysterically and you've created a different sound. Creating sound effects isn't so much what you do, it's what you hear. Therefore, no matter how you create your sound effects, manually, vocally, or electronically, make certain they add, not distract, from what the audience came to the audio theater to hear ... stories that create pictures in their minds.

Summary

1. The creation of sound effects is an art that requires both creative and technical skills.

2. Sound is caused by the vibrations of molecules.

3. Our perception of a sound is influenced by one or more of the following components: pitch, timbre, harmonics, loudness, attack, sustain, decay, speed and rhythm.

4. The timbre of a sound is its unique quality that sets it apart from all other sounds.

5. Harmonics are multiple frequencies of the basic frequency.

6. The loudness of a sound depends on the intensity of the stimulus.

7. The manner in which a sound is initiated is its attack.

8. The sustain portion of a sound envelope is that period of time after a sound has reached maximum loudness level and before it begins to decay.

9. Changing the speed of a sound influences the pitch of the sound.

10. The actual time it takes for a sound to diminish to silence is its decay time. The rhythm of a sound is its recurring alternations between strong and weak elements.

11. The measurable velocity of a sound determines its speed.

12. Sounding boards are extremely helpful in enhancing the loudness of an effect as well as giving one effect a variety of sounds.

13. An audile has the ability to determine a sound an object will make simply by its appearance.

14. In searching for something that makes a difficult sound, think about the nine components of sound. Because no matter how difficult the sound is you're after, one of those nine can be mixed, matched, or left alone to satisfy your needs.

Glossary

Accent   To stress and make something important.

Acoustics   The science of the behavior and control of sound. Although this is a very technical field, the acoustics of any enclosure is that particular quality that allows a good "sound" for your particular needs.

Across the board   Shows normally played Monday through Friday on successive days, said of series and soaps.

Action   Specific physical activity specified by the director or script.

Ad lib   From the Latin "ad libitum," meaning "at one's pleasure." When you make up words rather than read them from a script. "Ad libbing" is spontaneous and unrehearsed.

ADR   Automatic Dialogue Recording.

Affiliate   An independent radio or TV station associated with a network.

AFTRA   Acronym for the actors' union American Federation of Television and Radio Artists.

Ambience   More of a psychological rather than technical description. A restaurant may have a warm and friendly "ambience" for its patrons, whereas the pianist playing music in the restaurant may complain about its "acoustics."

Amplifier   A device used to increase the level of a sound signal.

Amplitude   The strength of a sound signal (*see* Loudness).

Anticipate   To "anticipate" a sound, you must start the sound effect before it is called for in the script.

Attack   The manner in which any sound begins. A clap of thunder has a strong "attack," the rustling of leaves has very little.

Atmosphere   The mood of a story.

Atom   From a Greek word that means "unable to be cut" or "indivisible."

Audio   From the Latin "I hear." This is the sound portion of any electronic mechanism.

Audition   To try out, or show your talents for a particular job.

Background   Sound effects or music to establish the mood of a scene.

Back timing   Means what it says. Timing the show from the time it must be off the air (the ending) "back" to the beginning of the show. The timings are normally done in 15- and 30-second increments.

Baffles   Objects made of sound deadening materials used to isolate voice, musical instruments, or sound effects in a studio.

Balance   The relatives between different sound sources.

Beat   When an actor is told to wait a "beat" the duration of waiting time is approximately one second, or the time it takes to say "Mississippi."

Beef it up   Increase the energy.

Bending the needle   Sound is way too loud!

BG   Abbreviation for the term Background (*see* Background).

Bidirectional microphone   A microphone that picks up sound from two sides.

Billboards   To publicize. Often used by announcers to create interest, or excitement, at the beginning of the show regarding who the stars or special interests will be.

Billing   Credits for the performers.

Bit   A small part, often used by comedians. "I'll add this 'bit' to my monologue, or routine."

Biz   *see* Business

Blend   (1) Similar to balance. Said of a "good mixture" of sounds from the actors, music and sound effects. (2) As a special effect for voices from two different microphones. One voice fades in and quickly attains the same level as the other voice.

Block   Refers to a "dry" rehearsal without technical facilities. In cutting a script, taking out sentences rather than just words. "Make a block cut from Maggie's speech down to Ken's."

Board   The sound mixer control panel that operates all the microphones and technical equipment.

Board fade   Done by the audio engineer with two microphones to designate either a passage of time or a change of scenes. "It seems like only yesterday we were swimming in the Hackensack River..." (start fading out narrator and fade in the sound effects of river sounds and children laughing).

Boost   Raise the level of the sound.

Bounce   The amount of sound wave reflection of a surface.

Break   To end it quickly, or take a 5-minute recess.

Bridge   Normally a music term. Used as a transition of moods from one scene to another. Also used effectively with sounds. The pounding of a judge's gavel in one scene might be bridged to the hammering in of a nail in the next scene.

Brilliance   The treble (highs) quality of a sound.

Build   Increase the intensity, or loudness.

Bump   Raise the level of the sound slightly.

Business   Physical action.

Busy   Too many things going on at once.

Buy   The word used for acceptance.

Canned   Prerecorded music or audience reactions.

Cans   Headphones.

Cardioid microphone   The sound pattern resembles the heart.

Cartoon effect   Exaggerated sound effects in the fashion of a cartoon.

Cattle call   An open actors' audition for a part.

Channel   A single sound path.

Cheating   Making allowances to solve a problem.

Clean it up   Make necessary changes to assure a smooth air show.

Cliff-hanger   Ending an episode of a serial, such as a soap, with high suspense.

Climax   Is the "payoff," or ending, to all the emotional intensity of a story.

Cold reading   Reading a script without benefit of microphone, music or sound effects. Basically done only to get the sense of the script's words and not a formal rehearsal.

Contact microphone   A microphone that is attached to an object and depends on the vibrations of the object for its electrical energy. Because contact microphones are attached to the object itself, interferences from other sources are eliminated.

Crank it up   Increase the volume or intensity of the sound.

Cross-fade   The technique of fading in a new sound as you fade out an old sound without any noticeable difference (*see* Board Fade).

Cue   A signal to start (*see* Hand Signals).

Cushion   Allowing ample time.

Cycles   A wavelength of sound is made up of individual cycles (*see* Frequency).

Dampen   To restrict something from vibrating freely. Normally said of cymbals, or gongs. This is done by lightly touching the edge of the ringing object and gradually pressing your fingers closed.

Db   Decibel.

Dead air   Silence normally caused by a technical or cast error.

Dead pot   Means starting a sound or music at a certain time without opening the "pot" (potentiometer, or volume control).

Dead side   The side of the mike that is insensitive to direct sound.

Decay   The end portion of a sound.

Decay time   The time it takes for a sound to end.

Decibel   An acoustical measurement of sound.

Distortion   A sound signal too loud for the playback system.

Doppler effect   The pitch of a sound depends on the number of air waves that strike the eardrum. The more frequently they come, the higher the sound.

Doubling   Playing two parts in the same script.

Drag   Too slow.

Dramatic license   Asking an audience not to be too judgmental.

Drowns   Overpowers in volume.

Dry reading   Without music or sound effects.

Drying up   Unable to speak caused by "mike fright" (same as "stage fright")

Dynamic range   A difference between the loudest and softest sound a source can produce before distortion can occur.

Echo   The repetition of sound caused be early reflections (*see* Reverberation).

Echo chamber   Created by placing a loudspeaker and microphone in a special room with highly reflective walls.

Electron   The negative charge of an atom.

Electronic   An electronic sound is any sound made by an electronic impulse used by an electrical circuit.

Energy   Pertains to the enthusiasm that actors put into their performance.

Equalizing   Adjusting the frequency responses for a desired sound quality.

Estab. BG and Fade   Usually a written cue for sound effects. "Establish, Background and Fade."

Fade in   A smooth graduation of sound accomplished by turning your face towards the microphone, or walking towards a microphone.

Fade out   A smooth decreasing of sound level by turning your head away from the microphone.

Fading Off   Turn your head away from the microphone. It's up to the story and the director to decide how slow, or fast the fades on and off are to be.

Fading On   This doesn't require any movement away from the microphone. Simply turn your head over your shoulder. Then, when cued, talk while you turn and face the microphone. The larger the room, the slower the turn.

Feet   Getting a script on its "feet" means going to the mike for a rehearsal.

Fibber's crash   A long crash produced with pots, pans and anything else that makes noise. (Got its name from an old radio show, *Fibber McGee and Molly*.)

Filler   Something to use up time.

Filter   An electric network that alters the response of certain frequencies.

First generation   Original, not a copy.

Fluff   To misread a line, or make a mistake pronouncing a word.

Foleying   Manual sound effects done in syncronization with movement. Formerly called "production sounds." Named after Jack Foley, a Universal Studios sound effects artist.

Format   The nature of a particular show that sets it apart.

Frames   Successive pictures on film.

Frequency   The number of cycles completed in one second.

Gain   Refers to the output signal level.

Glottal   From the word glottis, meaning tongue. A sound given to words by not moving your tongue when speaking.

Hams   Amateur radio operators.

Hand signals   Because the live days of radio demanded silence when a show was on the air, the hands were used to signal instructions to the actors or sound effects.

Harmonics   Whole-numbered multiples of the fundamental signal.

Hefting   Feeling the weight of a script to see if there are too many pages.

Hertz   Another name for a cycle. Named after the nineteenth century physicist, Heinrich Hertz.

Hogging   Not allowing room for another actor to get close to the mike.

Hold it down   Sustain a sound in the background at a low level.

Holes   Silence. No sound effects or dialogue.

Hot mike   The microphone is on and in operation. Being too "hot" means it's too loud.

Hubbub The term used for background voices. By mouthing the word "hubbub" it gives the impression that people are actually carrying on conversations.

Impedance Electrical resistance.

Improvise To create.

In the clear Without distractions.

In the red When loudness causes the volume indicator meter's needle to go into the red, or the unacceptable loudness portion of the meter.

Input The signal coming into a piece of equipment.

Intensity A term used to indicate the amount of energy per second per unit area of a sound. A sound heard twenty feet from the source, will only be a quarter as intense at a distance of forty feet.

Jumping a cue Reacting before a cue is given. Applies to actors, music and sound effects. Most often refers to an over-anxious actor beginning his line before the other actor in the scene has spoken all the words in her line.

Killed Taken out of the script.

Layering Adding a number of sounds together to attain a certain effect.

Lead In Words spoken at the beginning of a story or scene.

Leaking An unwanted sound being heard by the microphone.

Level The "level" of a sound is measured by a VI (volume indicator) or calibrated in DBs (decibels). When done by ear alone, the sound should be neither too loud nor too weak.

Lines Words spoken or written in a play.

Live Not taped or recorded. Spoken in real time.

Lose Take out of the script (*see* Killed).

Loudness Inasmuch as we hear the amplitudes of sounds in accordance with our own hearing ability, this is the one word that has caused more arguments that any other word in audio ... certainly in sound effects. However, there are sounds so loud we can actually feel them. When this is the case, there is a real danger of hearing loss.

Loudspeaker A transducer that converts electrical energy into acoustical energy. Perhaps the most common loudspeaker is found in our telephone.

Make and sync Film term for manual effects prior to Foleying.

Manual effects Sound effects done with the hands or body.

Mark A television term meaning to go to a predetermined area on the set for purposes of camera angles.

Masking Covering one sound with another of greater amplitude.

Microphone   A transducer that converts sound pressure waves to an electrical signal.

Midrange   Those frequencies that fall into the 200 to 2,000 hertz frequency range (*see* Hertz).

Mike hog   An actor who doesn't leave room for other actors to speak their lines.

Mix   The term used to describe taking various sound sources and putting them together in such a manner so that they are all in the proper perspective.

Molecules   Are made up of tiny particles (atoms).

Muddy   When a sound is too low. Conversely, when a sound is too loud it is said to be in the "red." (That term refers to the unacceptable sound level that pushes the sound measuring needle into the red part of the meter.)

Noise   Any spurious sound disturbance.

Nondirectional microphone   A microphone that has a pickup pattern of 360 degrees.

Nucleus   The center of an atom.

Octave   Octaves are perceived as equal pitch intervals that have a frequency ratio of 2:1.

Off mike   Not facing the microphone, or too far back from the microphone.

Omni-directional microphone   Its sound pattern is circular.

On mike   Facing the microphone at a distance of approximately 12 inches back from the microphone.

On the nose   At the correct time.

Onomatopoeia   The naming of an object or action by a vocalization of the sound it produces. Examples include: quack, gobble, buzz, hiss and booing.

Open cold   To start a program without music.

Oscillator   An electronic device that generates tones.

Overlapping   Interrupting an actor by repeating the ending of their line and then continuing talking alone. This is a valuable technique in adding pace to a comedy.

Pace   The rate of speed in delivering lines. Pace is to dialogue what tempo is to music.

Padding   Slowing the tempo of the script for purposes of time.

Pause   A silence that indicates thought. It can either be cued by the director, or the actor can feel how long the silence should be.

Peak   The highest point. Often said of a VI meter's reading in regards to unacceptable loudness (*see* In the Red).

Perspective   The sound heard in relationship to the distance of the origin. It is always in relationship to the principal listener's viewpoint. In radio, it was the person speaking on mike.

Phon   A unit of loudness level related to the ear's subjective impression of signal strength.

Pickup   To resume from a certain point in the script.

Pitch   Determined by the frequency of the sound.

Play, or playing   To react. "Play the sounds" means to react to the SFX.

Presence   The natural sound you hear in a large, empty room that is devoid of any extraneous sounds. A slight, indefinite movement of air to give a sound-proofed area a feeling of naturalness. "Presence" frequencies are somewhere between 2,000 and 8,000 hertz. Presence makes a soft "shhh-hhhhhhhhhh" sound.

Punch it up   To emphasize.

Putting it on its feet   A microphone rehearsal.

Quick Study   Grasping the meaning of a script without hesitation.

Reacting   Showing emotions.

Readings   Indications to actors as to what emotions are needed for words or scenes.

Remote   A show done from a location away from the normal operating base.

Resonance   The condition when the applied frequency is equal to the normal frequency of vibration of the system.

Reverberation   Repeated sound reflections after the original signal is out.

Rhythm   Recurring sound that alternates between strong and weak elements.

Rough timing   An approximate timing.

Run through   An early rehearsal for a rough timing.

Segue   A transition from one thing to another smoothly and without interruption.

Sibilance   A "hissing" sound caused by an actor enunciating words containing Ss and Cs too harshly and too close to the microphone.

Skiffle   A form of music utilizing "things" rather than musical instruments.

Sound effect   Any sound used artificially to produce another sound.

Sound generators   Electronic equipment capable of creating sounds.

Sound Patterns   A series of uninterrupted sound effects.

Sounding board   Something that will add and amplify sound.

Source   The origin of the sound.

Speed   Quickening the pace.

Stable   Normally refers to writers experienced with the format of the show and with whom the director is familiar.

Stage wait   Unnecessary delay.

Stand by   The command given in preparation to a cue.

Sting   A short, high pitched, piercing music chord. Usually indicates danger, or a thought recognition.

Straight line   Not intended to get laughs.

Stretch   To slow the pace of the dialogue (*see* Hand Signals).

Sweeten   To improve.

Sync   Sound effects done at the same moment.

Tag   To bring something to an end.

Teasers   Used to gain attention and interest.

Telegraph   To indicate by word or action that something is about to happen.

Throw away   Nonessential words.

Timbre   A sound that sets it apart from other sounds.

Top   Beginning.

Transcribed   Recorded.

Transducer   An instrument that converts one form of energy to another.

Trappings   Various props used to create sound effects.

Uvula   Fleshy looking tongue on the roof of your mouth.

Vibrations   A back-and-forth motion.

Walla Walla   Same as "Hubbub."

Waves   A series of peaks and valleys that repeat themselves.

Bibliography

Butler, Daws, Ben Ohmart, and Joe Bevilacqua. *Scenes for Actors and Voices.* Boalsburg, PA: BearManor Media, 2003.

Creamer, Joseph, and William B. Hoffman. *Radio Sound Effects.* New York: Ziff-Davis, 1945.

Dunning, John. *On the Air: The Encyclopedia of Old-Time Radio.* New York: Oxford University Press, 1998.

Head, Sterling W. *Broadcasting in America: A Survey of Television and Radio.* Boston: Houghton Mifflin, 1972.

McGill, Earl. *Radio Directing.* New York: McGraw-Hill, 1940.

Mott, Robert L. *Radio Live! Television Live! Those Golden Days When Horses Were Coconuts.* Jefferson, NC: McFarland, 2000.

_____. *Radio Sound Effects: Who Did It, and How, in the Era of Live Broadcasting.* Jefferson, NC: McFarland, 1993.

Nisbett, Alec. *The Technique of the Sound Studio: For Radio, Recording Studio, Television, and Film.* London: Focal Press, 1979.

Turnbull, Robert B. *Radio and Television Sound Effects.* New York: Rinehart, 1951.

Index